T0305196

Managing in Dynamic Business Environments

Managing in Dynamic Business Environments

Between Control and Autonomy

Edited by

Katarina Kaarbøe

NHH – Norwegian School of Economics, Norway

Paul N. Gooderham

NHH – Norwegian School of Economics, Norway

Hanne Nørreklit

Aarhus University, Denmark (Affiliated with NHH – Norwegian School of Economics, Norway)

Edward Elgar
Cheltenham, UK • Northampton, MA, USA

Published by
Edward Elgar Publishing Limited
The Lypiatts
15 Lansdown Road
Cheltenham
Glos GL50 2JA
UK

Edward Elgar Publishing, Inc.
William Pratt House
9 Dewey Court
Northampton
Massachusetts 01060
USA

A catalogue record for this book
is available from the British Library

Library of Congress Control Number: 2013943233

This book is available electronically in the ElgarOnline.com Business Subject Collection, E-ISBN 978 1 78254 453 1

ISBN 978 1 78254 452 4

Typeset by Servis Filmsetting Ltd, Stockport, Cheshire
Printed and bound in Great Britain by T.J. International Ltd, Padstow

Contents

Contributors

Sebastian D. Becker, Assistant Professor, Department of Accounting and Management Control, HEC Paris, France.
ORCID: 0000-0001-5519-8243

Trond Bjørnenak, Professor, Department of Accounting, Auditing and Law, NHH – Norwegian School of Economics, Norway.
ORCID: 0000-0003-4089-5534

Bjarte Bogsnes, VP Performance Management Development, Statoil, Norway and Chairman of Beyond Budgeting Round Table Europe (BBRT).
ORCID: 0000-0002-3489-8133

Anatoli Bourmistrov, Professor, Bodø Graduate School of Business, University of Nordland, Norway.
ORCID: 0000-0001-9421-2781

Bino Catasús, Professor, School of Business, Stockholm University, Sweden.
ORCID: 0000-0003-0008-3937

Bjarne Espedal, Professor, Department of Strategy and Management, NHH – Norwegian School of Economics, Norway.
ORCID: 0000-0001-9749-573X

Paul N. Gooderham, Professor, Department of Strategy and Management, NHH – Norwegian School of Economics, Norway.
ORCID: 0000-0001-6397-5823

Daniel Johanson, Associate Professor, Department of Accounting, Auditing and Law, NHH – Norwegian School of Economics, Norway.
ORCID: 0000-0003-1644-8494

Katarina Kaarbøe, Professor and Head of Department, Department of Accounting, Auditing and Law, NHH – Norwegian School of Economics, Norway.
ORCID: 0000-0003-0095-9054

Teemu Malmi, Professor, Department of Accounting, School of Business, Aalto University, Finland.
ORCID: 0000-0002-1609-1926

Martin Messner, Professor, School of Management, University of Innsbruck, Austria.
ORCID: 0000-0003-0933-5918

Odd Nordhaug, Professor, Department of Strategy and Management, NHH – Norwegian School of Economics, Norway.
ORCID: 0000-0003-1427-1656

Hanne Nørreklit, Professor, Department of Economics and Business, Aarhus University, Denmark.
ORCID: 0000-0002-6636-786

Lars Jacob Tynes Pedersen, Associate Professor, Department of Accounting, Auditing and Law, NHH – Norwegian School of Economics, Norway.
ORCID: 0000-0001-5709-8780

Niels Sandalgaard, Assistant Professor, Department of Business and Management, Aalborg University, Denmark.
ORCID: 0000-0001-9583-5518

Alexander Madsen Sandvik, Assistant Professor, Department of Strategy and Management, NHH – Norwegian School of Economics, Norway.
ORCID: 0000-0002-3320-2595

Inger Stensaker, Professor, Department of Strategy and Management, NHH – Norwegian School of Economics, Norway.
ORCID: 0000-0002-5189-1769

Siri Terjesen, Assistant Professor, Department of Management and Entrepreneurship, Kelley School of Business, Indiana University Bloomington, USA.
ORCID: 0000-0002-2070-1942

Preface and acknowledgements

It seems a long time ago but I recall that at some point in early 2008 my colleague Trond Bjørnenak and I started having discussions with Bjarte Bogsnes, a senior executive at the Norwegian petroleum company Statoil ASA, about what was then the very novel concept of "Beyond Budgeting." Trond and I were quickly won over by the notion that Beyond Budgeting was potentially so significant for the management of large, complex organizations in dynamic environments that it deserved serious and protracted attention. Wheels were set in motion and within a matter of months Trond and I, with the support of Statoil, had established the five-year "Beyond Budgeting Research Program."

It has been an exciting journey, and five years later we are now a research group comprising some 20 researchers spread across a range of European business schools focusing on management control systems and their relationship to other fields of research such as leadership, organizational performance and individual motivation. This volume contains a selection of the most significant research findings from the program.

The Beyond Budgeting Research Program in general, and this volume in particular, would not have been possible without the assistance, support and commitment of many colleagues, associates and friends. First, on behalf of the research group, I would like to express our sincere gratitude to Statoil ASA and its generous funding of the program throughout its five years. In particular I would like to thank our contact at Statoil, Bjarte Bogsnes. Throughout the program Bjarte has played a number of highly significant roles. At Statoil he has been a door-opener enabling our researchers and students to gain access to Statoil's global operations. He has introduced us to the wider Beyond Budgeting community based around the Beyond Budgeting Round Table. At our workshops he has contributed with presentations of new developments at Statoil and his evolving views on Beyond Budgeting. In regard to our research as it has progressed, Bjarte has been a robust, lively and at all times immensely constructive commentator.

In addition to thanking my co-editors, Paul N. Gooderham and Hanne Nørreklit, for their astute and rigorous approach to organizing and shaping this volume, I also want to thank all of the authors for their effort, creativity and patience as their chapters proceeded through a demanding review process.

Finally I would like to thank the Beyond Budgeting Research Program coordinator, Christian Eide Andvik, for his dedication in keeping us on track with this volume and our language editor, Tina Pedersen, for her editorial efforts.

Katarina Kaarbøe

Research Director for the Beyond Budgeting Research Program

NHH – Norwegian School of Economics

April 2013

1. Control and autonomy – management challenges and tensions

Katarina Kaarbøe, Paul N. Gooderham and Hanne Nørreklit

INTRODUCTION

Let us start with the obvious. Organizations whose competitive advantage lies in attributes such as design, quality of service, customer focus, innovative products or novel solutions are dependent on their employees being willing and able to respond to new challenges and opportunities in fresh and inventive ways. The more turbulent their environments become, the less viable traditional command and control management is and the more critical it becomes that employees are self-regulated. However, what is very much less obvious is how to develop approaches to management control that actually promote and support creative and innovative autonomy rather than undermining it.

Management control is often divided into three main forms: hierarchical or regulative control, control based on financial incentives and social control based on peer pressure (Jaffee, 2001; Bemelmans-Videc et al., 2007; Gooderham et al., 2011). Each form of control imposes significant but different constraints on autonomy. "Regulations" are rules that top managers can use to mandate or prevent people in the hierarchy from acting in certain ways. They can be expressed in negative terms, such as demands on what you not are allowed to do. Alternatively, they may also be phrased in affirmative terms and prescribe in a positive way what measures need to be taken. The defining property of a regulation is that the relationship is authoritative, meaning that the controlled persons are obliged to follow the rules set by the controlling authority. Managers can choose to use threats or negative sanctions if rules are broken, and they can also decide not to use such sanctions (Bemelmans-Videc et al., 2007). McGregor (1957, 1960) refers to this approach, which involves obedience to authority in exchange for security, as Theory X. Clearly, too much hierarchical control can severely limit autonomy.

Management control based on financial incentives attempts to introduce market mechanisms in organizations (Bemelmans-Videc et al., 2007). They differ from regulation in the sense that they neither prescribe nor prohibit actions, but make certain actions more or less expensive. Managers can choose different forms of economic incentives as means of enforcing strategies. The notion is that the firm provides financial incentives to employees in order to ensure that employee behavior is aligned with the strategic needs of the firm. Examples of tools that rely on such financial incentives are budgets, balanced scorecards and other types of key performance indicators. Incentives that are too strong can limit autonomy because they trigger rewards only for pre-defined standardized activities – employees have no incentive to develop novel responses to new situations.

Social control aims to develop organizational identity and commitment through peer acknowledgement of professional achievements. This form of control, which McGregor (1957, 1960) refers to as Theory Y, relies on the assumptions that employees will seek out opportunities for professional development and creativity when given the opportunity, and that peer pressure and peer acknowledgement will provide sufficient motivation. The limitation of this approach is that conventional rules and objectives may not be challenged or questioned. Professional cultures can become overly wedded to their particular rules and objectives, meaning that novel behavior that falls outside the established path is viewed as "non-conformist" and illegitimate and is, therefore, stigmatized.

The different types of instruments and tools of control entail varying degrees of constraint and power that managers can exercise in order to enforce a strategy. Regulation is more constraining than economic incentives, and economic incentives are more directly constraining than social control. Furthermore, tools often come in "packages" (Malmi and Brown, 2008) or "bundles" (Crowley, 2012), such that one tool may be used to promote or restrain another. The main point is that the design of a management control approach, i.e., the decision to use one or several tools, as well as the type of tools that are chosen, can have a significant impact on organizational performance. Accordingly, it should be borne in mind that striking the right balance among the different tools is vital.

Historically, a core problem associated with management control systems has been their dysfunctional effects on human behavior. Argyris (1952) initiated a discussion of the behavioral issues related to control and argued that control can have negative implications for learning. In the 1970s, researchers (Hopwood, 1972; Otley, 1978) explored the non-intended effects of various types of performance evaluation on human interaction and decision making. More recently, Amabile (1996, 1998) pointed out that some management control practices can kill creativity and, thereby, innovation.

Dissatisfaction with measurement systems is also being voiced by managers, who are calling for a new set of tools that promote innovation in a dynamic business context. Such tools emphasize employee autonomy, and have their roots in McGregor's (1960) notion of Theory Y, which posits that control is de-motivating, and that most employees will be self-directing and seek responsibility if they are motivated. However, as Bogsnes (2008) argues, Theory X, with its assumption that employees have to be coerced and controlled by management, remains engrained in many business models. Nevertheless, companies cannot survive without some sort of control. As expressed by Simons (1995), organizations need to balance employees' motives of self-interest with their desire to contribute, and balance creative views of strategy with planned views of strategy. Accordingly, there is a need for control methods that go beyond mechanical approaches to management control.

The complexity of the management control task is further aggravated by four key trends in the contemporary business environment. The first is globalization. Globalization refers "to processes of change which underpin a transformation in the organization of human affairs by linking together and expanding human activity across regions and continents" (Held et al., 1999: 15). Thus, globalization makes it possible to engage with parties regardless of their geographical location and without interruption, which leads to de-territorialization. As a result, the management control framework must handle larger organizations consisting of more geographically dispersed business units and characterized by increased diversity.

The second trend concerns the erosion of collectivistic societies and an increasing focus on individualization. The primacy of community is giving way to a liberal conception of the individual that de-emphasizes community. Management control methods must therefore consider employee demands for substantial empowerment and self-leadership (Sandvik, 2011).

The third trend is the increased pace of technological innovation. Rapid technological change shortens the useful lifetime of product developments and manufacturing facilities. In addition, technology advancements drive shorter product life cycles and flexible manufacturing processes. Thus, on the one hand, management control has to be supportive of innovation and creativity. On the other hand, it must contribute to the efficient "shipping of products." In other words, management control is not only about developing new products but also about getting these products to market before competitors (Lindvall, 2009).

Finally, the increased use of information technology, which substantially improves communication, also has considerable implications for control. Social media offer massive potential for improved communication and, thereby, learning. At the same time, such technologies create opportunities for increased centralization and the standardization of business models. In other words, information technology can enhance learning through information-management systems, but these systems can also be applied as a means for achieving increased control (Lindvall, 2009). Management control must recognize these twin possibilities and take them into account.

From a theoretical vantage point, we can distinguish among a variety of initiatives aimed at developing a management control framework suited for achieving competitive success in today's context. One such initiative encompasses a number of "strategic-management accounting" tools, such as the balanced scorecard, ABC, benchmarking and target costing (Ax and Bjørnenak, 2005). Other types of tools include rolling forecasts, benchmarking and more dynamic resource allocation. Novel incentive systems that focus not just on delivery but also on the actions preceding delivery are an additional feature of this new landscape. In practice, these new types of management control tools have been combined in a variety of ways (Hansen et al., 2003; Libby and Lindsay, 2010). Nevertheless, some researchers argue that, regardless of how these tools are combined, they inevitably introduce new dilemmas with regard to balancing the need for employee autonomy and innovation with the need to secure organizational effectiveness (Malmi and Brown, 2008).

A second distinct initiative is the development of new management tools based on a particular notion of employee motivation. This initiative is based on the assumption that a response to contemporary business challenges requires approaches to management control based on "a richer notion of human behavior that invites analysis of economic organization not just in terms of opportunism and incentives – but also involves issues of organizational identification, loyalty, and even culture" (Augier and Teece, 2008: 1199). One example of this initiative is found in new types of personnel and social control concepts, such as empowerment and self-leadership (Sandvik, 2011). In other words, we can discern management control tools that are outside the realm of hierarchical control and control based on financial incentives. These tools can be categorized as social control mechanisms.

In practice, the extent to which the three generic management control mechanisms we have outlined – hierarchical, financial incentives and social – are applied varies considerably even within individual industries. For example, unlike most banks, Sweden's Svenska Handelsbanken pays no bonuses to individual managers, nor does it have any sales targets that are determined through an annual budgeting process. Instead, it has a pronounced focus on costs, which is based on external and internal benchmarking and peer pressure. When external benchmarking indicates that the bank as a whole has outperformed competitors, a contribution is made to a pooled fund, which is invested on behalf of employees. It is a retirement fund, that is, employees cannot take out their portion of the fund until retirement. The fruits of the bank's success are distributed equally, and gratification is deferred (Wallander, 1999). In the view of one commentator:

> Huge responsibility is devolved to branch managers: they have no set budget and have to work through any bad loans themselves. Cost control is achieved largely through peer pressure; managers seem to be driven by a sense of pride in balancing their books. Loan decisions are made by the branch, rather than by an algorithm. (*Financial Times*, 2013)

A more precise analysis would be that, while Handelsbanken makes only moderate use of financial incentives by industry standards, it has implemented highly developed social control mechanisms. This social control is made possible through a significant degree of transparency, including the regular ranking of branch performance. Social control is supported by hierarchical control in the form of financial monitoring: "Senior managers comb the whole loan portfolio four times a year and look at all documentation annually for loans greater than SEK 1m (USD 153 000). Any credit loss of more than SEK 5m is analysed by senior management" (*Financial Times*, 2013).

However, determining whether this degree of social control, combined with some degree of hierarchical control and weak financial incentives, actually encourages autonomy and innovation is difficult. In fact, this control system may breed in-house best-practice imitation and, ultimately, conformity.

Given the lack of certainty as to which combination of management control mechanisms is best suited to a dynamic business environment, there is a pressing need for research that addresses this issue. The aim of this book, therefore, is to offer insights into the design of new, more dynamic approaches to management control.

PART I – BUDGETING CONTROL AND BEYOND

Part I of this book focuses on budgeting control and on-going Beyond Budgeting. The chapters improve our understanding of the Beyond

Budgeting movement and how it contributes to changes in management control approaches in terms of design and use. This part examines how organizations are trying to change the balance between control and autonomy by changing management control tools and by introducing new types of tools.

Chapter 2 discusses the practitioner's view. Bogsnes addresses the problem of budget-based control from the vantage point of the practitioner and outlines the main elements of an alternative – the Beyond Budgeting model.

Chapters 3 and 4 discuss the dominant tool used in management control today – budgets. In Chapter 3, Sandalgaard discusses contingency approaches and their limitations in order to help us appreciate the conditions under which budgets may serve a useful function. Furthermore, Sandalgaard analyzes the relationship between environmental uncertainty and different reasons for budgeting. In Chapter 4, Bjørnenak broadens the perspective to include not only budgets but also other tools, such as balanced scorecard and activity-based costing, that aim to exert control over activities. The chapter is based on a survey of Norwegian banks and highlights the performance effects of different tools.

In Chapters 5 to 7, the new Beyond Budgeting movement is analyzed. In Chapter 5, Johanson discusses corporate-governance and management control approaches. The Beyond Budgeting rhetoric in the US and Norway is analyzed and compared with governance models in the two countries. In Chapter 6, Kaarbøe, Stensaker and Malmi explore the implementation of Beyond Budgeting ideas. Their discussion improves our understanding of Beyond Budgeting as a practice. One important point is that Beyond Budgeting is not about new tools. Rather, it is a new way of thinking about management control approaches. In Chapter 7, Nørreklit and Kaarbøe introduce a new way of acting as a controller in a Beyond Budgeting setting. The chapter shows that the work of a controller is shifting from a more mechanical management control approach toward a paradigm of realism in which the work is based on a more dialectic perception of the business environment. In the latter situation, the controller's role is more reflective and interactive.

PART II – PERSPECTIVES AND CONTROL DIMENSIONS

In Part II, we broaden the scope to discuss wider perspectives on control, such as self-control, time control, transparency as control, ethical control and cultural control. In this regard, we focus more on social control and on how social control influences management control approaches. In Chapter 8, Becker and Messner discuss how management control approaches can be organized in order to meet the real-time needs of managers. In Chapter 9, Bourmistrov and Kaarbøe provide three examples of how budgeting activities are connected to the behavior of actors located in specific settings. They define the concept of a "planning regime" in order to emphasize the importance of social and temporary embeddedness for understanding why companies use certain forms of budgeting.

Given that organizations must increasingly address the need to enable employees to develop timely, relevant and, above all, creative responses to new challenges and opportunities, to what extent do employees actually seek "autonomy-creativity"? In response to this question, Espedal and Sandvik challenge the assumption that leadership that operates under clear organizational rules is inflexible, and unable to engage in learning and change, in Chapter 10. In Chapter 11, Gooderham, Sandvik, Terjesen and Nordhaug examine the degree to which key employees of the future desire autonomy-creativity in their future work. Their analysis is based on a study of students at elite business schools in Norway and North America. Many of these students are destined to become leaders who will have a profound influence on creativity and innovation in the future. Their findings indicate that both Norwegian and North American students value autonomy-creativity similarly, as do males and females. They also find that pay-for-performance schemes do not augment autonomy-creativity. Instead their research indicates that employers aiming at enhancing autonomy-creativity should concentrate on developing work environments characterized by supportive management and good social relations. Finally, in Chapter 12, Pedersen points to the need to resolve the potential tension between organizational systems of accountability and the individual's sense of personal responsibility. His chapter discusses the possibility and the problems of promoting the personal responsibility by means of accountability systems. The chapter argues that this involves facilitating organizational members' self-determination, which necessitates designing systems of accountability that provide fruitful conditions for self-determined, communal and engaged organizational action.

REFERENCES

Amabile, T.M. (1996), *Creativity in Context: The Social Psychology of Creativity*, Boulder, CO: Westview Press.

Amabile, T. (1998), "How to kill creativity," *Harvard Business Review*, September/October, 76–87.

Argyris, C. (1952), *The Impact of Budgets on People*, Ithaca, NY: School of Business and Public Administration, Cornell University.

Augier, M. and D.J. Teece (2008), "Strategy as evolution with design: The foundations of dynamic capabilities and the role of managers in the economic system," *Organization Studies*, **29** (8–9), 1187–1208.

Ax, C. and T. Bjørnenak (2005), "Bundling and diffusion of management accounting innovations culture," *Management Accounting Research*, **16** (1), 1–20.

Bemelmans-Videc, M.-L., R.C. Rist and E.O. Vedung (2007), *Carrots, Sticks and Sermons: Policy Instruments and Their Evaluation*, Comparative Policy Analysis Series, Piscataway, NJ: Transaction Publishers.

Bogsnes, B. (2008), *Implementing Beyond Budgeting: Unlocking the Performance Potential*, Hoboken, NJ: John Wiley & Sons.

Crowley, M. (2012), "Control and dignity in professional, manual and service-sector employment," *Organization Studies*, **33** (10), 1383–1406.

Financial Times (2013), "Sweden's back-to-the-future banker," January 14.

Gooderham, P.N., D.B. Minbaeva and T. Pedersen (2011), "Governance mechanisms for the promotion of social capital for knowledge transfer in multinational corporations," *Journal of Management Studies*, **48** (1), 123–50.

Hansen, D., T. Otely and W.A. Van der Stede (2003), "Practice developments in budgeting: An overview and research perspectives," *Journal of Management Accounting Research*, **15** (1), 95–116.

Held, D., A. McGrew, D. Goldblatt and J. Perraton (1999), *Global Transformations: Politics, Economics and Culture*, Stanford, CA: Stanford University Press.

Hopwood, A.G. (1972), "An empirical study of the role of accounting data in performance evaluation," *Journal of Accounting Research*, **10** (3), 156–82.

Jaffee, D. (2001), *Organization Theory: Tensions and Change*, Singapore: McGraw-Hill.

Libby, T. and R.M. Lindsay (2010), "Beyond Budgeting or budgeting reconsidered? A survey of North American budgeting practice," *Management Accounting Research*, **21** (1), 56–75.

Lindvall, J. (2009), *Controllers nya roll – om verksamhetsstyrning i informationsrika miljöer*, Stockholm: Akademiska Förlag.

Malmi, T. and D.A. Brown (2008), "Management control systems as a package – opportunities, challenges and research directions," *Management Accounting Research*, **19** (4), 287–300.

McGregor, D. (1957), "The human side of enterprise," *Management Review*, **46** (11), 22–8.

McGregor, D. (1960), *The Human Side of Enterprise*, New York: McGraw-Hill.

Otley, D. (1978), "Budget use and managerial performance," *Journal of Accounting Research*, **16** (1), 122–49.

Sandvik, A. (2011), "Leadership of knowledge workers," Ph.D. thesis, NHH – Norwegian School of Economics, Bergen.

Simons, R. (1995), *Levers of Control: How Managers Use Innovative Control Systems to Drive Strategic Renewal*, Boston, MA: HBS Press.

Wallander, J. (1999), "Budgeting – an unnecessary evil," *Scandinavian Journal of Management*, **15**, 405–42.

PART I

Budgeting control and beyond

2. Taking reality seriously – towards a more self-regulating management model at Statoil

Bjarte Bogsnes*

INTRODUCTION

Statoil is a Norwegian oil and gas company with activities in 36 countries, 23 000 employees and a turnover of USD 130 billion. The company is listed in New York and Oslo. On the Fortune 500, it ranks number 40 on size but number 1 on social responsibility and number 7 on innovation. Transparency International has named Statoil the most transparent listed company globally.

At Statoil, we try to take reality seriously, not just a dynamic and unpredictable business environment, but also all the competent and responsible people in the company. It sounds obvious, but requires fundamental changes in how we lead and manage. In 2005 we started on a journey of radically changing our management processes, which included abolishing traditional budgeting. In 2010 we also decided to "kick out the calendar" wherever possible. These were both key steps towards a more dynamic, flexible and self-regulating management model.

BACKGROUND

Statoil has always been a values-based and people-oriented organization, but during the years of growth, since its foundation in 1972, traditional management processes were introduced brick by brick, causing increasing bureaucracy and rigidity. The gap widened between what we said in our leadership principles and what we did in our management processes. This is poison in any organization, making leadership messages hollow, because process messages always are stronger. What we do always weighs so much more than what we say. "You are all great, and the company would be nothing without you, but we still need to control you through detailed budgets, rules and regulations." It does not help to have Theory Y leadership visions if you have Theory X management processes.

We wanted to close such gaps. We also wanted to find our way back to the agility and flexibility we had as a smaller company. The growth journey of companies shares many similarities with the aging process of humans. As we grow older, we lose more and more of what we took for granted in our younger days: the agility, flexibility and spontaneity of youth. Having passed 50, I am starting to get some personal experience! As age takes its toll, some also get weary of life and lose their spirit and that twinkle in the eye. This development in the human body and mind is unavoidable and irreversible, at least the physical part. It can be delayed through a healthy lifestyle or through other "interventions," but in the end age takes us all. We have no choice.

Companies, however, do have a choice. Companies are not destined to become slow and sad places to work because they grow and become older. Most of what causes this is decisions that companies make themselves, which cannot be blamed on destiny or on any aging process.

For humans, *older* normally also means *wiser*. For companies, this is not necessarily the case, as they struggle to capitalize on a mountain of collective wisdom and experience acquired during the growth journey. The solution is often another new process, "knowledge management." Many employees experience instead a "dumbing-down" trend, as they observe more and more strange decisions made further and further away from their own reality.

Of course, one cannot manage a big company exactly like the small company it used to be. But could there be alternatives? Could there be other ways, ways which better balance the benefits of being big – which of course are both real and important – with the benefits of being small?

The big question for any large organization should be: "How can we revitalize the agility of the past without having to go back and start all over again? How can we be small and big at the same time, young and old, brave and wise?"

The budget and the whole mindset behind it might be a good place to start.

LEAVING THE TRADITIONAL BUDGET

Real and sustainable change requires a solid case for change. While almost everybody complains about the budgeting process, fewer understand that their problems are only symptoms of a much bigger and more serious problem, rooted in the entire management model. Some complain about all the work involved; some worry about the gaming and the sub-optimization, some about the budget being a meaningless yardstick for performance, and some about how it prevents them from responding fast on value-adding opportunities. But these and many other problems are all connected. These are all consequences of a traditional management approach that ignores reality, both inside and outside our organizations, both what motivates the "knowledge worker" and what the implications of a dynamic and unpredictable business environment really are.

But these are big and hairy issues, and for many hard to grasp or address. So we started out with something more tangible and logical and also less threatening. We simply asked "Why do we budget?"

Most companies make budgets for three very different reasons: *target setting, forecasting* and *resource allocation*. Those budget numbers represent a set of targets, a forecast of what the future might look like, and an allocation of resources for next year. But these are all different things. The three purposes can't meaningfully be handled in *one* process resulting in *one* set of numbers. A target is what we want to happen. A forecast is what we think will happen, whether we like what we see or not. And resource allocation is about trying to use our resources in the most optimal and efficient way.

An ambitious sales target can't at the same time also be an unbiased sales forecast. And you rarely get a good cost forecast if the organization believes this is its one shot at access to resources for the next year.

Our solution to this serious problem was dead simple. We *separated* the three purposes, which made it possible to optimize each one in much more tailored processes. This allowed for instance for different numbers, updated on different frequencies and time horizons in each of the three processes.

But, more importantly, the separation was a catalyst for all those bigger issues that we need to address. It leads us into important discussions, whether we want it or not. How can we find targets that really inspire and stretch without feeling stretched, while avoiding all the gaming and negotiation that add no value at all? How can we make simple and unbiased forecasts, free of all the hidden agendas? How can we make people spend money as if it came from their own pocket? How can we move towards a management model which works more with and less against human nature? How can we be big and small at the same time? How can we take reality seriously? These are important questions for any large company. We have absolutely not solved them all, but we have definitely started (see Figure 2.1).

Where possible, we try to use *relative* instead of absolute and decimal-loaded targets. Relative targets redefine performance. They address how

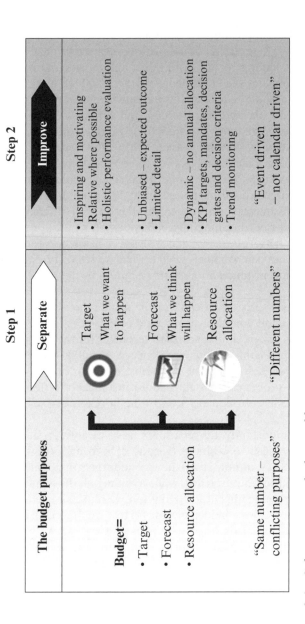

Figure 2.1 Solving a serious budget problem

we are doing compared to others, internally or externally, instead of a myopic focus on fixed and decimal-oriented numbers.

The power of comparison is fascinating. I have yet to hear a team coming out low (given they find the benchmarking fair and relevant) announce that they have no ambitions about climbing on the ranking. This is a much more *self-regulating* approach compared to the traditional budget game, which stimulates the very opposite mindset, the one that drives managers to negotiate for the easiest achievable number. Michelangelo put it like this: "Our problem is not that we aim too high and miss, but that we aim too low and hit."

Benchmarking is of course nothing new, with its purpose of learning from each other. This should still be the main purpose. But we believe we actually get more learning by combining the two, by increasing the focus on those comparisons through also using them more directly to gently stimulate performance.

Statoil's main financial targets are set against a peer group of 15 other oil and gas companies. We aim to be in the first quartile on return on capital employed, above average on shareholder return, and in the first quartile on unit production cost. These are the kinds of financial targets our board approves. They do not approve a budget. The two first metrics also drive our common bonus scheme. Everybody is in the same boat: us against the competition.

The quality of our *forecasting* has also improved, because we have taken out much of the gaming bias that came from target setting or resource allocation. Our forecasting process is now leaner and with much less detail, although there is room for even more simplification. Some still believe that their cost forecast is their "budget application" for resources. Some also mix target and forecast, and believe they need to "deliver" on their forecast. What we want to deliver on is our targets, and forecasts are there to help us. They might for instance show that we are heading in the wrong direction, towards places that we absolutely don't want to go.

We also introduced a *dynamic resource allocation* which provides much bigger and more flexible decision authorities to local teams, and a much more dynamic rhythm. Imagine a bank informing its customers, "We have now changed our hours, so if you want to borrow money we are now only open in October." It sounds ridiculous – but isn't this exactly what people in companies experience every year in the budget process?

We want the bank to be open 12 months a year. A funding request might still be refused; we should be just as good at saying no as yes. Cost is of course still very important for us. But why should we make all our cost decisions in the autumn, before we have to? Isn't it better to make them as late as possible, when we have better information – not only about the new project or activity up for decision but also about our capacity to fund it or staff it?

For operational or administrative cost, with fewer discrete decision points than projects, we offer a menu of alternative mechanisms for the business to manage its own costs. These include a "burn rate" guidance ("Operate within this approximate activity level"), unit cost targets ("You can spend more if you produce more"), benchmarked targets (e.g., "unit cost below average for peers"), profit targets ("Spend so that you maximize your bottom line) or simply no target at all ("We'll monitor cost trends and intervene only if necessary") (see Figure 2.2).

In the corporate staff I am based in we have no cost targets at all, but we discuss cost all the time. There is no travel budget, but a colleague of mine just spent days considering if he should send two of his team members on a business trip from Norway to Houston. With an eye on the team's cost trend, he ended up saying yes, because of a strong plea for help from the Houston office. Next time, it might be a no. Pre-approval of travel is normally required only for intercontinental flights.

In short, we try to make decisions at the right time, at the right level and with the right mindset. Being a capital-intensive and value-chain-organized company, every single decision can't be made at each platform or plant. But, given this industrial setting, we try to make decisions as far out in the organization as possible. In many other businesses decision authorities can be delegated even further out.

Here is our CFO Torgrim Reitan:

> We could easily put in place a cost program instructing all business areas to reduce costs by a given number. I believe this would work against our intention of building a cost-conscious culture. If we want to become more fit, a crash diet does not work. It takes a change of lifestyle. I believe Statoil is made up of competent, responsible and commercially oriented people who will make the right cost decisions. This means always working hard to reduce bad cost, while protecting good cost. You know better than me what these are and where they are.

The question we want everybody to ask when making cost decisions is not "Do I have a budget for this?" but:

- Is this really necessary?
- What is good enough?
- How is this creating value?
- Is this within my execution framework?

(See Figure 2.3.) In addition, we must always consider capacity, both financial and human. As things look today, can we afford it, and do we

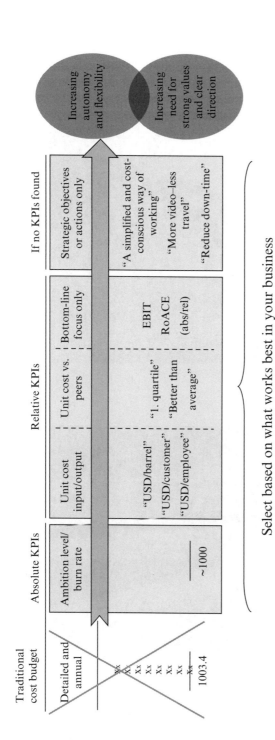

Figure 2.2   Cost management – the KPI menu

17

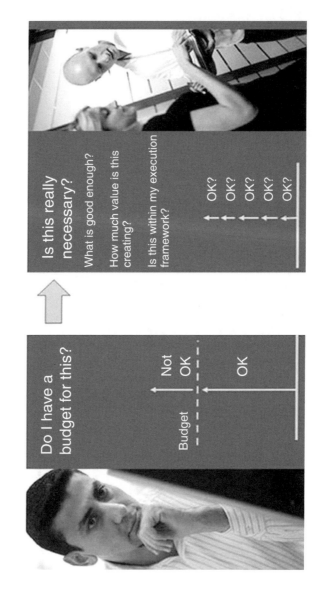

Figure 2.3   A different cost mindset – cost-conscious from the first penny

have the people to do it? This information would typically come from our latest forecasts.

Last, but not least, we have introduced a more holistic *performance evaluation*, with hindsight insights as a key component, and with *how* we have achieved our business results counting for 50 percent. How can we claim to be a values-based organization (as we do) if our values and people and leadership principles are completely absent in target setting and performance evaluation?

We also "pressure-test" measured business result. Key performance indicators (KPIs) are *indicators* only; they often struggle with telling us the full truth. As Albert Einstein put it, "Not everything that counts can be counted, and not everything that can be counted counts." We therefore use hindsight insights – the wealth of information unavailable for us at target-setting time. We ask, for instance: Have we really moved towards our longer-term objectives? Was there a significant tailwind or headwind that should be taken into account? Are results sustainable? Will they stand the test of time?

Some might say that this involves too much subjectivity, and that targets should be set in stone. But let us not fool ourselves. There is a lot more subjectivity involved at target-setting time, with plenty uncertainty about what good performance will look like 15 months down the road. This subjectivity does not magically transform itself to full objectivity just because we finally nail the target to "29.2." And why should we not apply subjectivity at the point in time when we are much more qualified to do so: after the fact, when uncertainty has become certainty?

These performance evaluation principles are examples of how we try to address the entire process, not just the "finance" part. I am based in finance, but we have worked closely with HR to make it all hang well together. This is not always the case. Both finance and HR would claim to work with "performance management," but in many companies they don't talk well together. The two are much to blame for gaps between what is said and done. Finance is pushing management, while HR is preaching leadership. Both need to climb out of their silos and start talking with each other and not just about each other.

I actually don't like the expression "performance management." Put yourself on the receiving end. How does it feel if someone wants to "manage" your performance? Most people feel over-managed and under-led, and for good reasons. Also, our ability to manage performance in today's business realities is actually quite limited. Fortunately, there are a lot of other great things we can do, but this has more to do with *creating conditions* for high performance to take place. This requires a very different mindset, both from managers and from their finance and HR people.

BEYOND BUDGETING AND AMBITION TO ACTION

We do all of what you heard about above in "Ambition to Action," our management process which runs all the way from strategy to people, ending up in what we call "People@Statoil." Ambition to Action is based on the balanced scorecard concept, but combined with the Beyond Budgeting principles the result is a much more unique and robust management model, solving many of the problems often seen in more conventional balanced scorecard implementations (see Figure 2.4).

Beyond Budgeting is a coherent set of leadership and management principles. The name is actually misleading. The purpose is not to get rid of budgets. The purpose is to create more agile and human organizations. This requires significant changes in our management models. But changing how we think about management and leadership also requires a radical overhaul of the budgeting process and the budgeting mindset, because it sits at the core of traditional management. It is about taking reality seriously, not just a dynamic world around us but also people in the organization. You have actually been introduced to many of the Beyond Budgeting principles already (see Table 2.1).

Take a look at bbrt.org for more information about this great model, which has inspired and guided so much of the Statoil journey.

Statoil's Ambition to Action has three purposes:

- to translate strategic choices into more concrete objectives, KPIs and actions (see Figure 2.5);
- to secure flexibility and room to act and perform;
- to activate our values and our people and leadership principles.

Almost all our competitors have management systems which in some form or shape aim to meet the first purpose: creating strategic alignment. But so many ignore or forget the other two purposes, and lose what is key for success: autonomy and agility, trust and transparency, ownership and commitment. If your own Ambition to Action becomes nothing but a landing ground for instructions from above, both ownership and quality tend to walk out the door.

An Ambition to Action starts with an ambition statement, a higher purpose. Call it a vision; call it a mission. We don't care, as long as it ignites and inspires. The Statoil ambition is to be "Globally competitive – an exceptional place to perform and develop." This is translated into different versions across the company. One of our technology teams chose for instance "Execution for today, solutions for the future." In our team, we "challenge traditional management thinking."

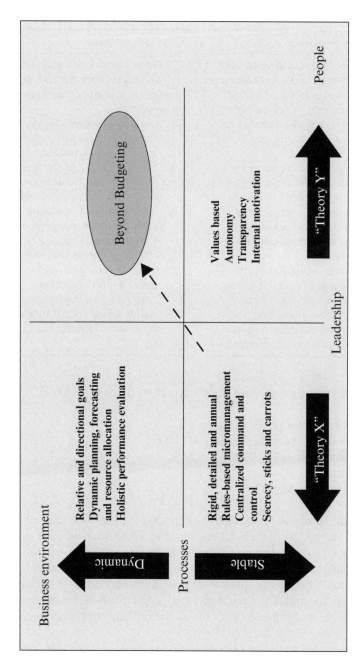

Figure 2.4   We must change both processes and leadership

21

Table 2.1   The Beyond Budgeting principles

Change in leadership	Change in processes
1. Values – Govern through a few clear values, goals and boundaries, not detailed rules and budgets.	7. Goals – Set relative goals for continuous improvement; don't negotiate fixed performance contracts.
2. Performance – Create a high-performance climate based on relative success, not on meeting fixed targets.	8. Rewards – Reward shared success based on relative performance, not on meeting fixed targets.
3. Transparency – Promote open information for self-management; don't restrict it hierarchically.	9. Planning – Make planning a continuous and inclusive process, not a top-down annual event.
4. Organization – Organize as a network of lean, accountable teams, not around centralized functions.	10. Coordination – Coordinate interactions dynamically, not through annual planning cycles.
5. Autonomy – Give teams the freedom and capability to act; don't micromanage them.	11. Resources – Make resources available as needed, not through annual budget allocations.
6. Customers – Focus everyone on improving customer outcomes, not on hierarchical relationships.	12. Controls – Base controls on relative indicators and trends, not on variances against plan.

Ambitions and strategies are translated across five perspectives:

- people and organization;
- health, safety and environment (HSE);
- operations;
- market;
- finance (or results).

You might recognize these from the balanced scorecard concept. We have added HSE because of the business we are in. In addition we have switched the order ("finance" is typically on top), because we know what happens in business review meetings when the agenda is tight and time is limited: "Let us come back to people and organization next time." Those are not the signals to send if we claim to be a people-focused organization. So now "people and organization" sits at the top: another small gap closed between what we say and what we do.

Today, we have around 1400 Ambition to Actions across the company. We try to connect and align all these through *translation* (each team

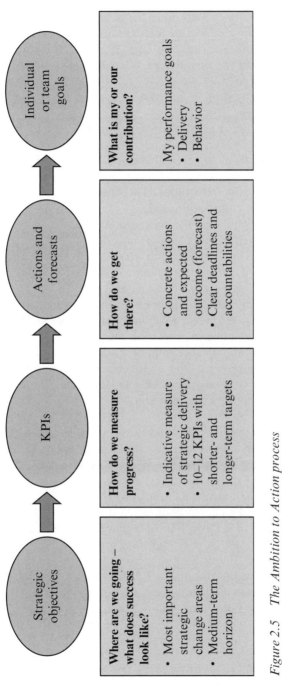

Figure 2.5   The Ambition to Action process

translating relevant Ambition to Actions, typically the one above) instead of cascading (corporate instructing). What should our Ambition to Action look like in order to support other relevant Ambition to Actions, including the one above? What kind of objectives, KPIs and actions do we need? Can we borrow from others or from above, or do we need something sharper because we are one step closer to the front line?

There are of course situations where instructions and cascading from above are necessary. But this should be the exception and not the rule, which also makes it more acceptable when it happens. We are starting to find the right balance between the two, even if some managers still rely too much on cascading. If a translation should go "wrong," which seldom happens, this is of course addressed.

Used in the right way, the balanced scorecard can be a great tool for supporting performance and helping teams to manage themselves. Unfortunately, many scorecard implementations seem to be about reinforcing centralized command and control. It is both tempting and easy to abuse that much bigger menu of management levers for Theory X-driven micromanagement, actually much easier than if you only have a financial budget available for that job. Many managers (and finance people) also bring an accounting mindset with them into these important issues. Alignment is not about target numbers adding up on the decimal; it is about creating inspiring clarity about which mountain to climb. Never forget the power of words in making this happen, even if it is so much easier to let the numbers only do the job.

To help the translation, there is full transparency around all 1400 Ambition to Actions. With a few exceptions of share price-sensitive information, everything is open for all. In most enterprise resource planning (ERP) systems, transparency seems to be reserved for the top. They boast about fancy drill-down functionality, allowing senior executives to monitor the smallest local detail. But why should these people spend time investigating travel and entertainment cost in every local team? What we need is much less of such drill-down, and much more of *drill-across* (what are those people over there doing?) and *drill-up* (what was that strategy again?).

In short, we want Ambition to Action to be something that helps local teams to manage themselves and perform to their full potential, while we at the same time secure sufficient alignment. This means using a different type of glue, and smaller doses: translation instead of cascading. The main purpose should not be centralized command and control.

Here is our CEO Helge Lund:

We have a management model which is very well suited to dealing with turbulence and rapid change. It enables us to act and reprioritize quickly so that we can fend off threats or seize opportunities. This is much more difficult in a traditional "budget world." One of the main principles in Ambition to Action is that Statoil consist of mature, responsible and able people who both can and want to accept responsibility.

IMPLEMENTATION

The years following our 2005 decision were a period of experimenting and learning. We have had some simple implementation principles:

- Design to 80 percent and jump. Not everything can be planned or fully designed up front. Get started, experiment, learn and improve.
- Make sure the case for change and the problems with the old way are well understood before talking about the new way.
- Go for pull, not push. We have no detailed roll-out schedule; we never even used the word. So many are fed up with being on the receiving end of corporate "roll-outs," again and again. Instead, we focus on teams who invite us. Not once did we put our foot in the door because "this is decided." It takes longer, it looks messier, but change becomes real and sustainable.
- We are however present in most of Statoil's leadership programs and also in all introduction programs for new employees.

We continuously experiment with and improve Ambition to Action, on content, on process and on the IT system behind it. In 2007 we merged with a competitor (Hydro). It was a very successful merger and we are absolutely a stronger company today, but it did mean starting almost over again. Still, the number of Ambition to Actions kept increasing, despite not being mandatory. This was a conscious decision, driven by our obsession with making Ambition to Action something that primarily helps teams to help themselves. You can't make that mandatory.

Of course there are skeptics. They come in two groups. The first is the bigger, but also the one that concerns us the less. These are managers who simply are confused. They probably learned very much the opposite during their business studies, and they might have honed these practices over many years. It can be painful to change old ways and your belief system, and we need to respect this. These people just need time, and we give them time. Being confused is part of real change. We are challenging accepted truth and entering unfamiliar territory, which actually is one of the Statoil values, and my favorite!

The second group is smaller, and this is where we find the real skeptics. They are not confused. They fully understand what this is all about, and they don't like it. This is so much against everything they believe in. Some may also pay lip service to the new principles, so you can't even engage in a discussion. This group still exists, but is getting smaller and smaller. Some leave, some retire, and every day that passes makes it more difficult for those still with us to abort the journey.

THE JOURNEY CONTINUES – LEAVING THE CALENDAR YEAR

On the contrary, we are moving on. In 2010 we were ready for the next step: escaping the calendar straitjacket. The purpose was to make Ambition to Action even more useful and relevant for all our business teams.

In April we went to the executive committee with our proposal to kick out the calendar wherever possible. We got a strong and clear green light. On our way out of the meeting, one of the executive VPs whispered to us: "Closer to a standing ovation you will not come in this room." It was a good day, but only the start of another mountain to climb!

January–December is an artificial construct from a business point of view. For some it is too short, for others too long. Even when a business has seasonal rhythms, the winter season is cut in two because we pass "year-end." Imagine a finance person meeting a fisherman and asking him about the rhythm of his work. "Well," the fisherman replies, "I am at sea for five months, and then I am home for five months." "So what do you do then the rest of the year?" the finance person wonders. Something is wrong, right? Absolutely, but maybe more in the head of the finance person than in the working rhythm of the fisherman.

Our statutory accounting and our communication with external parties and the capital markets will of course still need to be calendar oriented, but our internal processes could still have more natural rhythms. We want to free ourselves from the artificial, annual "stop/start/stop/start." We want to give our teams the opportunity to run their business more continuously, with update frequencies, time horizons and evaluation points driven by their own business flow.

We have however an industry-specific challenge. A license to explore and produce oil and gas in a defined geographical area is for risk-sharing and learning purposes typically awarded to a joint venture of companies. One of them acts as the "operator," which according to industry standards has to provide the other partners with a traditional, annual budget. Statoil has this role for around 80 percent of total production in Norway. We have been able to make this process towards our partners somewhat less rigid than before, but we envy companies that don't have to operate in such a set-up. It is a complication, but not a showstopper. So everything you read about here is how we try to manage internally, despite such external requirements.

The main principles in our new and fully dynamic process are as follows:

- *No annual versions* of Ambition to Action. Strategic objectives, KPIs, KPI targets and forecasts can be changed when deemed necessary by teams themselves.
- *Event-driven changes*, not calendar-driven. Events can be external or internal, and the definition is simple: "whatever is important for your team."
- *Simple change and coordination controls.* Big changes should be approved one level above, smaller changes only informed about. Big or small, always inform other affected units if necessary. Teams sort out between themselves what is big and what is small.
- *Target and forecast horizons* should reflect lead times, urgency, uncertainty and complexity in the different businesses.

What has triggered most questions is the possibility of changing targets at any point in time because something happened and they lost their meaning. That could mean "impossible to achieve" or "a piece of cake," or also "not relevant anymore." A target should motivate and inspire. It is not a goal in itself, but one way of achieving the ultimate goal of the best possible performance, given the circumstances. Targets set by teams themselves typically do this job much better than those coming as instructions from above.

Some have concerns about this possibility of changing targets being abused. There is just one way to find out, and that is to try it out. We have provided some help and guidance. First, there is full transparency; it won't happen in darkness. Second, you still need approval for big changes. And, third, we remind people about the fairness of the holistic performance evaluation, where changes in assumptions can be taken into account. You don't need to change your target every time assumptions change. A relative target is, by the way, much more robust and self-regulating in this respect. If conditions change, they typically do so for your peers as well. We also ask teams to look at their track-record of changing targets. If it always is about reducing ambition levels and never the opposite, that is an issue the team should reflect on.

It is still early days, and we don't yet have enough cases to learn from. What we do know is that there will be incidents which might smell of "abuse." Those should be firmly dealt with, but are no evidence of failure requiring a return to the old way.

The *dynamic forecasting* we are introducing is different from what is often called *rolling forecasting*. A rolling forecast is done on a fixed frequency and on a fixed time horizon across the company, typically quarterly and five quarters ahead. We were about to introduce this in Statoil as well. Then it struck us that rolling forecasting (which is much better than traditional "against the wall forecasting") still has a "fixed" frequency and time horizon, which might be too often and too long for some and the opposite for others. We wanted forecasts to be updated on an event-based and not a calendar-based rhythm, *when something happens*, and *as far ahead as relevant* for each unit. We called this dynamic forecasting.

If a unit one level up needs a forecast with a longer time horizon, it should normally be their responsibility to "fill the hole" with a "good enough" forecast. Why should all teams be forced to look ten years ahead because aggregated this is a relevant time horizon for an oil company? For our oil trading people, anything beyond three weeks can be quite foggy, while three years is very much on the short side for those bringing new oil and gas discoveries into production.

Also targets can now have shorter or longer time horizons, from months to years, again driven by lead times and complexity.

Note that "dynamic" doesn't necessarily mean more often. It means at the right time. For some it could actually mean less often.

Performance against Ambition to Action is reviewed monthly or quarterly in business review meetings. An individual performance evaluation will still take place at year-end. Some would then look back on a very dynamic Ambition to Action, others on the opposite. A log of Ambition to Action (which actually is an internally developed web interface sitting on top of a global SAP solution) keeps an overview of changes made.

Some have however questioned the annual review. Why is once a year in January always the natural point for evaluating performance? Is it only because of the link to pay? Is that a good enough reason? Are there alternatives, again driven by natural business milestones, project completions and so on?

We hope our new and more dynamic process (see Figure 2.6) also will make the current autumn planning much leaner and one day even obsolete. This planning work, which is not about budgets but about action planning and understanding the consequences of actions through unbiased and expected outcome forecasts, is still too time-consuming. Our goal is more of a "living" forecast where those needing forecast information

More event-driven
— less calendar-driven
More translation
— less cascading
More relative
— fewer absolute KPIs
More cost-conscious
— less cost-cutting

Figure 2.6   Towards a simpler, more dynamic and self-regulating Ambition to Action process

can tap into the latest information available. This can be done both regularly and ad hoc.

It is still early days and we still have many questions. All those situations which were so well regulated and understood in the old process, how should they now be handled? How often? How far out? What is "big" and what is not? All this uncertainty has however been well accepted. People are enthusiastic about the learning and adjusting phase we now are in. They would rather be part of finding out than just being told. There was actually more anxiety back in 2005 when we abolished traditional budgeting, even if a number of companies already had taken that step before we did.

Getting out of the calendar year will undoubtedly take time. Many are still cautious about utilizing these new opportunities. The calendar is not just "hard-wired" into our brains; it is also still highly present in a number of other processes in the company, many of which we now also are addressing. Some of these will need to continue on an annual cycle, with our statutory accounting as the obvious example. But, again, this is not a showstopper.

When we started out in 2011, our assumption was that we could still produce a business plan document for the board once a year. This would be done at a corporate level. We would "protect" the business areas and simply "tap into" their dynamic forecasting updates.

This was a mistake. The sheer knowledge in the organization that such a prestigious document still existed triggered a lot of unnecessary work. Many went into annual planning mode with a "next year and blank sheets" mindset. So in 2012 we agreed with the board to drop this document. Now we use the monthly performance report to keep the board more continuously informed about changes in longer-term forecasts and about strategic business issues that previously were addressed once a year in the business plan document. We recently renamed it as "performance perspectives" to underline its even stronger forward-looking focus.

We have tried to find other companies that have taken similar steps of radically challenging the calendar rhythm. We are convinced there is someone out there, but we are still searching. Many have introduced rolling forecasting, but we are aiming for a much more fundamental break with the calendar year.

There are other exciting things happening. Our IT colleagues actually started out on their own, inspired by the great lean and agile thinking which now is transforming how system development projects are run across the world. One such approach, "Scrum," was introduced in Statoil several years ago. We stay in close contact because there is so much common ground, both in what we rebel against and in what we are trying to do instead. They also realize that a company can never be fully successful with agile software development unless "agile" also becomes the way the whole organization is run.

LEADERSHIP IMPLICATIONS

Our new and more dynamic principles are in no way *easier* than those we are trying to leave. We have spent countless hours in management teams and on leadership training, helping Statoil managers to reflect on the leadership implications, not just from leaving the calendar year but from all the other steps taken on this journey. Here are some of our key messages:

- You have more autonomy and flexibility, but also higher accountability for results.
- Use your autonomy; don't delegate upwards – and let it pass on to your teams.
- Don't give up when trust is abused, but react firmly to those who do.

Some managers struggle with their new freedom. If you don't like to make decisions, then a detailed, annual budget and tiny decisions authorities are actually a great thing. Decisions are made for you, both what to do and how much it should cost. While the vast majority of Statoil managers highly appreciate the new and increased room to act and perform, some struggle with passing it all on to teams in their own organization. "I can of course be trusted, but . . ." We can't instruct them to do so; at least we shouldn't start there. You can't get rid of command and control through command and control. They need to find out themselves why passing on is a good idea. Eventually, most do, even if it can take time. For some, the excuse for not letting go can be incidents they have experienced which they believe prove that "this trust thing doesn't work." This is the wrong conclusion. We should deal resolutely with those who abuse trust, but should not take the tempting and easy option of retreating to the old way. In a free society, we are not sending everybody to jail because someone violates the rules of the game.

DOES IT WORK?

It is still early days for measuring sustainable results, even if we are convinced that there are positive performance effects. But it might not be a coincidence that we perform pretty well against a peer group of 15 other oil and gas companies that we set our targets against. We have actually performed better than the average of them for several years, except when we had our big merger in 2007. It might also not be a coincidence that we are Norway's most popular employer among technology, finance and IT graduates or that we did pretty well on Fortune 500, Transparency International and similar rankings.

We have however never attempted to calculate the business case. We simply know this is right and good for performance. It is a similar case to that of safety. There are things an organization should do simply because you know it is the right thing to do.

Everything you have heard about here is decided and described in our "Statoil Book," a small booklet given to all employees (on these kinds of important issues we believe in the physical paper format, but it is of course also available on our intranet). But, as you have heard, "decided and described" does not mean that everything has yet reached every corner and every head in Statoil. These are major changes. They will take time. This is no quick fix.

Our discussions are seldom about going back. They are about how to make it all work even better. Of course we have our dark days, when we hear words or observe behaviors echoing the past that we are trying to leave. We have however an effective medicine for those days. We just think back on where we were five or ten years ago. That always helps. If we make similar advances over the next five years, then . . .

I am proud to work for a company where we are encouraged to challenge accepted truth and enter unfamiliar territory. We are on an exciting journey, which is in no way over and where the direction is clearer than the destination, if there really is one.

Welcome on board!

NOTE

*   Credits: Jeremy Hope and Robin Fraser, founders of Beyond Budgeting Round Table (BBRT); Jan Wallander, former CEO of Handelsbanken, Beyond Budgeting pioneer; Peter Bunce, BBRT. This article was first published at Managementexchange. com, and won a 2012 Harvard Business Review/McKinsey award for Management Innovation.

BIBLIOGRAPHY

Bogsnes, Bjarte (2009), *Implementing Beyond Budgeting: Unlocking the Performance Potential*, Hoboken, NJ: John Wiley & Sons.

Hope, Jeremy and Robin Fraser (2003), *Beyond Budgeting*, Boston, MA: Harvard Business School Press.

Hope, Jeremy, Peter Bunce and Franz Röösli (2011), *The Leader's Dilemma*, Hoboken, NJ: John Wiley & Sons.

Morlidge, Steve and Steve Player (2009), *Future Ready*, Chichester: John Wiley & Sons.

3. Environmental uncertainty and the use of budgets

Niels Sandalgaard

INTRODUCTION

In recent years, the use of budgets has been criticized as a management control tool, and an alternative – the Beyond Budgeting model (Hope and Fraser, 2003) – has been presented. As pointed out by Hansen et al. (2003), critics claim that the assumptions underlying the budget are often quickly outdated, making budgets less useful in turbulent conditions. Likewise, Ekholm and Wallin (2000) note that environmental uncertainty is often used as an argument for abandoning budgets. Despite these criticisms, empirical studies indicate that budgeting is still the dominant method of profit planning and control (Libby and Lindsey, 2010; Sandalgaard, 2012).

The discussion of the relevance of budgeting in a competitive and uncertain environment is of great relevance. As pointed out by Hartmann (2000, 2005) and Ekholm and Wallin (2011), the findings are mixed and inconsistent regarding the connection between environmental uncertainty and reliance on accounting performance measures. Some studies find a positive relationship between uncertainty and the use of budgets (e.g., Ezzamel, 1990), while other studies find a negative relationship (e.g., Govindarajan, 1984). Notably, most studies focus only on the use of budgets for performance evaluation, while fewer studies focus on the use of budgets for other reasons (Hansen and Van der Stede, 2004).

This chapter, which is based on data from a cross-sectional survey of large Danish companies, focuses on the relationship between environmental uncertainty and the reasons for using budgets. This chapter takes the study by Hansen and Van der Stede (2004), which focuses on competition as an environmental variable, as its point of departure. This chapter contributes by giving an extra dimension to uncertainty by also focusing on the effect of unpredictability on different reasons for using budgets. The chapter also contributes to the contingency-based budgeting literature by investigating how different dimensions of environmental uncertainty affect the ways in which budgets are used. The results indicate that companies in more unpredictable environments use budgets for performance evaluation to a lesser extent. Furthermore, the results indicate that companies in more competitive environments are more likely to use budgets for planning-related purposes.

The chapter is structured in the following way. In the next section, the relevant literature on reasons to budget and the relevant literature within the contingency-based budgeting field are reviewed, and hypotheses are made. In the following section, the method is described, followed by a discussion of the empirical results. Finally, the conclusions are presented.

LITERATURE REVIEW AND DEVELOPMENT OF HYPOTHESES

Reasons to Budget

Numerous reasons to budget are mentioned in the textbook literature. For example, Anthony and Govindarajan (2006) state that budgets are used to fine-tune strategic plans, for coordination purposes, for assigning responsibility and as a basis for performance evaluation. Horngren et al. (2007) point out that budgets are used for re-evaluating existing activities, evaluating possible new activities, communicating objectives, coordinating actions across the organization and providing benchmarks for the evaluation of subsequent performance. In connection with their study of reasons to budget, Hansen and Van der Stede (2004) involve practitioners in order to derive a list of reasons to budget:

1. operational planning;
2. strategy formation;
3. communication of goals; and
4. performance evaluation.

Hansen and Van der Stede (2004) note that their study focuses on budget preparation in organizational units. They argue that additional reasons to budget could be found at higher organizational levels. In that connection, they mention two additional reasons:

5. allocation of resources; and
6. authorizing spending.

Perceived Environmental Uncertainty

According to Tymon et al. (1998: 35), Duncan (1972) was the first to use the term "perceived environmental uncertainty" (PEU). Tymon et al. (1998: 27) stress that it is the top managers' perception of uncertainty that is important. In other words, the *perception* of uncertainty, rather than *actual* uncertainty, affects decision making, and it is the perception of those able to affect decision making (e.g., top managers) that is important. Tymon et al. (1998) divide the behavioral accounting research within PEU into a group based on Duncan (1972) and another group based on Miles and Snow (1978) and Khandwalla (1972).

Duncan (1972) measures environmental uncertainty on two dimensions: complexity and dynamism. High complexity "indicates that the factors in the decision unit's environment are large in numbers," while dynamism relates to whether these factors "remain basically the same or are in a continual process of change" (Duncan, 1972: 315–16). In Miles and Snow (1978), environmental uncertainty focuses on the predictability of different dimensions of the environment, while Khandwalla (1972) focuses on the competition in the environment. Despite Khandwalla's focus on competition, Tymon et al. (1998: 38) still classify this as a measure of PEU.

However, according to Otley (1980: 423), one contingent variable "stands out, namely unpredictability (variously referred to as uncertainty, non-routineness, dynamism etc.). Even complexity and size may be important at least in part because of the unpredictability associated with them." Furthermore, unpredictability arguably becomes especially important in connection with budgeting. As pointed out by Chenhall and Morris (1986: 18), environmental uncertainty makes planning problematic and affects the usefulness of budgets for control purposes. The PEU view adopted in this chapter is based on Miles and Snow (1978) and on Khandwalla (1972) in the sense that the focus is on unpredictability and competition.

Competition and the Use of Budgets

Hansen and Van der Stede (2004) find a positive relationship between the degree of competition in the external environment and the use of budgets for strategy formation, and between competition and the use of budgets for communication of goals. Furthermore, they find a negative relationship between the degree of competition and the use of budgets for performance evaluation.

Khandwalla (1972: 275) focuses explicitly on the environmental uncertainty caused by competition and points out that greater competition leads to a greater need "to evaluate whether production, marketing, finance, etc. are operating according to expectations." Overall, Khandwalla (1972) finds a positive connection between competition and the use of the majority of the financial controls investigated, including those with the closest relation to budgeting (flexible budgeting and standard costing). Sharma (2002) finds that competition is mainly positively associated with the use of budgets, even though the results are significant only for the forecasting element of budgeting. Similarly, Otley (1978) notes that tight control may be suitable for difficult conditions and that a rigid evaluation style gives the most accurate budget estimates in a tough environment.

These empirical findings are in line with arguments found in contingency theory. For example, Pfeffer and Leblebici (1973), who specifically focus on competition, point out that a company facing a high degree of competition has a greater need for coordination and control, as it "cannot afford to make many major mistakes, nor can it be substantially less efficient than its important competitors" (Pfeffer and Leblebici, 1973: 270). Likewise, Miles and Snow (1978: 44) argue that, "given its emphasis on stability and efficiency, the defender cannot afford deviations from prescribed behaviors."

If we apply these contingency arguments to management accounting, the resulting hypothesis is that when competition is high, there is a focus on efficiency and, therefore, a greater need for planning and control, that is, budgeting. This is in line with the propositions made by Chenhall (2007) in his review of the contingency-based management accounting literature. Chenhall (2007) proposes that the more hostile and turbulent the environment, the greater the emphasis on formal controls and traditional budgets.

Based on the empirical studies discussed above, it is hypothesized that competition will lead to greater use of budgets, regardless of the reason for using budgets. The first hypothesis is therefore formulated as follows:

H1. There is a positive relationship between competition in the environment and the use of budgets for all reasons to budget.

Unpredictability and the Use of Budgets

Research also shows that increased uncertainty leads to a decreased focus on budgets. As argued by Chenhall and Morris (1986: 18), environmental uncertainty makes planning problematic because future events become more unpredictable, and unpredictability also affects the usefulness of static budgets for control purposes because the initial goals become outdated. Along these lines, Ekholm and Wallin (2011) find a negative relationship between unpredictability and the perceived usefulness of fixed annual budgets, while Govindarajan (1984) finds that managers facing higher unpredictability use a subjective evaluation style rather than a formula-based approach to performance evaluation. Sharma (2002) finds that companies in an unpredictable environment use budgets less for communication purposes.

Early contingency theory (Burns and Stalker, 1961) pointed to a fit between an organization's environment and its structure, suggesting that an organic structure was more appropriate in an uncertain environment. The contingency argument in this regard was that an organization needs to be more adaptive to changing conditions in an uncertain environment. Similar arguments are made in the Beyond Budgeting literature (e.g., Bunce et al., 1995; Hope and Fraser, 2003; Bogsnes, 2009) and, according to Otley (1999), increasing environmental uncertainty is one of the main arguments for the abandonment of traditional annual budgets.

Based on his review of the contingency-based management accounting literature, Chenhall (2007) proposes that a more uncertain environment is associated with a management accounting system that is more open and externally focused. This proposition implies relatively less use of budgets in an uncertain environment. Furthermore, Hartmann (2000) points out that uncertainty is often believed to make it difficult to set budget targets or to apply the controllability principle when evaluating performance. Based on these arguments, the following hypothesis is made:

H2. There is a negative relationship between unpredictability in the environment and the use of budgets for all reasons to budget.

METHOD

This study is based on data from a survey distributed to large Danish companies (companies with more than 200 employees). The sample was randomly selected from the GreensOnline database, which is a Danish database containing contact information and financial data for the largest Danish companies. A sample of 50 percent of the relevant companies was randomly selected, which gave a sample size of 608 companies.

Prior to its distribution, the questionnaire was tested on three practitioners and on academic colleagues, and adjustments were made based on the feedback received. The questionnaire was sent to the CFO in each of the selected companies. There were 246 usable questionnaires returned, which gives an overall response rate of 40.5 percent. As not all respondents answered all questions in the questionnaire, the response rate for the individual questions differs.

As one follow-up round was undertaken to enhance the response rate, a test for non-response bias was conducted by comparing the answers of first-round respondents (early respondents) to those of second-round respondents (late respondents). An independent samples t-test gave no indication of non-response bias. The questions used for this study are listed in the Appendix. The questionnaire also contained questions not used in this study. Details of the measures used in this study as well as respondent characteristics are provided in Tables 3.1 and 3.2.

Measure of Perceived Environmental Uncertainty

As previously discussed, perceived environmental uncertainty is the main independent variable in this study. Gordon and Narayanan's (1984) method for measuring PEU was used as the starting point. As pointed out by Chenhall (2007), this measure includes questions focusing on competition and unpredictability. Accordingly, I have separated the measure used by Gordon and Narayanan (1984) into one measure focusing on competition and one measure focusing on unpredictability. Furthermore, some of the questions were rephrased so that they better fit these two groups, and two new questions were added: one concerning competition in distribution channels and one concerning the predictability of raw material availability. The respondents were asked to indicate the levels of competition and unpredictability using a seven-point Likert scale.

As argued by Ekholm and Wallin (2011), measures of perceived environmental uncertainty should typically be regarded as formative measures rather than reflective measures. Therefore, the use of Cronbach's alpha is inappropriate. Accordingly, the low Cronbach's alphas for competition and unpredictability in Table 3.1 should be ignored.

Measures of the Control Variables

Size and decentralization are included as control variables, as are dependence and comparability among budgeting units. The degree to which the organization is organic (rather than mechanistic; see Burns and Stalker, 1961) is also included.

Size was measured as the natural logarithm of the number of employees, as Chenhall (2007: 184) points out that number of employees is the appropriate measure when considering the effectiveness of budgets for coordination of activities. The decentralization measure used by Gordon and Narayanan (1984) was used in a modified version, in which the questions were rephrased to make them fit into the questionnaire. Furthermore, a question focusing on the delegation of authority with regard to decisions

Table 3.1   Details of the measures and respondent characteristics

Details of measures used			Distribution of respondents by size			Distribution of respondents by industry		
Independent variables	Number of questions used	Cronbach's alpha	Size	Frequency	Percentage	Industry	Frequency	Percentage
PEU: Competition	5	0.521	<301	69	28%	Production	94	38%
PEU: Unpredictability	6	0.553	301–500	60	24%	Construction	24	10%
Decentralization	7	0.723	501–1000	62	25%	Retail	14	6%
Organic	2	0.655	1001–5000	45	18%	Other trading	24	10%
Comparability of budget units	1	–	5001–	10	4%	Transport	26	11%
Dependence of budget units	1	–	Total	246	100%	Consulting	15	6%
Size	1	–				Other	49	20%
						Total	246	100%

Table 3.2 Descriptive statistics and correlations

	N	Theoretical range	Actual range	Mean	Std. deviation	Pearson correlations					
						1	2	3	4	5	6
1. PEU: Competition	245	1–7	2.0–7.0	4.91	0.90						
2. PEU: Unpredictability	244	1–7	1.7–6.5	3.66	0.71	0.094					
3. Decentralization	245	1–7	1.0–6.6	3.45	0.97	−0.007	0.003				
4. Organic	245	1–7	1.0–7.0	2.75	1.39	0.037	0.035	0.021			
5. Comparability	242	1–7	1.0–7.0	4.16	1.86	−0.032	−0.057	−0.104	0.031		
6. Dependence	240	1–7	1.0–7.0	4.50	1.59	0.057	0.119	−0.192**	−0.146*	0.035	
7. LNsize	246	–	–	6.43	1.05	0.112	−0.053	0.220**	−0.093	0.099	−0.004

Notes:
* Significant at the 0.05 level(two-tailed test).
** Significant at the 0.01 level(two-tailed test).

41

on budget overruns was added. In order to enhance reliability, three questions were left out of the decentralization measure: one concerning managerial style, one concerning whether the company had an employee's manual and one concerning whether formal descriptions of job tasks existed. The latter two of these questions were used to compose a measure of the extent to which the organization is organic.

Comparability and dependence among the budgeting units were measured using simple one-item measures. The respondents were asked to indicate the degree of comparability and the degree of dependence among the budgeting units on a seven-point Likert scale.

Measure of the Dependent Variable

The reasons to budget listed above were used in the questionnaire with modifications based on feedback from the pre-test on practitioners and colleagues. "Operational planning" was reformulated as "planning, coordination etc." and "resource allocation" was reformulated as "investment and resource allocation." Furthermore, "strategy formation" was changed to "implementation of a strategy plan." The respondents were asked to indicate the extent to which they used each of these reasons to budget on a seven-point Likert scale. The descriptive statistics for the reason to budget are provided in Table 3.3.

In order to investigate the possible presence of underlying dimensions regarding the reasons to budget, a factor analysis (with varimax rotation) was conducted on the six reasons to budget. As shown in Table 3.4, "performance evaluation" loads on factor 2, while the other reasons load on factor 1. As the variable "authorization of spending" has a low loading, it was removed from the remainder of the analysis. As a result, the Cronbach's alpha for factor 1 increased from 0.663 to 0.734.

One might argue that all of the reasons to budget related to factor 1 are concerned with planning. In this regard, Hansen and Van der Stede (2004) suggest that "operational planning" and "strategy formation" relate to short-term planning, while "communication of goals" relates to the communication of plans. As "allocation of resources" could also be regarded as a planning activity, factor 1 is labeled "planning." Factor 2 is labeled "performance evaluation."

THE RESULTS

Two linear regressions were undertaken to test the hypotheses. One regression used the performance evaluation factor as the dependent variable,

Table 3.3 Descriptive statistics for reasons to budget

	N	Theoretical range	Actual range	Mean	Std. deviation	Pearson correlations					
						1	2	3	4	5	6
1. Planning, coordination, etc.	245	1–7	1–7	5.16	1.24						
2. Implementation of strategy plan	245	1–7	1–7	4.84	1.45	0.461**					
3. Communication of goals	245	1–7	1–7	5.24	1.26	0.293**	0.423**				
4. Performance evalution	245	1–7	1–7	4.81	1.55	0.151*	0.181**	0.288**			
5. Investment and resource allocation	245	1–7	1–7	5.26	1.30	0.529**	0.459**	0.280**	0.171**		
6. Authorization of spending	245	1–7	1–7	4.64	1.55	0.150*	0.099	0.076	0.005	0.187**	

Notes:
* Significant at the 0.05 level (two-tailed test).
** Significant at the 0.01 level (two-tailed test).

Table 3.4   Factor analysis of reasons to budget

Reason to budget	Factor	
	1	2
4. Performance evaluation	0.258	0.705
1. Planning, coordination, etc.	0.775	−0.008
5. Investment and resource allocation	0.786	−0.038
2. Implementation of strategy plan	0.744	0.191
3. Communication of goals	0.568	0.458
6. Authorization of spending	0.422	−0.607

while the other used the planning factor as the dependent variable. The variables related to PEU (competition and unpredictability), and the control variables were included as independent variables in the regressions. Consequently, the following regression was used:

$$Y = a + b_1X_1 + b_2X_2 + b_3X_3 + b_4X_4 + b_5X_5 + b_6X_6 + b_7X_7 + e \quad (3.1)$$

In the first regression, Y was the performance evaluation factor, while Y was the planning factor in the second regression. In both regressions, X_1 was competition, X_2 was unpredictability, X_3 was decentralization, X_4 was organic, X_5 was comparability, X_6 was dependence and X_7 was LNsize. Finally, e and a were the error term and the constant, respectively.

The results of these regressions can be seen in Table 3.5. There is a significant positive relationship between the degree of competition in the environment and the use of budgets for planning purposes. This result provides partial support for Hypothesis 1. Contrary to Hansen and Van der Stede (2004), the degree of competition is not negatively related to the use of budgets for performance evaluation. Furthermore, there is a highly significant, negative relationship between the degree of unpredictability in the environment and the use of budgets for performance evaluation. However, there is no sign of a significant relationship between unpredictability and the use of budgets for planning purposes. Thus, the results are only partially supportive of Hypothesis 2.

In terms of the effects of the control variables, there is a highly significant negative relationship between the use of budgets for planning purposes and the extent to which the organization is organic. As budgets are mechanistic by nature (Chenhall, 2007), it is not surprising that a more organic organization has fewer formal planning procedures.

Table 3.5 Regression results

	Unstandardized coefficients:		Standardized coefficients::	t	Sig.
	B	Std. error	Beta		
Y = Use of the budget for performance evalution					
(Constant)	5.263	1.036		5.083	0.000
PEU: Competition	0.029	0.116	0.016	0.252	0.801
PEU: Unpredictability	-0.529	0.143	-0.239	-3.701	0.000
Decentralization	-0.072	0.110	-0.044	-0.652	0.515
Organic	-0.055	0.073	-0.049	-0.760	0.448
Comparability	0.096	0.054	0.114	1.758	0.080
Dependence	0.063	0.065	0.064	0.972	0.332
LNsize	0.161	0.101	0.106	1.595	0.112
$R^2 = 0.099$; Adj. $R^2 = 0.071$; F = 3.567; p = 0.001					
Y = Use of the budget for planning					
(Constant)	3.677	0.595		6.184	0.000
PEU: Competition	0.170	0.066	0.166	2.567	0.011
PEU: Unpredictability	0.017	0.082	0.013	0.205	0.838
Decentralization	0.042	0.064	0.045	0.666	0.506
Organic	-0.139	0.042	-0.216	-3.338	0.001
Comparability	0.046	0.031	0.096	1.485	0.139
Dependence	0.048	0.037	0.084	1.279	0.202
LNsize	0.045	0.056	0.053	0.795	0.428
$R^2 = 0.096$; Adj. $R^2 = 0.068$; F = 3.446; p = 0.002					

CONCLUSION

The results presented here indicate that different forms of environmental uncertainty affect the way in which budgeting is used. The results indicate that a higher degree of unpredictability is related to less use of budgets for performance evaluation, while a higher degree of competition is related to greater use of budgets for planning-related purposes. Therefore, the results are in line with the typical argument found in the literature that "Uncertainty causes predictions to be difficult and thus hinders budgetary target setting" (Hartmann, 2000: 471). The practical implication is that organizations operating in unpredictable environments should find ways of evaluating performance other than comparing performance against budget targets.

One potential solution could be adopting a greater degree of subjective performance evaluation, which could take the changing circumstances into consideration (see Govindarajan, 1984). Another possibility might be to use relative performance evaluation, thereby filtering out the effect of common uncertainties (see Holmstrom, 1982). This is in line with the suggestion found in the Beyond Budgeting model (e.g., Hope and Fraser, 2003), which proposes abandoning budget targets and relying on relative performance evaluations with some element of subjectivity.

The result indicating a positive relationship between competition and the use of the budget for planning purposes shows that, as competition increases, formal planning procedures are needed to a greater extent. This is in line with Chenhall's (2007) proposition that the emphasis on formal controls and traditional budgets will be greater in environments that are more hostile. Notably, however, there is no significant relationship between competition and the purpose of performance evaluation. I therefore suggest that future research should focus on the entire management control package (Malmi and Brown, 2008) in order to investigate whether increased competition leads to an increase in the use of other performance evaluation methods.

As mentioned above, contingency theory provides mixed evidence concerning the relationship between uncertainty and the use of budgets. This chapter indicates that one possible explanation for this inconclusive evidence could be that the different studies measure perceived environmental uncertainty in different ways. Some studies use a measure focusing on competition (e.g., Khandwalla, 1972; Hansen and Van der Stede, 2004), while others focus on dynamism and complexity (e.g., Chenhall and Morris, 1986) or on predictability (e.g., Govindarajan, 1984; Ekholm and Wallin, 2011). The results in this chapter indicate that different forms of environmental uncertainty affect budget use in different ways. Therefore, future research should be focusing on the effects that different elements of environmental uncertainty have on the use of budgets.

REFERENCES

Anthony, R.N. and V. Govindarajan (2006), *Management Control Systems*, Boston, MA: McGraw-Hill.

Bogsnes, B. (2009), *Implementing Beyond Budgeting: Unlocking the Performance Potential*, Hoboken, NJ: John Wiley & Sons.

Bunce, P., R. Fraser and L. Woodcock (1995), "Advanced budgeting: A journey to advanced management systems," *Management Accounting Research*, **6**, 253–65.

Burns, T. and G.M. Stalker (1961), *The Management of Innovations*, London: Tavistock.

Chenhall, R.H. (2007), "Theorizing contingencies in management control systems research," in C.S. Chapman, A.G. Hopwood and M.D. Shields (eds.), *Handbook of Management Accounting Research*, vol. 1, Oxford: Elsevier, pp. 163–205.

Chenhall, R.H. and D. Morris (1986), "The impact of structure, environment and interdependence on the perceived usefulness of management accounting systems," *Accounting Review*, **61**, 16–35.

Duncan, R.B. (1972), "Characteristics of organizational environments and perceived environmental uncertainty," *Administrative Science Quarterly*, **17**, 313–27.

Ekholm, B.-G. and J. Wallin (2000), "Is the annual budget really dead?," *European Accounting Review*, **9** (4), 519–39.

Ekholm, B.-G. and J. Wallin (2011), "The impact of uncertainty and strategy on the perceived usefulness of fixed and flexible budgets," *Journal of Business Finance and Accounting*, **38** (1), 145–64.

Ezzamel, M. (1990), "The impact of environmental uncertainty, managerial autonomy and size on budget characteristics," *Management Accounting Research*, **1**, 181–97.

Gordon, L.A. and V.K. Narayanan (1984), "Management accounting systems, perceived environmental uncertainty and organization structure: An empirical investigation," *Accounting, Organizations and Society*, **9** (1), 33–47.

Govindarajan, V. (1984), "Appropriateness of accounting data in performance evaluation: An empirical examination of environmental uncertainty as intervening variable," *Accounting, Organizations and Society*, **9** (2), 125–35.

Hansen, S.C. and W.A. Van der Stede (2004), "Multiple facets of budgeting: An exploratory analysis," *Management Accounting Research*, **15**, 415–39.

Hansen, S.C., D.T. Otley and W.A. Van der Stede (2003), "Practice developments in budgeting: An overview and research perspective," *Journal of Management Accounting Research*, **15**, 95–116.

Hartmann, F.G. (2000), "The appropriateness of RAPM: Toward the further development of theory," *Accounting, Organizations and Society*, **25**, 451–82.

Hartmann, F. (2005), "The effects of tolerance for ambiguity and uncertainty on the appropriateness of accounting performance measures," *Abacus*, **41** (3), 241–64.

Holmstrom, B. (1982), "Moral hazard in teams," *Bell Journal of Economics*, **13** (2), 324–40.

Hope, J. and R. Fraser (2003), *Beyond Budgeting: How Managers Can Break Free from the Annual Performance Trap*, Boston, MA: Harvard Business School Press.

Horngren, C.T., G.L. Sundem, W.O. Stratton., J. Schatzberg and D. Burgstahler (2007), *Introduction to Management Accounting*, 14th edn., Upper Saddle River, NJ: Prentice Hall.

Khandwalla, P.N. (1972), "The effect of different types of competition on the use of management controls," *Journal of Accounting Research*, **10** (2), 275–85.

Libby, T. and R.M. Lindsey (2010), "Beyond Budgeting or budgeting reconsidered: A survey of North American budgeting practice," *Management Accounting Research*, **21** (1), 56–75.

Malmi, T. and D.A. Brown (2008), "Management control systems as a package – opportunities, challenges and research directions," *Management Accounting Research*, **19**, 287–300.

Miles, R.E. and C.C. Snow (1978), *Organizational Strategy, Structure and Process*, New York: McGraw-Hill.

Otley, D.T. (1978), "Budget use and managerial performance," *Journal of Accounting Research*, **16** (1), 122–49.

Otley, D. (1980), "The contingency theory of management accounting: Achievement and prognosis," *Accounting, Organizations and Society*, **5** (4), 413–28.

Otley, D. (1999), "Performance management: A framework for management control systems research," *Management Accounting Research*, **10**, 363–82.

Pfeffer, J. and H. Leblebici (1973), "The effect of competition on some dimensions of organizational structure," *Social Forces*, **52** (2), 268–79.

Sandalgaard, N. (2012), "Uncertainty and budgets: An empirical investigation," *Baltic Journal of Management*, **7** (4), 397–415.

Sharma, D.S. (2002), "The differential effect of environmental dimensionality, size and structure on budget system characteristics in hotels," *Management Accounting Research*, **13** (1), 101–30.

Tymon, W.G., D.E. Stout and K.N. Shaw (1998), "Critical analysis and recommendations regarding the role of perceived environmental uncertainty in behavioral accounting research," *Behavioral Research in Accounting*, **10**, 23–46.

APPENDIX

1. Questions concerning reasons to budget
   Budgets are used for different purposes. Indicate the degree to which the budget is used in your company for the listed purposes. (Respondents were asked to indicate their answers using a seven-point Likert scale, where 1 = "Not at all" and 7 = "Very much.")

   a. Planning, coordination, etc.
   b. Implementation of strategy plan
   c. Communication of goals
   d. Performance evaluation
   e. Investment and resource allocation
   f. Authorization of spending

2. Questions concerning the competitive environment
   How intense do you experience the competition for your company in the following areas? (Respondents were asked to provide their answers using a seven-point Likert scale, where 1 = "Negligible" and 7 = "Highly intense.")

   a. Purchase of raw materials and semi-manufacture
   b. Recruiting and retaining employees
   c. Price
   d. Distribution channels
   e. Development of new products/services

3. Questions concerning the predictability of the environment
   How do you experience the predictability of the following conditions in the company's environment? (Respondents were asked to provide their answers using a seven-point Likert scale, where 1 = "Totally predictable" and 7 = "Totally unpredictable.")

   a. Competitors' market activities
   b. Customers' needs and preferences
   c. Availability of raw materials and semi-manufacture
   d. Technological development
   e. Macroeconomic conditions
   f. Legislative and political conditions

4. Questions concerning decentralization
   To what extent has the actual decision-making authority been centralized in each of the following areas? (Respondents were asked to provide their answers using a seven-point Likert scale, where 1 = "Very decentralized" and 7 = "Very centralized.")

    a.   Development of new products and services
    b.   The hiring and firing of managerial personnel
    c.   Decisions on large investments
    d.   Budget allocations
    e.   Pricing decisions
    f.   Decisions on budget overrun
    g.   Daily operating decisions

5.   Questions concerning dependence and comparability of budget units
To what extent are the following statements true for your company?
(Respondents were asked to provide their answers using a seven-point
Likert scale, where 1 = "Not true at all" and 7 = "Fits completely.")

    a.   The activities in the individual budget units are directly compa-
rable.
    b.   The activities in the individual budget units are very dependent on
each other.

6.   Question concerning the number of employees
Please state the number of employees in the company (approximate
number including subsidiaries).

7.   Questions concerning the extent to which the organization is organic
To what extent are the following statements true for your company?
(Respondents were asked to provide their answers using a seven-point
Likert scale in which 1 = "Not true at all" and 7 = "Fits completely.")

    a.   There are no formal descriptions of job tasks/procedures.
    b.   The employee's manual contains only the most basic tenets
leaving many questions unanswered.

4. Management accounting tools in banks: are banks without budgets more profitable?

Trond Bjørnenak

INTRODUCTION

The book *Relevance Lost: The Rise and Fall of Management Accounting*, which was published more than 20 years ago, introduced a debate and sparked academic interest in new forms of management accounting, new management control ideas and potential solutions (Johnson and Kaplan, 1987). The main argument was that information provided by typical management accounting and control systems came too late, and was too aggregated and distorted by financial reporting to be relevant for decision making. Furthermore, the book suggested that these systems did not support communication or the implementation of strategies. In response, a number of new management accounting tools were introduced, including activity-based costing (ABC) systems and balanced scorecards. Table 4.1 contrasts the traditional systems (before *Relevance Lost*) with the modern solutions (after *Relevance Lost*).

After the publication of *Relevance Lost*, textbooks were changed, and

Table 4.1   Changes in management accounting and control systems

Dimension	"Traditional systems"	"Modern systems"
Costing	Simplified full costing	Advanced ABC systems
Cost objects	Departments and products	Multi-dimensional: customer, markets and distribution channels
Data sources	Internal	Internal and external
Time perspectives	Ex post	Ex ante (rolling forecasts, target costing)
Performance measures	Financials	Combinations of financials and non-financials, e.g., balanced scorecards

the new concepts and tools were given significant attention. More than 50 percent of the concepts listed in the 1982 edition of Horngren's *Cost Accounting: A Managerial Emphasis* (Horngren and Foster, 1982) were not included in the 2005 edition (Horngren, Foster and Datar, 2005) and vice versa. A dominant share of these changes related to concepts and tools discussed in the *Relevance Lost* debate, such as activity-based costing and balanced scorecards (Ax and Bjørnenak, 2007).

In the past decade, a new debate has emerged. This time, the movement, which is known as "Beyond Budgeting," is driven by a group of practitioners and consultants. Beyond Budgeting is a practice-defined concept that has taken many different forms. However, all instances of Beyond Budgeting have a common platform in that they serve as a critique of budgets. One of the pioneers in this movement was the Swedish bank Svenska Handelsbanken, which abandoned budgets as early as the 1970s.

These two critical movements in management accounting practice and research motivated this study. This study is informed by the success of Handelsbanken. Although other Scandinavian banks have followed Handelsbanken's example, the use of budgets in the Norwegian banking sector has not previously been investigated. In this regard, we identify the number of banks that do not rely on budgets and the characteristics of these banks, and we investigate how budgets are used and found useful in other banks. We also address the use of other tools in the industry with the purpose of understanding which tools are used and the extent to which they are found useful. Finally, we explore the association between the tools used and various measures of performance effects.

The chapter is organized as follows. First, the Handelsbanken case is presented. Second, the research method and variables are discussed. The findings from the survey study are then presented, while finally limitations and ideas for future research are discussed.

SVENSKA HANDELSBANKEN – A SUCCESSFUL BANK WITHOUT BUDGETS

In 1970, Jan Wallander took over as CEO of Sweden's Svenska Handelsbanken (hereafter Handelsbanken). One of his first moves was to abandon budgeting (Wallander, 1994, 1999). The decision did not receive much attention until the 1990s when Wallander published the book *Budgeten: Ett onödigt ont* [Budgets – an unnecessary evil] (1994). The book was written in Swedish, but a shorter version was published in English in the *Scandinavian Journal of Management* in 1999 (Wallander, 1999). This case has since been cited in a number of books and articles as a classic case of Beyond Budgeting, and Wallander is often described as a Beyond Budgeting pioneer (Hope and Fraser, 2003a, 2003b; Lindsay and Libby, 2007; Bogsnes, 2009).

Wallander's inspiration for abandoning budgets arose from his years as a professional economist. Prior to coming to Handelsbanken, he worked at a research institute specialized in providing long-term forecasts for different variables (e.g., demand for electronics). These forecasts were based on historical trends, and breaks in the curves could not normally be foreseen. He saw this as one of the main problem with budgets, as they prevented management from identifying the important issues that made a difference.

The alternative outlined by Wallander was to keep the management control system simple:

> It is evident that the kind of information I am talking about are the figures that to a large extent you already have or should have in your profit and loss account and balance sheet and your ordinary information systems. What you have to do is to organize and construct them in such a way that they fit the demand. (Wallander, 1999: 413)

Handelsbanken's solution was to focus on relative financial performance (benchmarking branches on costs, profit and losses) and a profit-sharing bonus plan (see Lindsay and Libby, 2007, for more details). The simple system was not kept secret in any way. The bank did not implement balanced scorecards, rolling forecasts or advanced activity-based costing systems. Nevertheless, Handelsbanken has continually outperformed other Scandinavian banks. The bank has reported an ROE above the industry average for almost every year since 1972, while its total annual shareholder return has been more than 20 percent over the same period. The most obvious profit driver has been cost-efficiency, with the cost/income ratio at approximately 45 percent (the industry average is above 60 percent).

The existence of a high-performing bank without budgets in which "modern" advanced management accounting tools are not used motivated this study of Norwegian banks for several reasons. First, although Handelsbanken is Swedish, it is one of the largest banks in Norway, and its success and its control system are well known in the industry. Second, some Norwegian banks have followed Handelsbanken in abandoning budgets (see bbrt.org). Third, the high number of different banks within the Norwegian banking industry, all generally operating in the same market, may give us interesting insights into the use of different tools in management control systems.

THE STRUCTURE OF THE STUDY

The study started with an investigation of the control system in Handelsbanken, which is described in detail in different books and articles (Wallander 1994, 1999; Lindsay and Libby, 2007). In addition, one of Handelsbanken's larger branch offices was visited and its managers were interviewed. Two Norwegian banks were also visited in order to collect background information.

The survey was then sent to 118 of the largest Norwegian banks. The largest Norwegian bank (DnB) was excluded because it works under different (more international) conditions, while the other banks mainly focus on the domestic market. Foreign banks active in the Norwegian market, such as Handelsbanken, were not included.

The Norwegian economy has experienced stable growth in recent decades, mainly driven by the booming oil industry. Although Norwegian banks were affected by the financial meltdown in 2008, all of the banks in the dataset showed a surplus in 2010 and 2011, and losses on bad loans were rather low in the period of investigation (2009–11). None of the banks included in the initial sample had problems fulfilling the capital requirement set by the financial supervisory authority (Basel II). Thus, all of the targeted banks were profitable and solid and faced relatively stable market conditions during the period of investigation.

Data were collected on three issues:

1. *The use and perceived usefulness of different management accounting tools, including budgets, benchmarking, activity-based costing, balanced scorecards, rolling forecasts and customer profitability accounting.* These were identified as the most important tools in the two banks analyzed in the pre-study. Respondents were asked to indicate the extent to which they used different tools using a five-point Likert scale (1 = "not at all," 5 = "to a very large extent") and the extent to which they found the tool useful (1 = "useful only to a very limited extent," 5 = "very useful").

2. *The degree to which respondents agreed with 18 different statements dealing with budgeting critiques.* This was measured on a five-point Likert scale (1 = "totally disagree," 5 = "totally agree"). The statements were consistently negatively loaded, and were mainly adopted from Libby and Lindsay (2010) and Ekholm and Wallin (2000).

3. *Measures of performance.* Three measures of success or bank performance were used. First, the perceived usefulness of different management accounting tools was included in the questionnaire (as shown in 1). The other two – the cost/income ratio (an important perform-

ance measure in Handelsbanken and used by the industry) and return on equity (used in the industry) – were measured using accounting data collected by the Norwegian Saving Banks Association (Sparebankforeningen). The data were publicly available on the association's webpage. Reliability was tested using accounting data for ten of the banks. The test did not identify any reliability problems.

The survey was undertaken in the spring of 2010 and specifically asked respondents to focus on the tools used in 2009 (Johansen, 2010). Performance measures were based on accounting figures for 2009.

In total, 81 banks returned the questionnaire. Ten of the 37 non-responding banks indicated that they did not have time to complete the questionnaire. This gives a response rate of 69 percent, which is relatively high when compared to similar studies (e.g., Naranjo-Gil et al., 2009; Libby and Lindsay, 2010). Each bank's CFO was asked to answer the survey, because decisions to adopt any of the investigated tools are often made by the top management team and because the CFO is a key person in the introduction or implementation of changes, for example the abandonment of budgets. The focus on CFOs is in line with other studies of management practices (Young et al., 2001; Naranjo-Gil et al., 2009). We tested for possible non-response bias with regard to size, profitability and cost-efficiency, but found no significant differences.

FINDINGS

This section presents the results of the survey. First, there is a description of the adoption rates for different tools and how different tools were used in combination. Second, the CFOs' responses to different statements on potential problems with budgets are presented. Third, the link between the use of different management accounting tools and two performance measures is explored.

The Use and Perceived Usefulness of Management Accounting Tools

Table 4.2 shows the use and perceived usefulness of different management accounting tools.

The adoption rate for activity-based costing (ABC) is very low. Only one of the banks had fully implemented ABC, while five others had done so to some degree and six had implemented it to a low degree. These adopters do not find ABC highly useful. The other tools are more common and, on average, seen as useful. Notably, 72 of the 81 banks used budgets. We

Table 4.2   Use and perceived usefulness of management accounting tools

Level of use	ABC	BSC	Benchmarking	Rolling forecast	Customer profitability analyses
Did not use (1)	85%	47%	21%	17%	16%
Low (2)	7%	11%	11%	14%	22%
Some (3)	6%	14%	24%	35%	35%
High (4)	0%	15%	36%	21%	26%
Fully implemented (5)	1%	14%	9%	14%	1%
Usefulness	2.56	3.68	3.87	3.56	3.57

Notes:
ABC = activity-based costing; BSC = balanced scorecard.
N = 81 for level of use, but only users are included in the calculation of usefulness.
Usefulness is an average on a Likert scale of 1–5.

Table 4.3   Use and usefulness of budgets for different purposes

Purpose	Planning	Coordination	Resource allocation	Motivation	Evaluation	Reward
Use	3.88	3.28	3.33	3.43	3.94	2.86
Usefulness	3.90	3.31	3.51	3.38	3.82	3.17

Notes:
N = 72.
Likert scale of 1–5.

asked these banks about the use and usefulness of budgets for different purposes. The results are show in Table 4.3.

Budgets are commonly used for planning and evaluation, and they are seen as highly useful for these purposes. Budgets are less often used in reward systems, but they are also viewed as useful for this purpose. The high proportion of users (89 percent of the total) and the level of perceived usefulness for the main purposes show that budgets hold a strong position in the management control systems of Norwegian banks.

Tools may be used in different combinations. An analysis of the correlations between the use of different tools is given in Table 4.4.

Only a few of the tools are significantly correlated. The use of ABC is correlated with the use of BSC. The uses of both tools are also significantly correlated with size, that is, larger banks are using ABC and BSC. Other tools are not strongly correlated with size. Thus size may be the underlying

Table 4.4 Correlations (Pearson) between the use of different tools

	ABC	BSC	Benchmarking	Budgets	Rolling forecast
ABC					
BSC	***0.333				
Benchmarking	*0.199	***0.311			
Budgets	0.085	0.076	0.052		
RF	0.16	0.111	***0.336	0.032	
Customer profitability analyses	0.038	0.053	**0.219	0.175	0.149

Note: Significance levels * $p < 0.1$, ** $p < 0.05$, *** $p < 0.01$.

Table 4.5 Correlation (Pearson) between the use and usefulness of different tools

Use	Perceived usefulness					
	ABC	BSC	Bench-marking	Budgets	Rolling forecast	Customer profitability analyses
ABC	***0.498	0.046	0.103	0.101	−0.089	0.029
BSC	0.153	***0.836	0.163	−0.019	0.048	0.158
Benchmarking	0.055	**0.239	***0.720	0.072	*0.206	**0.277
Budgets	−0.017	−0.012	−0.044	***0.682	0.053	0.15
Rolling forecast	0.045	0.042	**0.255	0.143	***0.767	**0.253
Customer profitability analyses	0.063	0.026	***0.286	**0.248	0.072	***0.747

Note: Significance levels * $p < 0.1$, ** $p < 0.05$, *** $p < 0.01$.

factor for the correlation between ABC and BSC. Benchmarking is correlated with many of the other tools, which may be explained by the nature of the benchmarking, that is, benchmarking is typically integrated with performance measures, customer analyses or forecasting.

In order to investigate the link between the use and usefulness of different tools, we correlated use with perceived usefulness. The results are shown in Table 4.5.

Notably, use and usefulness are highly correlated for all tools. In other words, CFOs seem to perceive the tools used in their organizations as useful. We also tested for interaction effects, that is, the use of budgets combined with the use of other tools and the level of usefulness of other tools, but did not find any significant results. Most significant in this respect is the finding that the use of a budget is not correlated with the perceived usefulness of other tools. This may indicate that budgets are not highly integrated with other tools.

This study of the adoption of different tools shows that, with the exception of ABC, the tools investigated are used by Norwegian banks and that the banks that use them find them useful. The use of these tools is highly correlated with perceived usefulness, a finding that may question the validity of studies based on the perceived usefulness of different tools. Budgets are the most widely used and are believed to be very useful. This implies that the view held by Jan Wallander and Handelsbanken is not generally accepted in the industry.

The Relevance of Critiques of Budgets

The previous section showed that budgets play an important role in the control systems of Scandinavian banks, despite the problems covered in the Beyond Budgeting literature. In this section, we investigate whether the bank CFOs agree with some of the claims made in that literature. In total, 18 different statements were tested. We used an approach similar to that found in Neely et al. (2003)[1] in that we looked at problems related to: 1) the budgeting process, 2) organizational and individual behavior and 3) strategic focus and value creation. These areas are discussed in more detail below.

Problems or weaknesses in the budgeting process

The budgeting process as a whole is often an endeavor requiring considerable amounts of time and resources (e.g., Neely et al., 2003) from the different layers of an organization. Thus budgets need to be developed, redrawn when needed and approved. After approval, they are often revised and different types of analyses are performed, including prognoses and variance analyses. Top management (e.g., the board of directors) often requires monthly or quarterly reports, and updates regarding corrective efforts when budgets are not met. The sheer number of participants in the budgeting process tends to prolong the process. Along these lines, in their study of US and Canadian companies, Libby and Lindsay (2010) found that the budgeting process took slightly more than ten and six weeks (median), respectively. Similarly, Hope and Fraser (2003a) claim that the budgeting process absorbs up to 30 percent of management's time. The scope of the budgeting process is also supported by Neely et al. (2003), who claim that as much as 20 percent of management time is spent on (planning and) budgeting practices.

Other aspects of the budgetary process have also been questioned. Most critical, perhaps, is the process's reliance on underlying assumptions about the future. Although such assumptions are inevitable given the nature of budgeting, the frequency, reliability and extent of these assumptions can hamper the benefits derived from the budgeting process. According to Wallander (1994, 1999), a budget is often no more than an extrapolation of the past and present, as the organization finds it too difficult and time-consuming to analyze these assumptions in detail. Thus, according to Wallander (1999), companies tend to make their predictions by looking at the past or by assuming the "same weather tomorrow as today." According to Hope and Fraser (2003b), Bogsnes (2009) and others, this lessens the company's ability to adapt to the ever-changing business environment. Furthermore, although Wallander (1999) admits that forecasts are inevitable, he suggests that their value will ultimately rely on their accuracy. Such assumptions range from general forecasts made by external experts (e.g., governmental bodies) on factors such as prices and wages to the interpretation of those forecasts in the organization and in specific parts of the organization (e.g., departments). Thus there is uncertainty related not only to the general forecasts but also to how those forecasts are incorporated into the different layers of the organization.

Similarly, budgets and the assumptions made in the budgeting process have been criticized for quickly becoming outdated (Hope and Fraser, 2003b). Libby and Lindsay (2010) investigated this issue in detail in their US survey and found that 65 percent of respondents "somewhat" agreed that outdatedness was a problem, whereas 40 percent "agreed" or "strongly agreed." These figures suggest that this particular issue can indeed be problematic for many organizations.

Another critique relates to the calendar rhythm of the budgeting process. Wallander (1999) refers to the budget as a yearly ritual. The Beyond Budgeting literature calls for a more dynamic (flexible) process (Bogsnes, 2009) in which resources are allocated based on ongoing judgments, targets are adjusted according to changes in the environment and prognoses are updated more frequently than every 12 months. In this respect, Hope and Fraser (2003b) emphasize that decisions should be made on a continuous basis and not according to the calendar. Furthermore, the fact that budgeting is often viewed as a yearly ritual (Wallander, 1999) may be one reason why budgets are poor in signaling changes relevant to the management of organizations. Hope and Fraser (1999) suggest that, as budgets are unable to cope with the changing competitive environment, they lack the responsiveness and agility needed to meet customer needs.

Table 4.6   Average response to statements related to the budget process

	Mean (St. dev.)
Time and assumptions	
Too much time is spent on budget-related activities (e.g., developing, revising, reporting, variance analysis, etc.).	2.74 (1.14)
Budgets are heavily based on uncertain assumptions about the future.	2.91 (1.03)
The assumptions on which budgets are built are quickly out of date/outdated.	2.90 (1.02)
On flexibility and dynamics	
Budgets prevent responsiveness because they are poor in signaling changes in the surrounding environment.	2.89 (0.96)
Budgets prevent responsiveness to changes because they are difficult to alter after they are approved	2.57 (1.01)
Budgets prevent responsiveness to changes because it is difficult to get funds allocated outside the budget.	2.16 (0.93)
Budgets hamper responsiveness because they mainly/heavily focus on achieving budget targets rather than maximizing value creation	2.83 (1.15)

Notes:
N = 81.
Likert scale of 1–5.

Moreover, Hope and Fraser (1999: 18) describe the general features of the budgeting process as "such a slow, rigid and often highly 'political' process," which "is a major handicap in today's fast changing competitive environment."

Based on the above critiques, we asked respondents to indicate the extent to which they agreed with seven different statements. The results, which are shown in Table 4.6, indicate that these critiques find little support in practice. All statements have an average of less than 3 on the five-point Likert scale, and the medians were 2 or 3 for all statements. If we exclude the nine banks that did not use budgets, the averages were even lower. All banks provided responses.

The influence on organizational and individual behavior
According to Neely et al. (2003), budgets and, to some extent, the budgeting process can make room for, and even encourage, dysfunctional behavior that results in actions and decision making that do not add value to the company as a whole. More specifically, Neely et al. (2003: 22) state that traditional budgeting methods "are counterproductive in that they are

usually affected by gaming, corporate politics and horsetrading tactics."
Hope and Fraser (2003b) suggest that the budget serves as a "fixed-performance contract." Hope and Fraser (2003a: 113) take this part of the critique even further, claiming that "budgets can result in 'earnings management' or even outright fraud."

Thus budgets often lack incentives that would encourage employees and departments to act in the best interest of the company. Instead, employees or departments promote their own interests. Typical examples include instances when departments, divisions or similar units protect their own interests at the expense of the company, that is, by choosing projects and investments that benefit the department rather than the company, by negotiating budgetary targets that can easily be reached, by overestimating the resources needed to ensure that adequate resources are at their disposal or by using resources when such use is not necessary in order to ensure that the next period does not bring a cut in resources. Other examples involve deferring revenues or expenses in order to achieve budgetary targets. Many of these issues are also valid on an individual level. These problems are often referred to as budgetary gaming (Hope and Fraser, 2003b). In general, they are related to what Hope and Fraser (2003b) term the "budget contract," which contains a number of fallacies (see Hope and Fraser, 2003b: 6–8). Interestingly, Libby and Lindsay (2010) find a significant negative correlation between budgetary value and gaming, that is, more gaming reduces the value of the budget.

Given the problems inherent in budgeting with regard to detecting or signaling business changes, some researchers claim that budgets reinforce vertical control, leading to a situation in which relevant information on how to deal with emerging issues is lacking (Neely et al., 2003; Bogsnes, 2009). Thus advocates of Beyond Budgeting suggest that making room for decentralized decision making makes it easier for an organization to adapt to changes, which in turn favors organizations, as they encounter these issues at an early stage. In other words, they can be proactive when dealing with changes, rather than reviewing them in hindsight when it may be too late to respond properly.

In relation to dysfunctional behavior, the existence of departmental budgets and targets may have a negative impact on cooperation and the sharing of knowledge in the organization (Hope and Fraser, 2003b; Bogsnes, 2009). Information, experiences and ideas may not be communicated throughout the organization, as departments are focused on their own best interests and on protecting their advantages at the expense of the rest of the organization. A focus on achieving budgetary targets may even provoke elements of hostility among different parts of the organization. This also relates to budgets lacking the incentives necessary to ensure that

Table 4.7   Statements on behavioral effects of budgets

	Mean (St. dev.)
Budgets hamper cooperation and knowledge sharing between departments owing to the heavy focus on achieving own budgetary targets.	2.62 (1.03)
Budgets may lead to the negotiation of targets lower than those actually achievable to make it easier to reach budgets.	3.07 (1.10)
Budgets may lead to an overestimation of resources to ensure an adequate supply of resources.	2.93 (1.05)
Budgets may cause assigned funds to be spent before the end of one period in order to prevent reduced funding in the next period.	2.23 (1.14)
Budgets may lead to deferring revenues and/or costs to ensure that the period's budgetary targets are met.	2.63 (1.05)
Budgets may lead to expediting costs when budgets will not be met.	2.40 (1.02)

Notes:
N = 81.
Likert scale of 1–5.

the entire organization is moving in the same direction and to support consideration of what is best for the company as a whole. Thus the importance of learning and knowledge sharing, and the need to attend to human capital and other resources are pivotal to ensure the necessary innovations and ideas are being applied and adapted in everyday activities.

Six statements based on these critiques were included in the survey. The results are show in Table 4.7. Consistent with Libby and Lindsay (2010), we find indications of budgetary gaming among the banks' responses. However, there is a low level of agreement with all of the other statements.

Strategic coherence and value creation
Strategic coherence, and the link between strategy and performance measures have increased in importance and relevance in recent years. As discussed earlier, some researchers claim that budgeting has too many roles and purposes, and that it centers on short-term target setting and resource allocation. These factors inhibit the budget from being clearly linked to the overall strategy of the organization. Overall, an assertion has been made that budgets cannot be aligned with strategy, as these elements are prepared in isolation (Hope and Fraser, 2003b). This is partially related to the frequent emergence of goal conflicts, and the lack of superior goals or objectives that would help to resolve such conflicts. In the presence of

Table 4.8   Integration of budgets in the strategic process and value creation

	Mean (St. dev.)
Budgets are poorly linked to the organization's strategy.	2.42 (1.09)
Budgets add little value because they focus too heavily on financial performance measures at the expense of other strategically important indicators/measures.	2.58 (0.93)
Budgets add little value because they focus on cost reduction rather than value creation.	2.51 (0.94)
Budgets create little value because they focus on achieving budgets rather than creating value.	2.57 (1.11)
Budgets create little value because they focus on routines rather than creative thinking and value creation.	2.67 (1.04)

Notes:
N = 81.
Likert scale of 1–5.

dysfunctional behavior and an over-reliance on financial performance measures, goal conflicts may escalate. As financial performance measures are often short-term by nature, employees' attention in the absence of a strategic focus will tend to be on historical conditions rather than on strategic, long-term thinking subject to some concrete goals and objectives (Hope and Fraser, 2003b; Neely et al., 2003; Bogsnes, 2009).

Researchers also claim that, in today's ever-changing business environment, organizational cooperation and the importance of the ability to foster creativity and innovativeness contrast the bureaucratic nature and formalized routines inherent in budgeting ("command and control"; see Bogsnes, 2009). Furthermore, budgets focus on costs and on variance analyses rather than on the exploration of strategic opportunities. This may result in exploitation rather than exploration and a failure to recognize potential new sources of income. In total, a focus on costs may lower the firm's overall value creation. In relation to value creation, Hope and Fraser (1999) argue that future cash flows are likely to flow from intangible assets, which they claim that budgets are not designed to manage or control.

The empirical results for five statements related to these critiques are shown in Table 4.8. The results are not very supportive of the critiques.

In summary, the findings show that the use and usefulness of budgets are supported by the generally low agreement with claims found in the Beyond Budgeting critique. Only one of the 18 statements has an average of more than 3. However, the proportion of "strongly agree" (5) varies from 5 to 20 percent for the different statements, which shows that some CFOs have adopted a critical view.

The Link between Management Accounting Tools and Performance

The success of management accounting innovations can be measured in numerous ways. According to Cinquini and Mitchell (2005), the most common measure of the success of ABC is the adopter's perceived view of the tool. Ittner and Larcker (2009) question the reliability of this measure and call for more studies that link management accounting systems to actual financial performance.

In our study, we linked the survey data to two different performance measures:

- *Return on equity (RoE)*. ROE is the most commonly used measure of financial performance in banks. One important weakness is that this measure is not risk adjusted and it does not adjust for the leverage of the bank.
- *Cost/income ratio*. This ratio is used by the bank association for benchmarking. It is also one of the most important measures reported in Handelsbanken.

In order to investigate the associations between the uses of different tools we use OLS regression analyses using the performance measure as the dependent variable and different tools in use as independent variables. Use is measured on Likert scale of 1–5. Size (measured as total capital) is also included in the analyses. The results for RoE are shown in Table 4.9.

We see that budgets are significantly negatively associated with performance, while benchmarking, size and customer profitability are positively associated with RoE. The coefficient for BSC is negative, but not significant. In order to validate the results we asked the banks with budgets whether there had been any changes in the focus on budgets in the last years. None of the banks claimed to have increased the focus on budgets (some have reduced it, but the majority did not make any changes). Thus the potential explanation of banks increasing focus on budgets when financial performance is low was not supported.

Note that this does not prove that there is a negative cause-and-effect relationship between budgets and performance. However, it indicates that budgets are not necessary for high performance. It is also interesting to note that Handelsbanken is strongly using benchmarking and relative performance as a key factor in its control system. ABC, rolling forecasts, BSC and budgets are used only to a low degree or not at all in Handelsbanken.

Table 4.9   Association between ROE and different tools in use

Variable	R² (adj.) 26.90%	P-value <0.001
	Coefficients	P-value
Intercept	6.247	0.003
Budgets	−1.1033	0.021
ABC	−0.1544	0.822
BSC	−0.3703	0.258
Benchmarking	1.2247	0.002
Rolling forecasts	0.1095	0.766
Customer profitability analyses	0.8354	0.054
Size (1000 million NOK)	0.04726	0.046

Notes:
N = 81.
OLS regression.

Table 4.10   Association between tools and cost/income ratios

Variable	R² (adj.) 12.10%	P-value 0.02
	Coefficients	P-value
Intercept	56.84	0.001
Budgets	1.613	0.165
ABC	−0.397	0.813
BSC	1.421	0.078
Benchmarking	−2.065	0.033
Rolling forecasts	0.550	0.542
Customer profitability analyses	−1.223	0.246
Size (NOK 1000 million)	−0.11125	0.055

Notes:
N = 81.
OLS regression.

The key to Handelsbanken's success has been its low cost/income ratios (around 40 percent; see, for example, Lindsay and Libby, 2007). The results of the OLS regression for cost/income ratios are shown in Table 4.10. The model explains less of the total variation than the RoE analysis. Benchmarking and size are associated with lower costs. One interpretation might be that benchmarking and size are positively associated with higher

Table 4.11   Association between performance and tools

Tools	RoE		Cost/income		Usefulness (adopters)
	Coefficients	P-value	Coefficients	P-value	
Benchmarking	1.17	0.004	−2.07	0.033	3.87
Budget	−1.10	0.021	1.61	0.165	3.17–3.90
BSC	−0.37	0.258	1.42	0.078	3.68
Customer Profitability analyses	0.84	0.054	−1.22	0.246	3.57
ABC	0.15	0.822	−0.40	0.813	2.56
Rolling forecasts	0.11	0.766	0.55	0.542	3.56

profitability through lower costs. The coefficient for budgets is positive (higher costs) but not significant. Note that the use of balanced score-cards is also associated with higher costs (significant at the 0.1 level).

In summary, we have three indicators of success, which are shown in Table 4.11. Benchmarking is widely adopted, and is perceived as very useful by the adopters. It is positively associated with higher profitability and lower costs. Budgets are the most used tool among banks, and are seen as very useful for different purposes. However, budgets are negatively associated with RoE. Balanced scorecards are also used by a high number of banks and are seen as very useful. The more they are used, the greater the perception that they are useful. However, the tool is negatively associated with cost-efficiency. Customer profitability analyses are seen as very useful, and they are positively associated with higher RoE. For rolling forecasts and ABC, we find no significant associations between use and financial performance. Furthermore, for ABC, the adoption rate and the perceived usefulness are low.

CONCLUSIONS AND FUTURE RESEARCH

This study of the adoption of different management control tools by Norwegian banks shows the Handelsbanken model has not been widely copied. Only nine of the 81 responding banks did not use budgets. A simple test of differences between banks without budgets and banks with budgets showed that the former had higher RoEs and lower cost/income ratios than banks with budgets in all years from 2006 to 2010. Furthermore, the difference was significant in 2006, 2007 and 2008. Therefore, Norwegian banks without budgets appear to be more profitable than banks with budgets. However, this conclusion is based on only one differentiating factor (budgets or no budgets).

The study presented in this chapter includes the size of the bank and the use of other tools. It also includes the extent to which budgets are used and the use of budgets for different purposes. When we include the level of use, we find a significant negative relationship between the use of budgets and financial performance. However, this does not serve as proof of a cause-and-effect relationship. The study does not control for the point at which a specific tool was adopted or the time at which budgets were removed. It is therefore difficult to trace the effects of such changes. However, the results show that there is not a conflict between a lack of budgets and cost-efficiency and profitability.

Beyond Budgeting is a practice-defined concept that takes many forms. Some companies that remove budgets replace them with other tools, such as rolling forecasts and versions of the balanced scorecard. Others, such as Handelsbanken, do not implement the new, more advanced tools introduced after the publication of *Relevance Lost*. The results of this study do not support the utility of the advanced solutions, as we do not find positive associations for balanced scorecards and rolling forecasts.

The nine banks without budgets differed to a statistically significant extent with regard to the use of two tools – benchmarking and customer profitability analyses – which they used to a greater degree. These tools are also significantly associated with higher profitability. Thus it is difficult to separate the effects of removing budgets from the effects of introducing benchmarking or customer profitability analyses.

It may seem paradoxical that budgets still are among the most important tools in banks' control systems – the more they use budgets, the less profitable they are. This paradox should be addressed in future research. The results of such research may give us an indication of how systems work. In order to better understand the cause-and-effect relationships, we need a deeper understanding of how the different tools are used and how the functions are filled when budgets are removed. This requires more field studies of banks with and without budgets.

NOTE

1. Neely et al. (2003) conducted a thorough literature review and undertook interviews with representatives of cutting-edge or leading companies to identify the most commonly cited problems or weaknesses inherent in budgeting. Neely et al. (2003) used three main categories: 1) competitive strategy, 2) business process and 3) organizational capability.

REFERENCES

Ax, C. and T. Bjørnenak (2007), "Management accounting innovations: Origins and diffusion," in T. Hopper, R.W. Scapens and D. Northcott (eds.), *Issues in Management Accounting*, Harlow: Pearson Education, pp. 357–76.

Bogsnes, B. (2009), *Implementing Beyond Budgeting: Unlocking the Performance Potential*, Hoboken, NJ: John Wiley & Sons.

Cinquini, L. and F. Mitchell (2005), "Success in management accounting: Lessons from the activity-based costing/management experience," *Journal of Accounting and Organizational Change*, 1 (1), 63–77.

Ekholm, B.G. and J. Wallin (2000), "Is the annual budget really dead?," *European Accounting Review*, 9 (4), 519–39.

Hope, J. and R. Fraser (1999), "Beyond Budgeting – building a new management model for the information age," *Management Accounting*, 77 (11), 20–23.

Hope, J. and R. Fraser (2003a), "Who needs budgets?," *Harvard Business Review*, 81 (2), 108–15.

Hope, J. and R. Fraser (2003b), *Beyond Budgeting: How Managers Can Break Free from the Annual Performance Trap*, Boston, MA: Harvard Business School Press.

Horngren, C.T. and G. Foster (1982), *Cost Accounting: A Managerial Emphasis*, Englewood Cliffs, NJ: Prentice Hall.

Horngren, C.T., G. Foster and S.M. Datar (2005), *Cost Accounting: A Managerial Emphasis*, Englewood Cliffs, NJ: Prentice Hall.

Ittner, C.D. and D.F. Larcker (2009), "Extending the boundaries: Nonfinancial performance measures," in C.S. Chapman, A.G. Hopwood and M.S. Shields (eds.), *Handbook of Management Accounting Research*, Oxford: Elsevier, pp. 1235–51.

Johansen, M. (2010), "Beyond Budgeting – noe som passer for meg? En studie av spredningen av Beyond Budgeting i Norge," Master's thesis, NHH – Norwegian School of Economics, Bergen.

Johnson, H.T. and R.S. Kaplan (1987), *Relevance Lost: The Rise and Fall of Management Accounting*, Boston, MA: Harvard Business School Press.

Libby, T. and R.M. Lindsay (2010), "Beyond Budgeting or budgeting reconsidered? A survey of North American practice," *Management Accounting Research*, 21 (1), 56–75.

Lindsay, R.M. and T. Libby (2007), "Svenska Handelsbanken: Controlling a radically decentralized organization without budgets," *Issues in Accounting Education*, 22 (4), 625–40.

Naranjo-Gil, D., V.S. Maas and F.G.H. Hartmann (2009), "How CFOs determine management accounting innovation: An examination of direct and indirect effects," *European Accounting Review*, 18 (4), 667–95.

Neely, A., M. Bourne and C. Adams (2003), "Better budgeting or Beyond Budgeting?," *Measuring Business Excellence*, 7 (3), 22–8.

Wallander, J. (1994), *Budgeten: Ett onödigt ont*, Stockholm: SNS Förlag.

Wallander, J. (1999), "Budgeting – an unnecessary evil," *Scandinavian Journal of Management*, 15 (4), 405–21.

Young, G.J., M.P. Charns and S.M. Shortell (2001), "Top manager and network effects on the adoption of innovative management practices: A study of TQM in a public hospital system," *Strategic Management Journal*, 22, 935–51.

5. Beyond Budgeting from the American and Norwegian perspectives: the embeddedness of management models in corporate governance systems

Daniel Johanson

INTRODUCTION

The Beyond Budgeting idea is receiving an increasing amount of attention, especially in the Scandinavian countries (Hansen et al., 2003; Østergren and Stensaker, 2011; Henttu-Aho and Järvinen, 2013). Simply stated, Beyond Budgeting is concerned with the dysfunctions of budgeting and proposes alternative management tools, such as relative performance measurement.

Beyond Budgeting models (BB models) are not yet as widely diffused as many other management accounting and control models (MAC models), such as balanced scorecards.[1] Nevertheless, Beyond Budgeting has spread in many different countries, as seen from the membership lists of the Beyond Budgeting Round Table (BBRT, 2011). Furthermore, its spokespersons (e.g., writers, consultants and business leaders) come from a range of countries, including the Scandinavian countries, the UK, the US and German-speaking countries.

The purpose of this chapter is to explore the relationship between MAC models and corporate governance systems (CG systems) from an international, comparative perspective. The chapter uses the case of Beyond Budgeting to theorize about the links between MAC models and CG systems. Beyond Budgeting is suitable for the purpose of this study for at least two reasons. First, its proponents originate from many different countries with different governance systems. Second, apart from its firm dedication to removing budgets, the implementation of Beyond Budgeting can take many forms. This leaves the idea relatively open for translation to specific settings.

Specifically, this chapter analyzes texts on Beyond Budgeting published by two leading writers. The writers come from two different countries (Norway and the US), they operate as managers and/or consultants in their home countries, and their texts are mainly practitioner oriented. One can identify significant differences in their expression and formulation of the Beyond Budgeting idea, which leads in turn to two versions or models of Beyond Budgeting (BB). They target specific audiences of organizations and individuals in their respective countries. This leads to the research questions that this study addresses:

1. What are the main differences and similarities between BB models in Norway (or, in a broader sense, Scandinavia) and the US?
2. Could these differences and similarities be explained by differences in the corporate governance systems of Norway and the US?

Thus, this chapter seeks to contribute to the literature about the transferability of management models to different national contexts (Bourguignon et al., 2004; Fiss and Zajac, 2004; Ax and Bjørnenak, 2005, 2007; Nørreklit et al., 2006). In focusing on the discursive level of ideas, this chapter does not deal with practice or with implementation issues associated with management models. The focus is on the design and rhetoric of the models as expressed in writings. Nevertheless, it seems plausible that the way in which a model is expressed in writing (e.g., in books, journals and the business press) affects the diffusion, translation and implementation of the model at the organizational level.

The chapter starts by presenting a conceptual framework for analyzing the texts. First, the extant literature about the diffusion and translation of management models is briefly reviewed. A cross-national political model of corporate governance is then described (Aguilera and Jackson, 2003) as a framework for the study. A second model by Gourevitch and Shinn (2005) is also introduced as a basis for positioning the governance systems of Norway and the US. The chapter proceeds by describing the Beyond Budgeting idea, focusing on the 12 Beyond Budgeting principles. The ensuing sections thoroughly examine and reflect upon the writings of Bjarte Bogsnes (of Norway) and Steve Player (of the US). The chapter then turns to analyzing the differences and similarities between the texts produced by Bogsnes and Player. The findings of this analysis are examined in the light of the political corporate governance framework, and theoretical links between the BB models and the respective CG systems are suggested. The chapter concludes with a discussion of the findings and raises some questions for future research.

CONCEPTUAL FRAMEWORK

The Diffusion and Translation of Management Models

One of the most common definitions of "diffusion" states that diffusion occurs when "an innovation is communicated through certain channels over time among the members of a social system" (Rogers, 1983: 14).[2] The rate of diffusion depends on efficiency gains resulting from the adoption of the diffusion and on how well the model fits the social context (Strang and Meyer, 1993; Bourguignon et al., 2004).

MAC models can have varying degrees of "interpretive viability" (Ortmann, 1995; Benders and Van Veen, 2001), which refers to the ambiguity inherent in certain management fashions, models or concepts. When a concept or model is characterized by ambiguity, users can eclectically adopt those elements that appeal to them (Benders and Van Veen, 2001). A moderate level of interpretive viability is considered important for the diffusion and adoption of MAC models (Benders and Van Veen, 2001; Ax and Bjørnenak, 2005; Becker et al., 2010).

Value-based management models (VBM models), such as economic value added (EVA™), contains a relatively solid core of finance theory and a norm of shareholder-value maximization (Stewart, 1991; Young and O'Byrne, 2001). This leaves limited room for translating the model to fit different contexts. In the 1980s and 1990s, Japanese MAC models, such as "target costing," "*kaizen*" and "lean production," diffused to US-based companies. However, some researchers argue that these models underwent significant translation and were adopted in a different way in the US (e.g., Hopper, Koga and Goto, 1999). Similarly, Ax and Bjørnenak (2005) find that the employee perspective in "balanced scorecards" is pronounced in Swedish firms. In the context of Ax and Bjørnenak's (2005) findings, the strong position of organized labor might serve as an explanation of the emphasis on the employee perspective in Swedish balanced scorecard models.

Concepts and models have been found to be adapted or translated to be more consistent with the organizational and/or socio-political context (e.g., Westney, 1987; Czarniawska-Joerges and Sévon, 2005; Johanson and Østergren, 2010).[3] However, changes in control systems may influence the balance of power among stakeholder groups and can have wealth-distributing effects. Therefore, influential coalitions of stakeholders may oppose the adoption of new MAC models. For example, it has been shown that a seemingly objective model, such as activity-based costing (ABC), can be implemented to cut costs, downsize operations and reduce the number of employees (Armstrong, 2002; Jones and Dugdale, 2002).

Finally, MAC models have been found to gain worldwide popularity to the extent that firms feel pressured to adopt them. However, this raises the question of how the models are implemented. Surface compliance or decoupling, rather than deep implementation, is often a more accurate picture of reality. In Germany and Japan, for example, the shareholder-value concept has been substantially translated and recombined with local practice (Fiss and Zajac, 2004; Ahmadjian and Robbins, 2005). Nevertheless, changing coalitions of stakeholders can enable more deeply entrenched implementations of new MAC models. Institutional investors from, for example, the US or the UK may pressure firms in other countries to use more transparent shareholder metrics and implement models based on shareholder value (Davis and Thompson, 1994; Gourevitch and Shinn, 2005). Once implemented in a large number of firms, a MAC model may enable additional changes in the business systems of countries.

A Political Corporate Governance Framework

The Aguilera and Jackson model
In contrast to financial accounting research, few studies in management accounting rely on a corporate governance framework. Nevertheless, the relevance of such a framework to these studies seems clear. For example, the work of boards of directors, stakeholders and capital market regulators could have important impacts on the design, use and adoption of MAC models. In this study, the broad issue of corporate governance is located at the macro and systemic level of countries, regions and business systems (e.g., O'Sullivan, 2000; Aguilera and Jackson, 2003; Guillén, 2004). As stated by Davis (2005: 143), "corporate governance describes the structures, processes, and institutions within and around organizations that allocate power and resource control among participants."

Aguilera and Jackson's (2003) cross-national governance model is used in this chapter as a framework for examining the Beyond Budgeting idea. This framework covers a broad spectrum of the institutional environment, and considers not only economic but also political, social, historical and legal factors. At the same time, it does not deal with unnecessarily ambiguous and controversial concepts, such as culture. Furthermore, it downplays simplistic market- and efficiency-driven explanations for the diffusion of concepts and innovations, including MAC models. The framework usefully combines important institutional arrangements or configurations with a focus on actors or groups of actors (stakeholders). Thus, the interplay between institutions and various actors is central. This is in contrast to many other governance frameworks that focus on abstract structures and neglect how coalitions of powerful actors shape the business systems.

Aguilera and Jackson define corporate governance as "the relationships among stakeholders in the process of decision making and control over firm resources" (2003: 450). They develop a synthetic model of CG systems with the purpose of explaining diversity across advanced capitalist economies. From their perspective, this entails going beyond simplifications of: 1) an Anglo-American shareholder model with dispersed ownership, equity financing, active markets for corporate control and flexible labor markets; and 2) a Continental European stakeholder model with concentrated ownership, long-term debt financing, weak markets for corporate control and rigid labor markets.[4]

Aguilera and Jackson's (2003) point of departure is the three groups of stakeholders: capital, labor and management.[5] On the basis of examples from the CG systems in the US, the UK, Continental Europe and Japan, they develop a number of propositions relating to the three stakeholder groups and institutional configurations. This chapter is confined to discussing those insights of their model that are assessed to have implications for MAC models. The model is illustrated in Figure 5.1.

First, *capital* differs in terms of its concentration, identity and commitment. Aguilera and Jackson (2003) draw on the distinction between "financial" and "strategic" capital. In Anglo-American countries, ownership is dispersed, mainly held by individual or institutional investors, and weakly committed to the firms. The objectives of firms are closely linked to maximizing shareholder value, and capital is referred to as "financial." Legally, shareholder rights are stronger in the US than in Europe. In the Continental European model, capital is concentrated among firms, banks and families. Commitment to the firm is argued to be strong, and value is defined in terms of a set of stakeholders that extends beyond shareholders. Thus, the nature of capital differs between the two regions.

Second, *labor* participation in corporate governance is much weaker in the US than in Continental and North European countries. In the latter countries, strong unions and representation of employees at the corporate board level provide labor with stronger rights. These rights are related to a higher degree of firm-specific skills among employees. For example, in Japan, skill formation takes place in firms, whereas skills are acquired externally in the US. Consequently, the US favors a more flexible labor market with portable skills.

Third, *management* differs with respect to both hierarchy and ideology. In the US, top management has relatively high authority and is more inclined to impose hierarchical structures. In contrast, German and Japanese management teams are more dependent on firm-specific relationships with various stakeholders, which encourage a stronger commitment to the firm. In the latter firms, managerial dominance is balanced by large

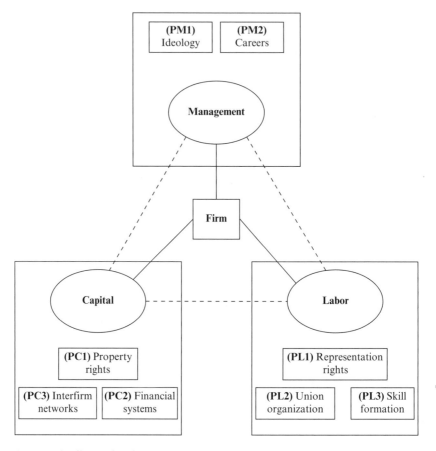

Source: Aguilera and Jackson (2003: 452).

Figure 5.1 Institutional domains shaping corporate governance

shareholders, strong unions and a tradition of consensus. Furthermore, functional orientations differ. US managers typically have a general management background, often with a strong emphasis on finance. German managers, on the other hand, typically have degrees in technical fields, such as engineering. Aguilera and Jackson (2003) therefore distinguish between a financial orientation and a functional orientation of management, stating that "the diffusion of shareholder value as management ideology in the last decade reinforces the power of financial orientations within the firm" (Aguilera and Jackson, 2003: 458).

These three groups of stakeholders (capital, labor and management) are used later in this chapter to structure the analysis of the relationship between BB models and CG systems.

The Gourevitch and Shinn classification

Gourevitch and Shinn (2005) developed a classification of different political corporate governance systems based on different coalitions and the power of those coalitions. In similarity to Aguilera and Jackson (2010), Gourevitch and Shinn's (2005) classification is based on a political perspective of corporate governance with three groups of stakeholders: owners (O), managers (M) and labor (W). These stakeholders form different coalitions, and different political models emerge on the basis of the relative strength of the coalitions. As shown in Table 5.1, Gourevitch and Shinn (2005: 23) identify six models, which are useful for positioning the CG systems of Norway and the US.

Politically, the United States exemplifies a liberal market economy. In the classification described in Table 5.1, the US corporate governance model belongs to the "investor" model. Owners and managers are stronger than labor. The latter group is weakly organized, as trade unions have never been strong in the US. In addition, employee skills are portable, which encourages a flexible labor market. Importantly, however, there is also a significant conflict between owners and managers. Agency theory's assumption of a divergence of interests between owners and managers underlies much of the research about US corporate governance (Jensen and Meckling, 1976; Shleifer and Vishny, 1997). This is in accordance with the dispersed ownership structure of US companies, where it is rare to find large shareholders exercising direct control over management. This has led to periods of "managerism" (model 6), in which top managers have looked after their own interests rather than the interests of owners. To mitigate managerial agency problems, individualized performance

Table 5.1   A political classification of governance systems

Coalitional lineup	Coalitional outcome	Political coalition label	Ownership concentration
Owners + managers vs. labor	O + M > W	1. Investor model	Diffusion
Owners + managers vs. labor	O + M < W	2. Labor model	Blockholding
Owners vs. managers + labor	O < M + W	3. Corporatist model	Blockholding
Owners vs. managers + labor	O > M + W	4. Oligarchy	Blockholding
Owners + labor vs. managers	O + W > M	5. Transparency	Diffusion
Owners + labor vs. managers	O + W < M	6. Managerism	Diffusion

Source: Based on Gourevitch and Shinn (2005).

contracts with market-based incentive schemes have become important in the US. The well-developed, soundly regulated capital market also plays a role in US corporate governance, as it transmits valuable signals and information, and puts pressure on management through the market for corporate control (e.g., hostile takeovers).

In Norway, which is geographically part of both the Nordic and the Scandinavian countries,[6] the political system is a social market economy, which is similar to the systems found in the other Scandinavian countries. It is typically governed by a coalition of parties (a non-majority system). The Scandinavian countries have a history of corporatism and consensus, which to some extent remains part of economic and political life (Campbell and Pedersen, 2007). The balance of power among capital, labor and the state is critical in the Scandinavian political model.

An important aspect in the context of this chapter is the influence of trade unions and organized labor in Scandinavia. The strong position held by organized labor and trade unions makes it difficult to radically restructure companies or to lay off employees (Thompson and Wallace, 1994). It has also been an obstacle to the far-reaching individualization of wage contracts (Frøland, 1997). As in several Continental European countries (e.g., Germany, Austria and the Netherlands), lower-level employees are represented on Norwegian corporate boards. In fact, the legally binding Companies Act in Norway requires that at least three of the board members be employee representatives.

In addition, there is the concept of "Scandinavian management," which refers to a particular style of leadership at the organizational level. Scandinavian management is characterized by the low mobility of the workforce, low power distance, teamwork and a democratic but relatively slow decision process (Grenness, 2003; Stensaker et al., 2008). Moreover, although shareholders have become an increasingly important stakeholder group in the Scandinavian countries, it is far from uniformly accepted that the goal of the public company is simply to maximize shareholder value (Högfeldt, 2005). However, it should be stressed that the Scandinavian countries differ in this regard. The importance of the state as a shareholder is most pronounced in Norway, where the state holds controlling blocks of shares in some of the largest firms. In particularly, the country's oil and gas resources are viewed as a common national treasure to be preserved for future generations.

In terms of Gourevitch and Shinn's (2005) model in Table 5.1, Norway shares similarities with the "labor" model (model 2). The presence of far-reaching employee rights and strong unions supports this conclusion. However, Norway also shares some characteristics with the "corporatist" model (model 3). Gourevitch and Shinn (2005) use a standard measure of corporatism: the Hicks–Kenworthy measure. The measure supposedly captures such elements as the degree of consensual decision making, centralized collective bargaining and ownership concentration. Of the 18 OECD countries, only Sweden and Austria score higher on corporatism than Norway.

BEYOND BUDGETING

The 12 Beyond Budgeting Principles

The best-known feature of the Beyond Budgeting movement is probably its strong opposition to budgets and budgeting. The dysfunctions of budgets described by supporters of Beyond Budgeting are many, as are the arguments for removing budgets. As other chapters in this book describe the Beyond Budgeting model in depth, this chapter is mainly concerned with the 12 Beyond Budgeting principles, which are often viewed as the core of the Beyond Budgeting idea. The 12 principles, as presented on the Beyond Budgeting Round Table's website, are provided in Table 5.2 (BBRT, 2011).

The first six principles are referred to as "leadership principles," while the last six are known as "process principles." The model is said to be holistic rather than a "menu of options" (BBRT, 2011). Thus, an organization is regarded as having gone Beyond Budgeting only when all of the principles have been followed and implemented. The principles in Table 5.2 are the most recent. Over the years, the principles have changed somewhat and they have been expressed in different ways.

The key persons behind the initial development of the principles were Hope and Fraser (e.g., Fraser, 2001; Hope and Fraser, 2003). Interestingly, Hope and Fraser avoid addressing issues relating to potential conflicts between shareholders in the 12 Beyond Budgeting principles. However, their concern with shareholder value and a finance approach is evident, at least in their early works. For example, in discussing share options, Hope and Fraser (2003) refer to Alfred Rappaport (1999) and state:

> He believes in the power of shareholder value measures to evaluate and reward executive performance provided that such measures are based on returns equal to or better than those earned by the company's peer group or by broader market indexes. This approach supports the general relativity principle of the Beyond Budgeting Model. (Hope and Fraser, 2003: 118)

Furthermore, the work of financial economist Michael C. Jensen is repeatedly acknowledged by Hope and Fraser (e.g., Hope and Fraser, 2003).

Table 5.2   The 12 principles of Beyond Budgeting

Governance and transparency

1. Values   Bind people to a common cause, *not a central plan.*
2. Governance   Govern through shared values and sound judgment, *not detailed rules and regulations.*
3. Transparency   Make information open and transparent, *don't restrict and control it.*

Accountable teams

4. Teams   Organize around a seamless network of accountable teams, *not centralized functions.*
5. Trust   Trust teams to regulate their performance; *don't micro-manage them.*
6. Accountability   Base accountability on holistic criteria and peer reviews, *not on hierarchical relationships.*

Goals and rewards

7. Goals   Set ambitious medium-term goals, *not short-term fixed targets.*
8. Rewards   Base rewards on relative performance, *not on fixed targets.*

Planning and controls

9. Planning   Make planning a continuous and inclusive process, *not a top-down annual event.*
10. Coordination   Coordinate interactions dynamically, *not through annual budgets.*
11. Resources   Make resources available just-in-time, *not just-in-case.*
12. Controls   Base controls on fast, frequent feedback, *not budget variances.*

Source: BBRT (2011).

Jensen is a well-respected, defender of agency theory and shareholder value (e.g., Jensen, 2010). Presumably, Hope and Fraser's shareholder orientation can, to some extent, be explained by their relationship with the UK, where management's fiduciary duties to shareholders are stated in company law.

Nevertheless, this chapter leaves this other rhetoric aside and defines the genuine Beyond Budgeting idea as being composed of the 12 Beyond Budgeting principles.

The Beyond Budgeting Model in Norway

Bjarte Bogsnes has worked as a manager in Norwegian firms, mainly in controller and finance functions. He has also been active in HR functions.

He has been a key player in the implementation of Beyond Budgeting in two Norwegian firms. Although Bogsnes writes in English, the main audience for his book – *Implementing Beyond Budgeting: Unlocking the Performance Potential* (2009) – is likely to be Norwegian practitioners (CFOs, HR specialists and consultants). In addition, Bogsnes has taken an interest in communicating and discussing his ideas with the academic research community.

In his book, Bogsnes is highly critical of budgets and budgeting. However, he seems to emphasize the behavioral effects of budgets, such as demotivation, more than the direct cost savings gained from removing budgets:

> Cost budgets tend to be spent, even when the initial budget assumptions change (which they almost always do). Managers do not necessarily behave like this to cheat; they do it because the system encourages them to do so. Managers see budgets as entitlements, as bags of money handed out at the beginning of the year. Nobody gets fired for spending their budgets. (Bogsnes, 2009: 15–16)

For Bogsnes, Beyond Budgeting is something more than, and perhaps even different from, rolling forecasts. He argues that rolling forecasts are based on fixed periods related to calendar rhythms:

> Why is the five-quarter horizon the right answer? And why should there be one fixed forecasting frequency and horizon for all the different businesses in the company? Our crude oil traders and geologists have very different time perspectives. Why should they all be forced into the same rhythm? The calendar also dictates when forecast updates should take place. (Bogsnes, 2009: 171)

Bogsnes proposes dynamic, event-based forecasting as an important alternative to rolling forecasts.

With regard to balanced scorecards, Bogsnes also expresses some concern. However, his criticism is not of scorecards as such, but of the top-down manner in which they are often implemented in organizations:

> Detailed budgets, supported by consequences people fear if the numbers are not met, are a proven and effective way of tying an organization's hands and feet. Implementing a scorecard does not necessarily solve this problem. It actually can make things worse. If such a control mind-set remains unchallenged and unchanged, scorecards often are used to tighten the control screw even harder. (Bogsnes, 2009: 160)

An important assumption in Bogsnes's book relates to human nature. He says that he firmly believes in the goodness of human nature and that people can be trusted, commenting that "trust is perhaps the most important word in the Beyond Budgeting vocabulary" (Bogsnes, 2009: 8) and "the model is based on trust, on the belief that the majority of people are mature and can be trusted to spend money wisely" (Bogsnes, 2009: 143).

Furthermore, Bogsnes is not overly enthusiastic about a purely financial approach to management. He recognizes a need to change the mindset of finance people, stating that: "This responsibility takes quite a different mind-set and competence from what we typically find in finance. It requires a holistic perspective, a broad understanding of strategy and organizational behavior, on top of the necessary business and financial competence" (Bogsnes, 2009: 166).

Bogsnes avoids defining the goal of the corporation only as maximizing shareholder value. Instead, he prefers to talk about "sustainable results" (e.g., Bogsnes, 2009: 139). In addition, his concern with different stakeholder groups is apparent: "if we want to create sustainable value, we cannot ignore any of the company's stakeholders" (Bogsnes, 2009: 164).

Whereas bonuses and the banking of bonuses based on the creation of shareholder value are important in VBM models, Bogsnes is critical of bonus systems, especially individualized bonus schemes. In this regard, he emphasizes that "I have totally lost my belief in individual bonus systems" (Bogsnes, 2009: 29). Instead, Bogsnes suggests the introduction of collective rewards that reward shared success based on measures of relative performance.

Finally, Bogsnes adopts a pragmatic stance towards the 12 Beyond Budgeting principles, as evidenced by his statements that "the relative importance of each principle might vary depending on the business in question" (Bogsnes, 2009: 56) and "As for the model, it is not perfect. We do not have all the answers. We are on a journey" (Bogsnes, 2009: 210).

The Beyond Budgeting Model in the US

Steve Player is a management consultant and program director for the North American Beyond Budgeting Round Table (BBRT). As Player is a US-based consultant, his audience is likely to be US-based practitioners (finance directors, controllers and CEOs). As a long-standing columnist for the magazine *Business Finance*, which explicitly targets financial executives, Player has a clear orientation towards finance. This section draws on two articles published by Player:[7] "Why some organizations go 'Beyond Budgeting'" (Player, 2003) and "New paths to dramatically improve your planning and control processes" (Player, 2007).

At first sight, what is most striking about Player's 2003 paper is that it does not include a description of the Beyond Budgeting principles. Ten principles had been set down a few years earlier (Becker et al., 2010), and

12 principles were presented as early as 2001 (Fraser, 2001).[8] The lack of principles in Player's 2003 paper could imply that he did not perceive a call for the full implementation of all principles as completely realistic. However, it is clear in the 2003 paper that Player perceives shareholders as the primary stakeholder. From his perspective, Beyond Budgeting serves as a means to increase shareholder value: "these key value drivers lead to the creation of shareholder value and sustained competitive success" (Player, 2003: 9).

Although he states that "Beyond Budgeting is a guiding set of principles" (Player, 2003: 8), Player seems highly preoccupied with management tools (MAC models). He argues that the full potential of these tools can be enabled only after budgets are removed. In order of importance, these tools are "shareholder-value models," "benchmarking models," "balanced scorecards," "activity-based management," "customer relationship management models" and "enterprisewide information systems" (Player, 2003: 8).

In the 2007 article, Player expresses his enthusiasm for balanced scorecard models. Interestingly, as argued by Player (2007), limited autonomy seems to be created through the use of balanced scorecards. The desirable element is that balanced scorecards enable everyone to understand their roles: "From a philosophical standpoint, the balanced scorecard tries to create a system of front-line empowerment where everyone knows what to do because the firm's strategy is explicitly mapped to the actions needed to execute the strategy" (Player, 2007: 42).

Another interesting aspect of Player's writings is the emphasis on the merits of rolling forecasts. For Player, Beyond Budgeting seems to be largely equivalent to rolling forecasts. In describing a case company in which rolling forecasts had been introduced, Player states: "Planning Transformation Leader Jamie Croake noted that their culture had changed to a much more forward-looking approach to driving their business" (Player, 2007: 41).

Player is also highly concerned with the capital market and legislation, stating that "investors and regulators are demanding higher standards of reporting. They will make life difficult for those that do not comply" (Player, 2003: 7). Player's preference for shareholder-value models and his preoccupation with the capital market imply an orientation towards finance.

In both of Player's papers, Beyond Budgeting is viewed as a means to revitalize organizations perceived to be bureaucratic and inefficient. Furthermore, Player focuses on the immediate cost savings achieved from removing the budget. He suggests that budgets simply cost too much, commenting: "your organization can never become a true lean enterprise if it continues to use a traditional push budgeting system" (Player, 2007: 42).

Table 5.3   The North American Beyond Budgeting principles

---

1. *Relative goals and rewards* – Set aspirational goals and reward performance based on continuous relative improvement rather than fixed targets.
2. *Continuous planning and controls* – Make planning and control an inclusive and continuous process based on relevant and open information rather than an annual (and highly political) budgeting process.
3. *Resources as needed* – Use resources and coordinate actions based on current customer demand rather than annual allocations and predetermined plans.
4. *High performance culture* – Lead by setting clear principles, boundaries and high performance standards rather than through detailed rules and budgets.
5. *Freedom and capability to act* – Transfer decision-making scope, authority and capability (including open information) to small front-line teams rather than direct and control operations from the center.
6. *Accountability for results* – Make terms accountable for improving (internal and external) customer outcomes and relative performance rather than meeting internally negotiated targets.

Source: http://www.bbrtna.org/principles.html (accessed April 15, 2013).

Notably, in his second paper, Player takes a pragmatic stance towards the 12 principles of Beyond Budgeting. He argues that an evolutionary approach is a safer way of achieving many of the benefits from Beyond Budgeting: "For most financial executives, the revolutionary approach seems far faster than they feel they can go" (Player, 2007: 41). Furthermore, when referring to practice in North America, Player (2007) argues that an evolutionary path may be preferred by many organizations: "This path includes an organization's move to adopt the Beyond Budgeting principles using a more gradual approach that seeks to try key parts of the Beyond Budgeting philosophy while continuing to utilize some form of traditional budgeting" (Player, 2007: 41).

Interestingly, the North American branch of the BBRT recently launched six principles of Beyond Budgeting. This means that the North American branch now has its own set of principles and, consequently, a different set of criteria for implementing Beyond Budgeting. These principles, which are presented in Table 5.3,[9] are further analyzed in the next section.

ANALYSIS

The previous section discussed the texts produced by two influential Beyond Budgeting writers. This section starts by sorting out the various dimensions along which the two writers have divergent views. In the next step, these dimensions are related to differences in the corporate governance settings. The analysis links each of the stakeholder groups (capital, labor and management) to elements in the two BB models.

Two Models of Beyond Budgeting

Bogsnes and Player approach the BB idea in different ways. Bogsnes adopts a visionary view in which BB is revolutionary and involves changing the mindsets of people. Player, on the other hand, adopts a more practical orientation. He focuses on the costs of budgeting and the technical benefits of various management tools, such as rolling forecasts.

The two writers' assumptions about human nature also differ. Bogsnes clearly states that he believes that people can be trusted. It follows that employees do not have to be monitored and controlled. From a theoretical perspective, Bogsnes's views have similarities with the "stewardship theory of management" (see, for example, Donaldson and Davis, 1991). Player is less explicit about his view of human behavior. He avoids the word "trust," and his top-down approach to balanced scorecards seems to indicate a belief that formal controls are needed. His endorsement of shareholder-value models based on incentive contracts designed to align the interests of shareholders, managers and lower-level employees also points in this direction. Player's BB model seems to resemble agency theory more than stewardship theory.

Furthermore, Bogsnes and Player have somewhat different views of the balance between autonomy and control, which seem to largely reflect their perspectives on human nature. Bogsnes favors radical decentralization and he is generally critical of incentive schemes, especially individual bonuses. Player also favors decentralization, but is reluctant to give up control by insisting on the inclusion of tools to align employees' interests with those of shareholders.[10]

In addition, the functional perspectives adopted by Bogsnes and Player differ. Bogsnes, who has worked with finance issues in practice, emphasizes a broader management perspective. Player, on the other hand, seems to understand Beyond Budgeting mainly through the lens of finance.

Finally, Bogsnes and Player differ in their perspectives on the organization and its goals. Player is explicit in expressing his view of shareholders as the most important stakeholder group and in stating that the goal of the firm is to maximize shareholder value. Bogsnes is more ambivalent. Although he may be in favor of maximizing long-term shareholder value, he also speaks of sustainable results. Furthermore, Bogsnes stresses that no stakeholders can be ignored if an organization is to achieve sustainable results.

Table 5.4   Comparison of the two BB models along five dimensions

Dimensions	Author	
	Bjarte Bogsnes	Steve Player
Approach to the BB idea	Visionary/to change the mindset.	Practical/technical focus on MAC tools.
Assumption about human nature	People can be trusted (stewardship theory).	Trust is downplayed; alignment through contracting (agency theory).
Autonomy versus control	Radical decentralization; incentive schemes are often dysfunctional.	Decentralization, but alignment through incentive schemes (contracting).
Functional perspective	Management/ organizational behavior (in addition to finance).	Finance.
Stakeholder focus	Focus on many different stakeholders to achieve long-term value.	Main focus on shareholders and maximizing shareholder value.

Table 5.4 summarizes the five dimensions along which Bogsnes's and Player's assumptions, thoughts and views differ. It is important to note that the two models share some important similarities. First, both Bogsnes and Player are critical of and opposed to budgets and budgeting. Second, they are both focused on markets and in favor of delegating responsibility to front-line managers.[11] Third, they both take a pragmatic stance with regard to implementing the 12 Beyond Budgeting principles.

BB Models and CG Systems

MAC models and management models in general are not neutral tools (e.g., Chua et al., 1989). By prioritizing some interests over others, they distribute wealth among stakeholders. In accordance with the political perspective on governance, the diffusion and successful adoption of MAC models are a function of the power held by various stakeholders. As the model by Aguilera and Jackson (2003; see Figure 5.1) indicates, the relative power and constellations of stakeholder groups differ among CG systems. This may explain variations in the patterns of MAC model diffusion across countries. In other words, MAC models are embedded in systems of corporate governance that are specific to countries and, to some extent, to groups of countries.

This section uses the political CG framework to theorize about this embeddedness by providing examples from the BB models. In line with Aguilera and Jackson's (2003) model, each of the three stakeholder groups (capital, labor and management) are addressed separately.

Capital

In the US, the shareholder-value norm is influential, and the capital market plays an important role. In this governance context, the fact that the 12 principles of Beyond Budgeting do not explicitly mention the creation of shareholder value as organizational objective may be viewed as a drawback. This may be one reason why shareholder value is emphasized by Player. Through his emphasis on the creation of shareholder value, Player translates the BB idea into a model that is more consistent with the US governance setting.

In contrast, the fact that the 12 principles of BB do not address conflicts between capital and labor might be an advantage in the Norwegian CG system of powerful unions and extensive labor rights. In Norway, owners are more committed, and they are often concerned with avoiding conflicts with labor or left-wing politicians in government. The stakeholder orientation in Norway may also explain Bogsnes's concern with addressing all stakeholders and achieving "sustainable" results.[12]

Labor

As skills are typically formed outside firms in the US, US firms are less dependent on employees and employees are less committed to their firms. This suggests that it is difficult for trusting relationships to develop. In the US BB model, as expressed by Player, trust has been downplayed or ignored. Furthermore, in the new principles of the North American BBRT, the word "trust" has been removed. Arguably, this could be related to the influence of agency theory in the US and its assumptions of opportunistic behavior. Thus, in the US context, it may be difficult to understand the rather abstract concept of trust.

In Norway, extensive employee protection makes it difficult to lay off employees. Employees often stay in firms for longer periods of time, and they typically have the opportunity to acquire new skills and to participate in decision making. The low power distance could also support the development of trust-based relationships. Furthermore, trust in employees may rhetorically appeal to labor in Norway. Accordingly, trust is strongly emphasized in the Norwegian BB model, as expressed by Bogsnes. Finally, the persistent criticisms of budgets and bureaucracy could also rhetorically appeal to lower-level employees and some managers.

Management

In the US, management has a significant amount of authority, and many organizations are relatively hierarchical. This may explain not only why the US BB model takes a top-down approach to implementing balanced scorecards but also why Player is more reluctant to radically decentralize organizations. Player favors decentralization, but he encourages the use of incentive contracts that align the interests of the agent with the principal. Bogsnes's position of giving up control in favor of decentralization is more consistent with the flatter structures of Scandinavian organizations.

Furthermore, the functional orientation of managers differs. In the US, top managers often have an educational background in finance. In Norway, they typically have a wider range of educational backgrounds. More generally, top managers are less likely to be finance professionals in Scandinavia than in the US. This may explain why Player emphasizes the role of finance in top managers' work. Finally, the orientation toward finance further reinforces the shareholder-value concept, which is central in finance theory.

Arguably, the Beyond Budgeting idea is more in line with the Scandinavian governance context than the US context. It might be difficult to incorporate certain elements, such as shared values, teamwork, radical decentralization and trust, into the "investor" model common in the US. These elements seem more compatible with "labor–corporatist" models in which consensus, collaboration and compromise are considered important.

The 12 Beyond Budgeting principles in Table 5.2 are more consistent with the writings of Bogsnes (the Scandinavian model) than with the writings of Player (the US model). The two models differ along a number of dimensions. This may be a minor problem, as the Beyond Budgeting idea has a high degree of interpretive viability. Translation can be achieved by pragmatically selecting or placing varying emphasis on the different BB principles. Furthermore, many of the principles are ambiguous enough to leave room for different interpretations. This may explain why BB has substantial coverage in terms of its distribution across various countries and regions. Nevertheless, this flexibility has not stopped the North American BBRT from developing its own set of principles.

What, then, are the differences between the six principles of the North American BBRT and the original 12 Beyond Budgeting principles? A comparison of the two sets of principles shows that concepts such as "shared values," "trust" and "peer reviews" have been excluded from the principles of the North American BBRT. These are the concepts that would seem less relevant in the US corporate governance setting.

CONCLUSION AND FUTURE RESEARCH

The purpose of this study was to contribute to the literature on the diffusion and transferability of management models (e.g., Abrahamson, 1996; Malmi, 1999; Bourguignon et al., 2004; Fiss and Zajac, 2004; Ax and Bjørnenak, 2005, 2007). This study has extended existing knowledge about how a given idea or basic model can be adapted or translated to a different economic, political, social or legal context. Furthermore, it has demonstrated that a comparative, political corporate governance framework can provide valuable insights into the transferability of management models.

This chapter shows that the two models of Beyond Budgeting (the Scandinavian model and the US model) differ along five important dimensions: 1) approaches to the BB idea, 2) assumptions about human nature, 3) views on autonomy versus control, 4) functional perspectives and 5) stakeholder focus. The differences are so substantial that it is justified to talk about two different models of the same idea.[13]

The relative power, constellations and supporting institutions of various stakeholder groups (capital, labor and management) provide good theoretical explanations for the translations of the Beyond Budgeting idea. This political governance framework may also be useful for examining the diffusion and translation of other MAC models.

It could be argued that this chapter does not address the interests of organizational actors further down in organizations. The counterargument is that, from a political CG perspective, those in power decide. The introduction of a new MAC model in a firm is a big decision, one which sometimes involves radical organizational change. The CFO, for example, can drive the process, but a decision to go Beyond Budgeting normally requires persuading and gaining acceptance from both the CEO and the board of directors.

Nevertheless, empirical studies at the organizational level seem to be important for the future. Such studies could focus on a number of questions: How do the perceptions of Beyond Budgeting in, for example, Norwegian organizations differ from those in US organizations? What elements of the respective BB models are adopted and what explanations do organizational actors provide for selecting those elements? Is the BB idea more appealing to Scandinavian organizations than those in the US, as suggested in this study? Furthermore, what part of the BB management literature is only rhetoric and how are the BB models actually implemented in organizations?

A political corporate governance framework could also be used to study the diffusion, translation and adoption of other MAC models. For example, it would seem difficult to introduce shareholder-value models, such as EVA, in some of the largest Norwegian firms. The Norwegian state owns controlling blocks of shares in many very large firms, such as Statoil (oil and gas), DnB (banking) and Telenor (telecommunications). Therefore, a shareholder-value model is likely to be met with political opposition, at least under the current left-wing government, as the model is not aligned with existing institutional norms as defined by powerful stakeholders. Conversely, in countries with a "shareholder model" of corporate governance, such as the US, we would expect to see models that are sensitive to the demands of the capital market. As mentioned, some of the more visionary ideas of Beyond Budgeting may be difficult to sell into US organizations. This highlights the importance of studying the supply side of MAC models. What models are most frequently used by consultants to sell in their services in different countries? Such questions are undoubtedly important for future research.

Finally, this chapter takes no normative stance on whether one of the two BB models is better. Rather, it can be argued that both writers have made the right decision in selecting the elements of the BB idea that appeal to their targeted audiences in the different governance contexts.

NOTES

1. The concept of "Beyond Budgeting models" is used in the plural because one of the main points in this chapter is that there is more than one model, or version, of the Beyond Budgeting idea. If we follow broader definitions of MAC systems, such as those proposed by MacIntosh and Quattrone (2010), Beyond Budgeting models can also be referred to as MAC models.
2. The wide range of literature about diffusion is beyond the scope of this study. This chapter is confined to addressing the concepts and findings that are assessed to be of relevance to this study.
3. Similar, although not identical, concepts such as translation, adaptation and imitation have been used in place of diffusion depending on for example the methodological orientation of the researcher.
4. It is assumed that the Scandinavian countries, including Norway, resemble the Continental European model. This assumption is supported later in this section.
5. The state is not directly present as a stakeholder, although it is implicitly considered to be part of the regulatory environment. As discussed later in this chapter, the state is important in the Norwegian context as owner of considerable blocks of shares in some large Norwegian firms.
6. There are clear differences among the Nordic countries. Nevertheless, this chapter adopts the well-grounded empirical position that there are also important similarities among the Scandinavian (Denmark, Norway and Sweden) and Nordic countries (Denmark, Finland, Iceland, Norway and Sweden).
7. These are the two main articles published by Player about Beyond Budgeting.
8. See Becker et al. (2010) for a detailed account and analysis of the development of the BB model.
9. The membership lists of the North American BBRT and the International BBRT differ

significantly. Most of the organizations on the North American list are based in North America. This supports the argument made in this study that the two Beyond Budgeting writers target different audiences.
10. Notably, even Bogsnes is reluctant to completely let go of control. His insistence on collective rewards based on shared success implies possible control of the individual through pressure from the group.
11. However, Bogsnes's model includes a more radical form of delegation and creation of autonomy.
12. The stakeholder orientation is especially relevant in some of the very large firms where the state is a major shareholder.
13. The term "housing concept" could be used in place of "idea" (Ax and Bjørnenak, 2007).

REFERENCES

Abrahamson, E. (1996), "Management fashion," *Academy of Management Review*, **21** (1), 254–85.
Aguilera, R.V. and G. Jackson (2003), "The cross-national diversity of corporate governance: Dimensions and determinants," *Academy of Management Review*, **28** (3), 447–65.
Aguilera, R.V. and G. Jackson (2010), "Comparative and international corporate governance," *Academy of Management Annals*, **4** (1), 485–556.
Ahmadjian, C.L. and G.E. Robbins (2005), "A clash of capitalisms: Foreign shareholders and corporate restructuring in 1990s Japan," *American Sociological Review*, **70** (3), 451–71.
Armstrong, P. (2002), "Management, image and management accounting," *Critical Perspectives on Accounting*, **13** (3), 281–95.
Ax, C. and T. Bjørnenak (2005), "Bundling and diffusion of management accounting innovations – the case of the balanced scorecard in Sweden," *Management Accounting Research*, **16** (1), 1–20.
Ax, C. and T. Bjørnenak (2007), "Management accounting innovations: Origins and diffusion," in T. Hopper, D. Northcott and R. Scapens (eds.), *Issues in Management Accounting*, 3rd edn., Harlow: Pearson, pp. 357–76.
BBRT (2011), "12 principles of Beyond Budgeting," available at http://www.bbrt.org/beyond-budgeting/bb-principles.html (accessed April 15, 2013).
Becker, S., M. Messner and U. Schäffer (2010), "The evolution of a management accounting idea: The case of Beyond Budgeting," Working paper, available at http://ssrn.com/abstract=1535485 (accessed April 15, 2013).
Benders, J. and K. Van Veen (2001), "What's in a fashion? Interpretive viability and management fashions," *Organization*, **8** (1), 33–53.
Bogsnes, B. (2009), *Implementing Beyond Budgeting: Unlocking the Performance Potential*, Hoboken, NJ: John Wiley & Sons.
Bourguignon, A., V. Malleret and H. Nørreklit (2004), "The American balanced scorecard versus the French tableau de bord: The ideological dimension," *Management Accounting Research*, **15** (2), 107–34.
Campbell, J.L. and O.K. Pedersen (2007), "Institutional competitiveness in the global economy: Denmark, the United States, and the varieties of capitalism," *Regulation and Governance*, **1**, 230–46.
Chua, W.F., T. Puxty and T. Lowe (1989), *Critical Perspectives in Management Control*, Basingstoke: Macmillan.

Czarniawska-Joerges, B. and G. Sévon (2005), *Global Ideas: How Ideals, Objects and Practices Travel in the Global Economy*, Malmö: Liber.

Davis, G.F. (2005), "New directions in corporate governance," *Annual Review of Sociology*, **31** (August), 143–62.

Davis, G.F. and T.A. Thompson (1994), "A social movement perspective on corporate control," *Administrative Science Quarterly*, **39**, 141–73.

Donaldson, L. and J.H. Davis (1991), "Stewardship theory or agency theory: CEO governance and shareholder returns," *Australian Journal of Management*, **16** (1), 49–64.

Fiss, P.C. and J. Zajac (2004), "The diffusion of ideas over contested terrain: The (non)adoption of a shareholder value orientation among German firms," *Administrative Science Quarterly*, **49** (4), 501–34.

Fraser, R. (2001), "Figures of hate," *Financial Management (UK)*, February, 22–5.

Frøland, H.O. (1997), "Refleksjoner rundt korporativ lønnsfastsettelse i Norge," in B.L. Basberg, H.W. Nordvik and G. Stang (eds.), *I det lange løp: Essays i økonomisk historie tilegnet Fritz Hodne*, Sandviken, Bergen: Fagbokforlaget.

Gourevitch, P.A. and J. Shinn (2005), *Political Power and Corporate Control: The New Global Politics of Corporate Governance*, Princeton, NJ: Princeton University Press.

Grenness, T. (2003), "Scandinavian managers on Scandinavian management," *International Journal of Value-Based Management*, **16**, 9–21.

Guillén, M.F. (2004), "Corporate governance and globalization: Is there convergence across countries?," in T. Clarke (ed.), *Theories of Corporate Governance*, Abingdon, Oxon: Routledge, pp. 223–42.

Hansen, S.C., D.T. Otley and W.A. Van der Stede (2003), "Practice developments in budgeting: An overview and research perspective," *Journal of Management Accounting Research*, **15** (September), 95–116.

Henttu-Aho, T. and J. Järvinen (2013), "A field study of the emerging practice of Beyond Budgeting in industrial companies: An institutional perspective," *European Accounting Review*, published online January 17, DOI: 10.1080/09638180.2012.758596.

Högfeldt, P. (2005), "The history and politics of corporate ownership in Sweden," in M. Randall (ed.), *A History of Corporate Governance around the World*, Chicago, IL: University of Chicago Press, pp. 517–80.

Hope, J. and R. Fraser (2003), "New ways of setting rewards: The Beyond Budgeting model," *California Management Review*, **45** (4), 104–19.

Hopper, T., T. Koga and J. Goto (1999), "Cost accounting in small and medium sized Japanese companies: An exploratory study," *Accounting and Business Research*, **30** (1), 73–86.

Jensen, M.C. (2010), "Value maximization, stakeholder theory, and the corporate objective function," *Journal of Applied Corporate Finance*, **22** (1), 32–42.

Jensen, M.C. and W.H. Meckling (1976), "Theory of the firm: Managerial behavior, agency costs and ownership structure," *Journal of Financial Economics*, **3** (4), 305–60.

Johanson, D. and K. Østergren (2010), "The movement toward independent directors on boards: A comparative analysis of Sweden and the UK," *Corporate Governance: An International Review*, **18** (6), 527–39.

Jones, T.C. and D. Dugdale (2002), "The ABC bandwagon and the juggernaut of modernity," *Accounting, Organizations and Society*, **27** (1/2), 121–63.

MacIntosh, N. and P. Quattrone (2010), *Management Accounting and Control Systems: An Organizational and Sociological Approach*, Chichester: John Wiley & Sons.

Malmi, T. (1999), "Activity-based costing diffusion across organizations: An exploratory empirical analysis of Finnish firms," *Accounting, Organizations and Society*, **24** (8), 649–72.

Nørreklit, H., L. Nørreklit and P. Melander (2006), "US 'fair contract' based performance management models in a Danish environment," *Financial Accountability and Management*, **22** (3), 213–33.

Ortmann, G. (1995), *Formen der Produktion: Organisation und Rekursivität*, Opladen: Westdeutscher Verlag.

Østergren, K. and I. Stensaker (2011), "Management control without budgets: A field study of 'Beyond Budgeting' in practice," *European Accounting Review*, **20** (1), 149–81.

O'Sullivan, M. (2000), *Contests for Corporate Control*, Oxford: Oxford University Press.

Player, S. (2003), "Why some organizations go 'Beyond Budgeting,'" *Journal of Corporate Accounting and Finance*, **14** (3), 3–9.

Player, S. (2007), "New paths to dramatically improve your planning and control processes," *Journal of Corporate Accounting and Finance*, **18** (3), 37–43.

Rappaport, A. (1999), "New thinking on how to link executive pay with performance," *Harvard Business Review*, March/April, 91–101.

Rogers, E.M. (1983), *Diffusion of Innovations*, New York: Free Press.

Shleifer, A. and R.W. Vishny (1997), "A survey of corporate governance," *Journal of Finance*, **52** (2), 737–83.

Stensaker, I.G., H.H. Larsen and J. Schramm-Nielsen (2008), "Adjusting organizational change processes to the Scandinavian context," Working paper, March 14.

Stewart, G.B. (1991), *The Quest for Value: The EVA Management Guide*, New York: HarperCollins.

Strang, D. and J.W. Meyer (1993), "Institutional conditions for diffusion," *Theory and Society*, **22** (4), 487–511.

Thompson, P. and T. Wallace (1994), "Trade unions and organizational innovation: British and Swedish experiences," *Employee Relations*, **16** (2), 53–64.

Westney, D.E. (1987), *Imitation and Innovation: The Transfer of Western Organizational Practices to Meiji Japan*, Cambridge: Cambridge University Press.

Young, S.D. and S. O'Byrne (2001), *EVA and Value-Based Management: A Practical Guide to Implementation*, New York: McGraw-Hill.

6. Putting Beyond Budgeting ideas into practice

Katarina Kaarbøe, Inger Stensaker and Teemu Malmi

INTRODUCTION

This chapter examines how management control practices aiming to move firms "Beyond Budgeting" are interpreted and implemented, and how they subsequently affect practice. Practitioners of Beyond Budgeting have criticized budgeting for some time (Wallander, 1999; Hope and Fraser, 2003a), claiming that the widespread dissatisfaction with budgeting results from the cost of preparing budgets, the gaming associated with the budgeting process and the increased environmental uncertainty that companies face. As a result, numerous companies have replaced annual budgets with alternative forms of management control. These approaches range from technical substitutes, such as rolling forecasts and benchmarking, to more comprehensive solutions, including team structures, empowerment, new policies and more philanthropic human resource practices, which some call Beyond Budgeting (BB) (Becker, 2011; Østergren and Stensaker, 2011). Indeed, the literature presents conflicting evidence on the benefits of budgeting practices and the extent to which companies are abandoning those practices. While the evidence shows that firms are increasingly implementing BB, one stream of research suggests that relatively few companies have actually abandoned budgets altogether or plan to do so (Ekholm and Wallin, 2000), and that budgets continue to be used for motivation and for performance evaluations (Libby and Lindsay, 2010).

One reason for the inconsistent findings may be that there are multiple conceptualizations of accounting and its use in organizations depending on the context and the groups of actors involved (Nahapiet, 1988; Mouritsen, 1999; Ahrens and Chapman, 2007). Furthermore, some studies examine budgeting in isolation from its organizational and social contexts. Such studies rely on limited frameworks and focus on only a few variables (Ihantola, 2006). Increasingly, budgeting research has sought to understand why budgeting practices work in some contexts but not in others. A number of studies have attempted to correct for the simplifications found in functionalist studies by arguing that accounting both shapes and is shaped by its context (Jönsson, 1987; Ahrens and Chapman, 2007).

Two streams have evolved in research emphasizing the importance of context. The first focuses on a proper fit among accounting, operations and strategic priorities (Chapman, 1997). The second deals with the practical understanding of management controls through their use by organizational members (Nahapiet, 1988; Mouritsen, 1999). In this latter line of research, often called "accounting as practice," accounting is understood as forming and being formed by the context and by those who use the system. This is where we aim to contribute.

The aim of this study is to explore how managers make sense of BB's ideas and put those ideas into practice. The development of such insights requires an interpretative perspective, which enables us to take a deeper look into how BB ideas inform and influence control activities within organizations. Only by probing how BB is actually used for control can we discuss the consequences and impacts of BB as a management control system.

In order to understand how companies work with BB as a management control practice, we draw on a comparative case study of how BB ideas were practiced in three different business units of a large multinational corporation. We find that, after BB ideas were introduced, organizational members practiced management control in a variety of ways. On the basis of sensemaking theory, we analyze how those practices were linked to individuals' sensemaking of new ideas and the perceived applicability of those ideas to the local circumstances. Our findings suggest that only one of the three business units practiced BB as prescribed at the corporate level. In the two remaining business units, organizational members struggled to see the benefits of the new system and to change their practices. In fact, one business unit formally reintroduced budgets as its official control system.

Organizational members struggled with BB implementation because BB requires making sense of complex information. For some managers, this complexity was overwhelming, and resulted in a fragmented view of the information and in perceptions of reduced control relative to the control offered by budgets and accounting. In contrast, managers who succeeded in changing their practices in line with BB generally felt that the more complicated informational picture was valuable. Typically, these managers held broader, more holistic views of their own roles in the organization, which were reflected in the decisions they made. As a result, the learning process became more important to them than the budgeted numbers.

This chapter is structured as follows. In the next section, we present the key ideas of BB and our theoretical point of departure. This is followed by a discussion of our methodological approach and an introduction of the focal company. We then show that different BB practices were prevalent within the three business units, and we contrast these practices with the corporate intentions. Our analysis shows how organizational actors made sense of and acted upon BB. The concluding section provides a summary of the main theoretical inferences of the study, and a discussion of the balance between control and autonomy.

BEYOND BUDGETING: A COMPREHENSIVE MODEL

"Beyond Budgeting" was initially used by the consultants Hope and Fraser (1997, 2003a, 2003b, 2003c) to describe a form of management that was not based on annual budgets. Hope and Fraser found their inspiration in the ideas of Jan Wallander, the former CEO and chairman of Sweden's Handelsbanken (Wallander, 1999; Hope and Fraser, 2003a). Hope and Fraser present BB as an integrated management model in which the goal is to abandon the budget-constrained style of management control without putting an end to financial planning. The broad scope of their ideas is illustrated by two groups of principles: 1) *aligning management processes with leadership actions*; and 2) *leadership action principles* (bbrt.org). As the term suggests, "aligning" principles seek to better align strategy with operational activities by introducing, for example, flatter hierarchical relationships, decentralized functions, increased autonomy and responsibility, increased transparency, and clear goals. In contrast, "leadership action" principles aim to strengthen the focus on customers by increasing autonomy at lower levels. This involves setting relative goals, rewarding shared successes, using continuous planning, avoiding control by variances against plan (no focus on deviations) and refraining from the use of annual budgets.

The BB initiative appears significantly more comprehensive than other developments within management control systems, such as the balanced scorecard (BSC) and activity-based costing (ABC). For instance, BSC and ABC were initially promoted in the literature as new tools for control. Later, these new tools were placed in a broader context and aggregated into something resembling a management philosophy (Jones and Dugdale, 2002; Bible et al., 2006). In contrast, BB is more abstract. From the beginning it has represented more of a philosophy or a way of thinking about control. It cannot, therefore, be viewed as a simple tool or technique.

BB, as described by Hope and Fraser (2003a), is a comprehensive model that requires a specific management style and culture. Such comprehensive models appear complex and may fundamentally challenge existing norms in organizations that have previously relied on budgets as their primary lever for control. The BB system comprises a number of ideas. The extant literature provides some indications of the basic assumptions and underlying ideas found within BB. However, although these principles are prescriptive, they do not include specific information about how to put the principles into practice or make them work. As general principles, therefore, they leave room for interpretation and can be put into practice in various ways.

A number of recent studies on accounting practices have explicitly aimed to develop theory on the variety of accounting and control practices (Mouritsen, 1999; Vaivio, 1999; Jørgensen and Messner, 2010). This interpretative stream of research suggests that, in many organizations, different understandings (or accounts) compete against each other as individuals attempt to make sense of and assess the desirability of a particular set of control practices (Mouritsen, 1999; Vaivio, 1999). For example, Vaivio (1999) illustrates that differences in functional backgrounds and local practices inform employees' customer orientations. Mouritsen (1999), on the other hand, shows how the term "flexible firms" was introduced as a notion for being customer oriented. Such studies suggest that different types of accounts of control practices may compete against each other as employees work to make sense of the desirability of a particular practice. However, we know little about how conflicting accounts affect management control practices.

This study intends to contribute to this stream of research by adopting a sensemaking perspective to analyze how different organizational members make sense of and act upon BB control systems. This sensemaking perspective appears appropriate, as it emphasizes the linkages between cognition and action, and can therefore provide information about how controllers and managers within the operational sphere of the organization interpret corporate BB ideas, and about the accounts they provide in relation to their control practices.

THE SENSEMAKING PERSPECTIVE

Sensemaking theory provides insight into how individuals make sense of ambiguous and novel situations (Gioia and Chittipeddi, 1991; Weick, 1995). Sensemaking can be defined as "the meaning construction and reconstruction by the involved parties as they attempt to develop a meaningful framework for understanding the nature of the intended strategic change" (Gioia and Chittipeddi, 1991: 442). Organizational members use sensemaking processes to attempt to resolve the uncertainty and ambiguity often associated with new ideas (Balogun and Johnson, 2004). On the one hand, therefore, sensemaking allows organizational members to create rational accounts of what, why and how to change, which in turn enables action (Maitlis, 2005). On the other hand, sensemaking is just as likely to occur after action in a retrospective manner, where individuals attempt to make sense of their own behavior or that of others (Weick, 1995).

Sensemaking is both a cognitive and a social process. Recent sensemaking research tends to emphasize the social aspects (Maitlis, 2005) by tapping, for instance, into ongoing conversations among organizational members. Accounts of what a new system is about and descriptions of how it has been put into practice provide evidence about how sense has been made, as opposed to information on the cognitive (and less available) processes that take place inside an individual's head. Through both cognitive and social sensemaking processes, individuals construct interpretations of the changes, which can be more or less in line with the corporate intentions and the rationale behind those changes.

In our study, we examine how organizational members interpret and make sense of BB by tapping into their control practices (actions), interpretations and accounts (expressed thoughts) concerning BB. We are interested in uncovering whether control practices appear unified across organizational units and the extent to which control practices coincide with corporate intentions. We expect BB practices to be more likely to lead to the outcomes desired by management if the BB system is viewed as favorable in the organizational context, and if management actively gives sense to the new system, shows how to put it into practice and provides a rationale for why doing so may be beneficial.

METHOD

An investigation of the issues we explore here requires access to an organization that has adopted BB ideas and attempted to change its management control system accordingly. The empirical study presented here involves a corporation that has been experimenting with the introduction of a more dynamic management control system that is clearly based on BB ideas.

The organization, "OilCo," operates within the oil and energy industry. Although this case is drawn from a single organization, multiple cases facilitate comparison, and can highlight similarities and contrasts. We therefore sought to obtain contextual variation by employing a comparative research design in which we selected three strategic business units that differed in terms of the nature of the business and the expected degree of implementation of BB ideas.

Our primary method of data collection was interviews, which were conducted during the autumn of 2008 and the spring of 2009. We conducted 30 semi-structured interviews with managers involved in operational, human resource and financial activities at different levels. We also interviewed several lower-level employees. Each interview lasted approximately one hour. We asked open-ended questions to allow interviewees to explain linked events. Several master's students helped us with the data collection (Haaland and Ytreland, 2009; Ribe, 2009).

THE CASE COMPANY AND THE BB CONTROL SYSTEM

OilCo – Background

OilCo is a public, limited listed oil and energy company based in Norway. At the time of our study, the company was organized into six strategic business units. The three business units that were selected for our case study were INT (international activities), EPN (Norwegian activities) and M&M (petrol stations).

Beyond Budgeting Becomes "Ambition to Action"

In this section, we describe the intentions of corporate headquarters with regard to BB. The development of a new, comprehensive control system implies sensemaking at the corporate level. However, for our purposes, we describe the corporate system as it was presented internally, without probing the interpretations and translations that took place at the corporate level.

OilCo[1] chose to label its BB project "Ambition to Action" (A2A). The move towards a more dynamic and holistic management control system had, according to the respondents, evolved over a period of 15 years. It comprised efforts to introduce more dynamic control systems, implement the BSC and implement BB in the form of A2A processes. While the first two changes paved the way for BB, we focus on the final step – the decision to move towards BB by introducing A2A. On October 1, 2008, OilCo officially abolished annual budgets.[2] From that day on, the board no longer accepted annual budgets.

Bjarte Bogsnes (2009: 114), the model's creator, described A2A as follows: "Ambition to Action is our version of the balanced scorecard and also the name of our integrated performance management process, which runs all the way from strategy to business management and into individual goals, evaluation, and rewards." A2A included four processes: 1) strategy and target setting, 2) planning, 3) dynamic resource allocation and 4) holistic performance evaluation.

A2A differed from OilCo's previous budgetary system in four key respects. First, the target-setting processes, which addressed *where* the company was heading, were separated from planning and resource alloca- tion. Previously, the company relied on a single budgetary process that took place once a year. The goal of this shift was to make targets more ambitious, and to base those targets on external expectations and competi- tor performance.

The second change was that forecasting or *planning processes* would take place continuously rather than annually. These new processes aimed to address *how* to reach the ambitious targets and to produce *realistic* financial forecasts. The separation of targets from forecasts was an explicit attempt to reduce incentives for gaming, which occurs when targets are set at a level where they can easily be reached.

The third change was a move toward continuous *allocation of resources* to the business units. Resource allocations were previously handled in a detailed, annual process. In the new system, resources were to be allocated whenever a business unit (BU) had a good project. Such allocations were to be made through a joint process involving all of the BU managers, forcing them to look beyond their own divisions and evaluate projects based on a number of criteria.

The fourth change consisted of the introduction of a *holistic perform- ance evaluation process* (known as People@OilCo), which focused on per- formance not only in terms of delivery but also in relation to behavior. The previous bonus system was based on objective criteria related to deviations between targets and outcomes. In A2A, the bonus system also included subjective dimensions and dialogue.

MAKING SENSE OF BB PRACTICES WITHIN THE THREE BUSINESS UNITS

Although A2A was officially implemented in October 2008, the system was still practiced in different ways in the three BUs at the time of our study. Our analysis indicates that only one of the three BUs successfully transformed its organization in line with the corporate A2A principles and ideas. Table 6.1 summarizes our main findings.

In this section, we illustrate how BU members practiced and made sense

Table 6.1   Interpretation of BB in the three business units

	INT	EPN	M&M
Business unit context	Long-term, high-risk, large investments in international, collaborative exploration projects.	Long-term investments in national exploration projects.	Downstream activities (refining and petrol stations). More short-term financial investments.
New management control practices – general perception at the business-unit level	Successful transformation to A2A.	A2A appears to be implemented, but old practices seem to have been reintroduced.	Dual practices coexist and little change is evident.
Four separate process 1. Target setting 2. Forecasting 3. Dynamic resource allocation 4. Evaluation based on delivery (KPIs) and behavior	Control is practiced in the form of four separate processes, which are described as logical and consistent.	The four processes are described according to corporate intentions, but they are not consistently put into practice.	The four processes are described according to corporate intentions, but they are not practiced, particularly at lower levels.

of the new control system. We examine the underlying reasons for the varied responses in the three BUs and argue that a number of challenges kept individuals in two of the BUs (EPN and M&M) from making sense of the new control system. As one BU (INT) successfully transitioned to the new system, we can also identify several conditions that facilitated the introduction of the BB-like system.

INT: Successfully Putting A2A into Practice

In the INT business unit, annual budgets were completely replaced with the four A2A processes. The respondents provided unified, coherent accounts of their management practices, which were generally in line with corporate intentions.

First, respondents indicated that INT set ambitious targets. However, if the targets became too ambitious (to the extent that they might negatively affect motivation), then there was a possibility to renegotiate them in a "target-review process": "Basically, you have the flexibility. You can adjust and modify actions during the process when you see that something needs to be changed in order to be optimized, improved or made more efficient. Therefore, I think that [A2A] is a good thing" (financial manager, INT).

Secondly, the planning process was also altered in accordance with intentions at the corporate level. After the introduction of A2A, forecasting took place during the autumn through a bottom-up process in which deliveries were specified and "expectation-oriented forecasts" were presented. As the forecasting process took place after the targets were set, forecasting served to illustrate expectations in relation to the targets. Forecasts were updated throughout the year, so that they resembled a rolling forecast.

The third change introduced in the new control system related to the resource-allocation process. Most respondents argued that resource allocation had become more dynamic as a result of A2A, as it was possible to obtain resources throughout the year. One respondent explained that previously one would have needed the right contacts to obtain the necessary resources, whereas the priorities had become clearer with the new system, making the need to know the "right" people less important. Several respondents described the new system as more flexible and stated that it enabled the organization to respond more quickly to new opportunities: "The good thing with BB is that you can get acceptance for relatively large projects that were not in the business plan. That gives you the possibility to create something new if you have a good argument and if it is related to the strategy of the company" (vice president, INT).

Finally, in relation to the fourth control process, our data suggest that, under the new control system, evaluations within INT were based on both delivery (key performance indicators, or KPIs) and behavior. However, some challenges related to evaluating individual behavior, particularly the issue of subjectivity, surfaced in our interviews: "[The] behavioral [dimension] is difficult, but we are more mature now. We have had this system for two years and we are much better at setting the behavioral goals" (vice president, INT).

As the above quotes indicate, organizational members in this business unit typically described their new management control system in favorable terms, referring to it as more flexible and dynamic. They argued that the new management control system resolved a number of challenges the unit had been dealing with for some time. Budget gaming and the resulting demotivation were resolved through the adoption of A2A, as the budget had been removed. Respondents also described how the IT part of

A2A had replaced several different systems, resulting in a lower number of steering documents and the inclusion of all elements in a single A2A IT system. This was viewed as an improvement. Furthermore, the management information system (MIS) within A2A was perceived as more action oriented: "We had an enormous amount of steering documents before . . .This [A2A] is a step towards making it easier" (manager, INT).

The superiority of the new control system was also apparent in respondents' references to increased system transparency. Some interviewees felt that this served to increase accountability and responsibility: "You can see how you [have an] influence on the bigger picture, step by step" (financial manager, INT).

Respondents argued that the A2A implementation finalized a process the organization had been working on for some time. Some managers referred to budgets as a rigid, silly tool that had been used in the past: "It is obvious that there is something unhealthy with budgeting. I remember when the focus was on using all of the existing resources before the end of the year. It was silly. I remember that – but it was a long time [ago] – in the 1970s or maybe the 1980s" (vice president, INT).

In sum, our evidence indicates that A2A was practiced within INT in accordance with the corporate intentions. In line with the corporate goals, the introduction of A2A practices in INT appears to have reduced gaming, lowered the level of bureaucracy, increased flexibility and resulted in a renewed focus on action.

Furthermore, organizational members in INT described the new system as a more standardized, homogeneous system developed through a continuous, incremental process that gradually replaced the more fragmented control systems. They also viewed A2A as more coherent. All in all, they not only accepted the A2A ideas, but also seemed to view them as widely accepted norms. Thus they had fully adopted the corporate views on budgetary and non-budgetary systems. The implications of the new control system for individuals in INT were also perceived as positive. The system was believed to have increased accountability and responsibility, which was motivational for most respondents. The role of the management control system can therefore be understood as a *mechanism for reflection*. The system created opportunities for individuals to reflect on their decisions instead of blindly focusing on budget figures.

EPN: Realizing that Beyond Budgeting Practices Are Also Constraining

In the EPN business unit, managers and controllers generally undertook management control in line with the new corporate intentions. However, we found evidence of a reintroduction of budget-like procedures. In fact, some managers speculated about whether the unit was still, in fact, following the A2A principles. The following quote illustrates one manager's attempt to make sense of the new system: "The difference is not all that great. BB, yes, but as long as we have KPIs and constraints – what do we have then? Do we have budgets or not?" (operational manager, EPN).

In line with corporate intentions, target setting was stretched (high ambition), and targets were set through dialogues with superiors and/or subordinates. These targets were linked to KPIs. Respondents reported that they could influence KPIs to a certain extent, but that some indicators were more difficult to influence. When asked whether performance measures were compared internally or externally, one respondent reflected on the need to develop more external benchmarks. This suggestion was in line with corporate ideas, and the need for such benchmarks appeared to be clearly understood:

> [Measures are] mostly internal . . . . There are some discussions about whether we could externally benchmark our exploration costs. If we find something at $10 a barrel, is it good or bad? [The CEO] does not know. No one knows. If our competitors find oil at $4 a barrel, then $10 is not good. However, if we find it at $4 or $6, then it is good. (Controller, EPN)

The planning process was not described to the same extent by EPN respondents as by the INT respondents. While corporate intentions included proactive, aggregated and action-oriented planning, we found limited support for (or against) such planning in EPN: "Previously, we were much more detail oriented. Now it is more about coaching, advising and challenging. It works well for us and I think it is an advantage, but we need time to do it. We have to be very visible" (controller, EPN).

In the new management control system, resource allocation was intended to be more dynamic and continuous. The respondents indicated that this goal fit with how EPN managers used the new control system: "We have gotten used to dynamic resource allocation. For example, you may have a project in which you attempt to identify the potential for oil and gas exploration. If the potential . . . is good enough and satisfies our criteria, then we say 'go'" (controller, EPN).

These statements suggest that resource allocation had become more dynamic. However, some managers argued that the criteria for resource allocation had not changed: "I do not really see the difference. When hard realities hit, it pretty much boils down to the same thing" (manager, EPN).

Finally, the fourth process, evaluation, appeared to be practiced largely in accordance with corporate intentions. In this regard, a combination of behavioral and performance indicators was evident: "With [the CEO], the focus on behavior has increased. It is not just what you deliver; it is also how you deliver" (operations manager, EPN).

At first glance, therefore, EPN appeared to practice the A2A control system according to corporate goals and guidelines. However, some respondents stated that they increasingly experienced budgetary constraints after the financial environment changed (as a result of the financial crisis), and some speculated about whether their business unit had returned to the previous way of reporting and controlling activities. Hence, managers and controllers in EPN initially successfully implemented and used BB. However, they then imposed budgetary constraints, which represented a reversal in practice but not on paper. Official descriptions of procedures and the control system still reflected a BB perspective, indicating a loosely coupled system in which formal descriptions did not match the actual practices.

Some discussions indicated that budgets were increasingly being used, which some EPN respondents viewed as positive:

Respondent: We miss a greater focus on budgets. . . . We start budgeting next week, so we are not entirely BB. (Manager, EPN)
Interviewer: Why do you say that you "miss" budgets?
Respondent: I see that they are returning. The first year, we did not have many budgets . . .. There was much less structure than I am used to. However, now it is becoming similar to what I am used to. (Manager, EPN)

For some EPN employees, especially those responsible for licensing agreements with other companies, budgets were required by their partners. Hence, BB as a control system was used in parallel with budgets employed in cooperation with other companies. This made it difficult for employees in EPN to understand the difference between budgets in the line organization, where the budget was decided by the board, and project budgets decided by their managers.

Others argued that, although budgets might not have been necessary, they offered clear advantages. In this respect, some claimed that the new control system was less precise and that it did not allow employees to do their jobs properly. These employees never actively began to use the new system. Such respondents showed little interest in attempting to put the new system into practice, and they referred to it as loose and sloppy: "It was a major transformation . . .. I am used to management based on budgets" (manager, EPN). "For us, BB was an unknown world. We experienced it as very loose . . .. There is less focus on detailed and accurate budgets" (manager, EPN).

The most negative responses to the A2A system came from managers who had joined OilCo in connection with a recent merger. These managers came from an organization in which budgets were the main control mechanism. They questioned the objectivity of the new system and argued that it was difficult to evaluate performance using such imprecise values as "hands on." In addition, they argued that, although behavior was important, it was more important to focus on delivery.

In summary, at first glance the practices in EPN appear to have moved toward BB and, by definition, towards A2A. However, a closer examination reveals that budgets were still used, and that organizational members in this division either defended the use of budgets or explained that budgets had to be reintroduced after the financial crisis. Particularly in later periods, there is evidence that the practices retained (and perhaps reintroduced) features from the previous system.

However, while some managers welcomed the return of budgets, other organizational members struggled to discern the difference between the old and the new management control systems. The most critical group of managers encompassed those who had come to OilCo from an organization that relied on a budgetary regime. Some of these employees did not attempt to understand or learn A2A. Instead, they employed their old systems and practices, as they felt the A2A system had no legitimacy. The various accounts provided by EPN managers about the new management control system differ, with these employees appearing to be divided into two groups: one arguing that the organizational reality had become fuzzier and less detailed, and the other describing the reality in terms of increased transparency.

M&M: Dual Systems in Practice

Management practices appeared to vary across organizational levels in the M&M business unit after A2A was introduced. At the managerial level, the new management control system was practiced in line with corporate goals, albeit with some frustration: "It took a year or two before we understood that we did not need to make detailed budgets. We continued to call them 'budgets,' but that has changed. Now we work with target setting, forecasts and KPIs" (country manager, M&M).

However, we failed to find coherent descriptions of the four new processes at lower organizational levels. Although a key goal of the project was to separate these processes in time, they were often described as occurring simultaneously. In particular, descriptions of the target-setting and forecasting processes were intertwined. In addition, budgets were still used, sometimes together with some of the BB processes.

Among the petrol stations, the new control system did not influence practice to a notable extent. Instead of moving towards BB and introducing the four new processes, annual budgets were still used in this part of the M&M division: "The sales organization is built on budgets, so we still use budgets for each petrol station, and we spend lots of time on them. We do not dare to stop" (controller, M&M).

Organizational members described the sequence of their control activities in the following way. A budget was derived through bottom-up budgeting. That budget was then translated into a number of KPIs. Targets were not set prior to forecasting. In fact, forecasting appeared to occur *before* targets were set. Respondents argued that this process fit the business context better.

Budgets were used internally in M&M, while KPIs were reported to the corporate level for control purposes. From the corporate-level perspective, therefore, it may have seemed that A2A had been implemented within the business unit. As the quote below shows, KPIs were also used within the business unit to a certain extent, although most respondents were more eager to talk about the limitations of KPIs. Hence, the tools for measuring and benchmarking were not viewed as constructive:

> You can use KPIs (to benchmark), but the problem is and was that, when we reach this level of aggregation, it is no longer possible to compare the different countries. Also, the fact that our own system [the IT system] does not offer the possibility to consolidate target setting and the KPIs that are used makes it difficult. (Finance manager, M&M)

The new forecasting process was also an issue of concern, as it was not synchronized between levels. For example, respondents explained that they often lacked information in their forecasting processes, as the processes in M&M Denmark and M&M Europe were not synchronized. Moreover, M&M employees could not see how dynamic resource allocation could be possible. They argued that the BB model was not dynamic because the targets for the following year were decided at an early stage and could not be changed afterwards.

M&M managers were measured on both delivery and behavioral factors, although this two-dimensional focus was not yet entirely in place in Denmark. There was some frustration about the specific KPIs, with some managers arguing that they were not within the individual's span of control and therefore unfair: "We have a way to go in relation to A2A. There should be goals that the manager can influence" (HR manager, M&M).

Clearly, management practices within M&M (particularly in the petrol stations) were not in line with the corporate intent. Rather, the previous, budget-focused control system guided the practices. Some elements of the new system could be found, but overall there were more traces of a budgetary control system than a BB system. When attempting to make sense of the new practices, organizational members in M&M focused on the shortcomings of the new system and argued that it was a poor fit for their business. Individuals in M&M also struggled to understand how A2A could be put into practice and presented arguments that served to legitimize the "old" practices.

In addition, some individuals were unsure about whether they had moved toward BB, as they still had budgets, stating: "I believe there are both [A2A and budgets] . . . because I do not know the difference between a budget and a forecast. We send our 'forecasts,' but they look like budgets to me" (HR manager, M&M).

There was also some uncertainty about whether budgets remained relevant. This ambiguity was apparent in the respondents' descriptions of the new management control system. When asked to describe A2A, one employee responded: "It is . . . hmmm . . . a much smaller budgeting process" (employee, EPN).

Another employee interpreted A2A as the IT system (MIS) and argued that, although it probably had value for others, it was not something that he used:

> I think it is good with these dashboards in MIS where you can see things. It is not personally anything I use. I use other tools to find out how things went last year . . . but, for managers or other people, it is fantastic that they have dashboards, so they can get an idea of how we are doing. However, it is *only* an idea. (Employee, M&M)

Several respondents expressed an inability to understand A2A, or its implications for practice and behavior. Such challenges in making sense of new systems tend to impede action, as most individuals require some level of understanding to change their behavior. In M&M, several employees simply relied on old practices and actively legitimized doing so, as illustrated in the following quotes: "I cannot see any problems with having a shadow budget, as long as a lot of time is not used on it, because people are driven by their own way of thinking. That is great – let them do that" (employee, M&M). "I think the idea and the whole concept of BB are good. It is a fascinating idea, but moving from idea to practice is difficult" (employee, M&M).

These respondents consistently referred to difficulties in understanding the purpose of the new system, and how it should impact their work behavior and management practices. Respondents failed to see how the different elements created a consistent, unified control system. Instead of viewing A2A as a holistic approach, they perceived the new management control system as insufficient and inappropriate. Sensemaking of existing practices predominantly centered on explaining why A2A did not apply to the business unit. This accentuated the idea of A2A as a management ideal rather than something that affected the work of employees in the division. Nevertheless, employees recognized A2A as important for top management, and they understood the importance of referring to the new labels and constructs.

In summary, A2A was not effectively put into practice in the M&M business unit. The descriptions of management practices indicate that few of the ideas within BB and the corporate A2A system influenced practice in M&M. Individuals struggled to make sense of A2A, and perceived the new ideas as irrelevant to or inappropriate for their activities. Some individuals saw merit in the new system, but primarily for others.

Those managers who struggled with the unresolved sensemaking resolved this conflict by attributing responsibility for the A2A information system to the controllers, while they themselves continued to rely on budgets. M&M managers perceived the management control system as a *mechanism for getting better information for planning.*

DISCUSSION OF FINDINGS

We have described how BB ideas adopted at the corporate level were put into practice in three business units. As previous implementation studies have shown, new management techniques tend to be used in various ways depending on how managers respond to those ideas (Oliver, 1991; Modell, 2009). Our findings suggest that the adoption of the new management practices varied based on how individuals made sense of those practices. Individuals in two of the BUs (EPN and M&M) clearly struggled to make sense of some of the ideas inherent in the A2A system, and found it difficult and, at times, not sensible to adopt A2A in their business contexts. In this section, we theorize about explanations for the competing practices.

Making Sense of Beyond Budgeting Ideas

We have presented BB as a comprehensive control system encompassing a number of elements. As BB is a fairly recent innovation, there are few examples to draw on with regard to the implementation of these ideas. As such, the A2A system is extremely ambitious. Although OilCo's corporate management had formulated the new management control system, there was no general consensus about what BB was – was it a tool, a philosophy or both? The term "Beyond Budgeting" itself does not answer this question. Instead, it suggests what BB is not –it is *not* budgeting. Moreover, OilCo labeled both the management control system and the supporting IT system as A2A, and Bogsnes (2009) referred to A2A as a form of balanced scorecard. In general, this ambiguity and the general debate about what BB actually means, which can be observed in both academic and practitioner communities (Becker et al., 2010; Libby and Lindsay, 2010), are likely to create confusion about the practices and implications associated with this new control system.

In addition, our findings suggest that the introduction of BB triggers various perceptions about the role of the control system. Some individuals apply a broader, more holistic view of their own roles in the corporation and are thus capable of generating value from widespread sources of information. However, organizational members who understand their context as having a single predominant goal – securing a balance in their books – and who operate within organizational contexts that emphasize a shorter-term focus struggle to make sense of the new ideas. They tend to view BB as a fragmented system that ultimately leads to a loss of control.

Constructing the Fit Is Also about Sensemaking

Previous research has shown that new ideas implemented in contexts where they are perceived to have a poor fit may become corrupted (Lozeau et al., 2002). Although certain systems may have a better fit with particular business contexts and logics, our analysis indicates that individual sensemaking is also important. Managers construct their perceptions of organizational contexts and the roles of new systems in a way that supports their notion of fit (or poor fit), as organizational fit itself cannot be objectively measured.

Among those OilCo organizational members who succeeded in making sense of A2A, the new system was perceived as responding to long-standing organizational challenges, such as budgetary gaming, bureaucratic decision-making, reporting and information-handling processes, and rigid resource-allocation processes. In this regard, A2A promised an improvement, particularly within INT. In such units, the new system was viewed as compatible with and beneficial for the organization, and managers believed that the role of the system was to enhance reflection in their decision-making processes. INT's managers argued that A2A provided them with valuable, multifaceted information, and stated that the system's dialogue and qualitative measures increased the quality of their decisions. Conversely, among the petrol stations operating within M&M, managers found it difficult to understand how a complex, comprehensive control system could be beneficial. Employees in this division appear to have expected the management control system to provide improved information about how to increase profitability. As the system included vast amounts of information, it was difficult for these organizational members to understand what to use or how to draw appropriate conclusions.

The Importance of Role Models

Role models can facilitate sensemaking by providing visual illustrations of how new ideas, such as non-budgetary control, can be put into practice. In this sense, role models allow other individuals to see the new system in action *before* they think about the relevance or appropriateness of that system. Previous research has shown that, in highly institutionalized contexts (such as hospitals), changes can be made from *within* the system if managers or employees in the organization are able to illustrate how the new system functions and how it might be superior to previous ways of working (Reay et al., 2006; Østergren, 2009). In our study, respondents who struggled to see how to apply A2A ideas lacked role models who could pave the way toward a better understanding and use of the new system. In contrast, individuals in INT had role models in close proximity, which made it easier for them to see how BB should be practiced.

In addition, new employees who do not have readily available role models, such as those in the EPN business unit, may be less inclined to adopt non-budgetary control systems. In our study, their idea of control was closely linked to a command-and-control philosophy and budgets, and they were typically unable to talk about control without referring to budgets. In other words, the fact that they lacked role models and that their experience and training were based on traditional budgetary control blocked their sensemaking. They were therefore unable to understand planning and control in a new way.

In sum, an understanding of the various elements of A2A, especially the need to replace ordinary budgets with the four new processes, the logic behind the different components, and ways of putting the ideas into practice, was facilitated by role models. Our findings also suggest that proximity to role models can offset a lack of sufficient time to make sense of ambitious (and sometimes ambiguous) new ideas.

CONCLUDING DISCUSSION

The BB control system comprises many different elements. As a result of its broad scope and comprehensiveness, BB is more open to interpretation and less clear cut in its design than other control tools such as target costing, ABC or BSC. Our study shows that, in contrast to ABC or BSC,

BB is not a readily available tool that can easily be implemented. Rather, it is a collection of ideas that materialize as different tools and processes, which makes sensemaking and coordinated action challenging.

We observed a variety of practices in three business units that had allegedly adopted and implemented a BB control system. We argue that variations in individual sensemaking about control practices and differing organizational contexts led to this range of practices. Interestingly, we find that a comprehensive BB system triggers sensemaking about the role of management control systems. BB seems to encourage managers to question their own decisions and to be continuously prepared to make changes in the desired path. Consequently, forecasts and benchmarks need to be continuously reviewed. Individuals who adopt top management's view of the problems associated with budgets and who agree that the new management control system can resolve existing challenges are better able to make sense of BB and change their control practices accordingly. As a result, some organizational members perceive the new control system as improving their decision making, while others essentially perceive a loss of control related to the introduction of non-budgetary practices. For the latter, the control system creates a conflict, even though it aims to allow for both control and autonomy by providing decision-making freedom.

Two contextual features figure in individual sensemaking. First, practices are influenced by how individuals view the nature of their work. Whereas previous research has tended to treat the fit between new organizational tools and the organizational context as an objective measure, we argue that the perception of fit depends on individuals' sensemaking. Organizational members with a single predominant goal – securing a balance in their books – and those operating within organizational contexts that emphasize the shorter term struggle to make sense of these new ideas. They tend to view BB as a fragmented management control system that leads to a loss of control. The second contextual feature that may influence the extent to which new techniques are understood as "fitting" is the availability of role models that can give sense to the new practices. Individuals who are surrounded by others who successfully use BB have numerous opportunities to learn from them.

These findings suggest the need for three interrelated refinements of the management control literature. First, the notion of practice variation in the use of control systems needs to be reconceptualized to illuminate how such variations are entangled with managerial and organizational sensemaking processes. While the extant contingency literature focuses on how budgeting systems fit with contingent variables (Chapman, 1997), our findings suggest that sensemaking entails important elements of serendipity when organizations experiment with various management control ideas. While the literature on management control has largely ignored such processes, it may be extended through an integration with investigations of how people make sense of new ideas and, thus, how they learn about and understand new systems. The successful adjustment of a new management control system to a particular organizational context may require the selective incorporation of design elements in order to create a clearer picture of what is being developed.

Second, in recognition of the fact that experimenting with management control systems entails important aspects of sensemaking, we need to abandon the view of such new systems and organizational innovations as relatively momentary phenomena with a limited long-term impact on practices. In line with Mouritsen (2005), our findings show the importance of engaging in a relatively long sensemaking process in order to understand the new ideas and how they can be implemented in a fruitful way given the context at hand. The design and use of the BB system are not separate. Rather, they are intertwined by the idea of continuous improvement. Furthermore, if new members in the organization can frequently interact with others who use and understand the system, they can make sense of BB more rapidly. A relevant issue for future research, therefore, is how management can facilitate making sense of new ideas and putting them into practice through sense giving.

Third, our study provides a language that helps us to talk about BB practice. As Ahrens and Chapman (2007) argue, the contribution of practice theory is that it provides a language for talking about skillful practical activity in context and for recognizing the constitution of context through action. BB practice is not a unidimensional concept. Its interpretation depends on how business units make sense of the practice as it develops.

The BB concept is based on the idea of balancing autonomy and control by using management control tools in a different way. By loosening up traditional budgetary control, companies attempt to increase autonomy and individual responsibility. The idea is to move away from pure accountability and make the managers more responsible for their decisions. However, our study shows that individuals within the company are likely to adopt very different interpretations of how to balance autonomy and control depending on when they were exposed to the new ideas of BB.

NOTES

1. We have chosen to call the company OilCo because the company's name in itself is not of importance. However, the company is Statoil, and it has not asked to remain anonymous.

2. See Østergren and Stensaker (2011) for an analysis of the pilot sites. The analysis shows how they participated in and continuously developed ideas on how to work with A2A.

REFERENCES

Ahrens, T. and C.S. Chapman (2007), "Management accounting as practice," *Accounting, Organizations and Society*, **32**, 1–27.
Balogun, J. and G. Johnson (2004), "Organizational restructuring and middle manager sensemaking," *Academy of Management Journal*, **47**, 523–49.
Becker, S.D. (2011), "The innovation, change, and implementation of budgeting techniques," Ph.D. thesis, WHU Otto Beisheim School of Management, Koblenz.
Becker, S., M. Messner and E. Schæffer (2010), "The evolution of a management accounting idea: The case of Beyond Budgeting," Working paper, Presented at the Beyond Budgeting Workshop, Bergen, September.
Bible, L., S. Kerr and M. Zanini (2006), "The balanced scorecard: Here and back," *Management Accounting Quarterly*, **7** (4), 18–23.
Bogsnes, B. (2009), *Implementing Beyond Budgeting: Unlocking the Performance Potential*, Hoboken, NJ: John Wiley & Sons.
Chapman, C.S. (1997), *Controlling Strategy: Management, Accounting, and Performance Measurement*, Oxford: Oxford University Press.
Ekholm, B.G. and J. Wallin (2000), "Is the annual budget really dead?," *European Accounting Review*, **9** (4), 519–39.
Gioia, D.A. and K. Chittipeddi (1991), "Sensemaking and sensegiving in strategic change initiation," *Strategic Management Journal*, **12**, 443–8.
Haaland, L.H. and G. Ytreland (2009), "Beyond Budgeting i Statoil" [Beyond Budgeting in Statoil], Master's thesis, SNF Report series, Bergen.
Hope, J. and R. Fraser (1997), "Beyond Budgeting: Breaking through the barrier to the 'the third wave,'" *Management Accounting*, **11**, 20–23.
Hope, J. and R. Fraser (2003a), *Beyond Budgeting: How Managers Can Break Free from the Annual Performance Trap*, Boston, MA: Harvard Business School Press.
Hope, J. and R. Fraser (2003b), "Who needs budgets?," *Harvard Business Review*, **81** (2), 2–8.
Hope, J. and R. Fraser (2003c), "New ways of setting rewards: The Beyond Budgeting model," *California Management Review*, **45** (4), 103–19.
Ihantola, E.M. (2006), "The budgeting climate concept and its application to case organizations' budgeting – an explorative study," *Scandinavian Journal of Management*, **22** (2), 138–68.
Jones, R. and D. Dugdale (2002), "The ABC bandwagon and the juggernaut of modernity," *Accounting, Organization and Society*, **27** (1–2), 121–63.
Jönsson, S. (1987), "Frame shifting, sense making and accounting," *Scandinavian Journal of Management Studies*, **3** (3–4), 255–98.
Jørgensen, B. and M. Messner (2010), "Accounting and strategizing: A case study from new product development," *Accounting, Organization and Society*, **35**, 184–204.
Libby, T. and R.M. Lindsay (2010), "Beyond Budgeting or budgeting reconsid-

ered? A survey of North American budgeting practice," *Management Accounting Research*, **21** (1), 56–75.

Lozeau, D., A. Langley and J. Denis (2002), "The corruption of managerial techniques," *Human Relations*, **55**, 537–64.

Maitlis, S. (2005), "The social process of organizational sensemaking," *Academy of Management Journal*, **48** (1), 21–48.

Modell, S. (2009), "Bundling management control innovations: A field study of organizational experimenting with total quality management and the balanced scorecard," *Accounting, Auditing and Accountability Journal*, **22** (1), 59–90.

Mouritsen, J. (1999), "The flexible firm: Strategies for a subcontractor's management control," *Accounting, Organizations and Society*, **24** (1), 31–55.

Mouritsen, J. (2005), "Beyond accounting change: Design and mobilization of management control systems," *Journal of Accounting and Organizational Change*, **1** (1), 97–113.

Nahapiet, J. (1988), "The rhetoric and reality of an accounting change: A study of resource allocation," *Accounting, Organizations and Society*, **13** (4), 333–58.

Oliver, C. (1991), "Strategic responses to institutional processes," *Academy of Management Review*, **16** (1), 145–79.

Østergren, K. (2009), "Management practices and clinician managers: The case of the Norwegian health sector," *Financial Accountability and Management*, **25** (2), 167–95.

Østergren, K. and I. Stensaker (2011), "Management control without budgets: A field study of 'Beyond Budgeting' in practice," *European Accounting Review*, **20** (1), 149–81.

Reay, T., K. Golden-Biddle and K. Germann (2006), "Legitimizing a new role: Small wins and microprocesses of change," *Academy of Management Journal*, **49** (5), 977–98.

Ribe, S. (2009), "Lederes bruk av informasjon i styringssystemet" [Managers' use of information], Master's thesis, SNF Report series, Bergen.

Vaivio, J. (1999), "Examining 'the quantified customer,'" *Accounting, Organizations and Society*, **24** (8), 689–715.

Wallander, J. (1999), "Budgeting – an unnecessary evil," *Scandinavian Journal of Management*, **15**, 405–21.

Weick, K. E. (1995), *Sensemaking in Organizations*, Thousand Oaks, CA: Sage.

7. A new way of being a controller – from bellboy to actor

Hanne Nørreklit and Katarina Kaarbøe

INTRODUCTION

In recent decades, it has been argued that the old values, thoughts and norms regarding the appropriate way of being a controller (the role of a controller) have been disturbed, requiring the formation of new ways (Burns and Baldvinsdottir, 2007; Østergren and Stensaker, 2011). In this chapter, we tie the way of being a controller to the choice of management control method, which encompasses the logical structuring of the control phases as well as the procedures and instruments used in each of these phases (Arbnor and Bjerke, 1997). The particular method says something about the perception of the material and social subjects involved in the control activities and the form of social relations among those subjects. Accordingly, the management control method makes assumptions about the management control phenomenon, including the controller's character, his or her way of doing and the relationships formed between controller and other actors in the firm. Ultimately, the contemporary business environment might even require a paradigmatic change in the way of being a controller. Therefore, this chapter explores whether a novel management control method in a contemporary business context entails a change in the paradigm for being a controller.

Based on the book *Implementing Beyond Budgeting: Unlocking the Performance Potential* by Bjarte Bogsnes (2009), our analysis follows the controller Bjarte Bogsnes[1] over 25 years, during which he changed his and two companies' approaches to management accounting, from one of traditional corporate budgeting to a new one labeled "Beyond Budgeting" (BB). The crucial part of BB is its focus on the processes around management accounting and planning rather than on techniques (Bogsnes, 2009: xi). In self-narrative form, Bogsnes writes and tells about how he mediated this change in management control method. Overall, he was successful.[2]

The self-narrative form of the book, which says something about the engaged and embodied human being's understanding of his or her historical existence and how that existence changes (Ricoeur 1990 [1992]), makes the book particularly interesting for further analysis. However, although Bogsnes communicates the account of his change experiences,[3] it would be wrong to argue that it authentically represents the actual event. A narrative can only pull fragmented episodes into a coherent plot – the choice of interpreted episodes and plot could have been different. However, a lack of faithful representation is not a problem, since the aim of a narrative is less about describing the factual way of being a controller than about prescribing it. Thus, a narrative mediates "the descriptive viewpoint" and "the prescriptive viewpoint" (Ricoeur 1990 [1992]: 114) and hence has normative implications for action. Communicating to a wider audience, the narrative conveys Bogsnes's thoughts of how a controller could or should carry out his or her functions. Accordingly, this self-narrative aims both to relate how he changed his role as controller and to prescribe change for controllers at large. These normative implications for other controllers make the book relevant for further investigation.

Because the communicative context of the book is unique, our aim is not to make quantitative generalizations from the analysis, but rather to explore and conceptualize the nature of an emerging trend in the management accounting area. However, the book appears to have a wider business interest and acceptance: the foreword is written by Robert Kaplan, the back cover of the book contains quotes from, amongst others, the CFO of Statoil, Jan Wallander from Handelsbanken, and Jeremy Hope, cofounder of the BB Round Table and co-author of another book on BB. Moreover, the book was published by the prestigious publisher Wiley & Son. This noteworthy interest suggests that a more penetrating analysis of its thoughts is relevant for both researchers and practitioners of management control.

Our analysis reveals that Bogsnes constructs himself in opposition to the mechanical management control approach, which is rooted in a paradigm of realism. As an alternative, he advocates a more dialectic perception of the business environment and a more reflective and interactive controller. Thereby, he is able to construct himself as a controller who manages the actual forces of doing business, and by doing so makes himself more powerful in practice. Overall, we find that he advocates a more individualized and practice-oriented paradigm, which comes close to a paradigm of pragmatic constructivism.[4]

The next section describes the theoretical and methodological foundation. Subsequently, we present an analysis of a change in the way of being a controller, as reflected in the book. We conclude our analysis and put the results into perspective by reflecting on whether the book represents a shift in the paradigm for the way of being a controller.

METHODOLOGY

Methodologically, this chapter draws on discourse analysis. Below we explain the theoretical foundation of our discourse analysis and hence clarify the chapter's discourse approach. Subsequently, we raise our more theoretically founded research questions. Finally, we describe our method for analyzing the discourses embedded in Bogsnes's self-narrative.

Discourse Theory

Our analytical approach to discourse is rooted in a moderate post-structuralist perception of language. Accordingly, we do not subscribe to the structuralist assumption that there is a pre-given language system of proper stable structured signs (langue), which the individuals can make use of but not change (Saussure 1960). In this view, the language system (langue) diverges from the more random use of signs in language practices (parole). In contrast, the more post-structural view of Wittgenstein (1953) does not make a distinction between the formal language system and language practices but argues that the meaning of language is linked to social practices.

Human practices are organized around the use of language games, which is the wholeness of the language and the activity it is woven into (Wittgenstein, 1953, §7), that is, language use and thoughts and actions are linked together. Language is like a toolbox, containing a multitude of types of words and types of sentences having different functions, such as giving orders, describing, storytelling, reporting and joking (Wittgenstein, 1953, §23).

How we put words together in sentences does not depend on a fixed external rule system, but on the language game within the social practice in which the language game is used and learned. One could imagine a language game that includes only sentences that question or joke. However, imagining such a type of language would also call to mind images of a form of life. Accordingly, the type of language embedded in a set of language games as driver of thoughts and actions is bound together with a form of life (Wittgenstein, 1953, §23).

Human practices include a multitude of language games linked to different forms of life. A specific language game is constituted by using specific types of compositions, arguments, semantics, grammar and so on, all of which make it possible to discover and unfold a particular form of life. Following Wittgenstein (1953), Ricoeur (1983 [1984]) argues that human beings have the ability to generate new types of language games and hence develop new forms of life.[5] The individual has choices within a language game and hence can influence and develop new types of life forms within a social practice. However, some social conditions are required for making an expression work (Austin, 1962), which implies that the space for language choice is limited.

From such a theoretical view, the meaningful principle for generalizing language games is the type of action linked to the sign. This is prudent for the purpose of this chapter, which is to uncover the construction of new forms of saying and doing management accounting and not to trace its institutional power structure. However, because one can imagine many language games and life forms, the conceptualization of language games is challenging. In this chapter, we consider two analytical levels for generalization (Ricoeur, 1990 [1992]: 61–7). On the first level, we analyze the types of signs in the language game and link them to existence and action, that is, to form of life. On the second level, we link the production of language game to the philosophical assumptions or rather to the paradigm. Because a paradigm includes basic presumptions about the nature of our material and human life world and how to obtain knowledge (Arbnor and Bjerke, 1997), it expresses the life form of the language game at a meta-level.

Research Questions

In this theoretical view, we take Bogsnes's book to be a self-narrative description of the change in the language games of management control methods in a particular practice. We explore the specific genre, types of argument and forms of language used in the book that produce the emerging management control method and hence the change in the controller's form of life, that is, way of being a controller. We explore the life forms embedded in the narrative descriptions of the management control methods, particularly the form of social interactions and the character of the controller they represent. Finally, we consider whether the change in the life form of being a controller at a meta-level advocates a new paradigm for being a controller. On this basis we raise our more theoretically profound research questions:

1. What types of language games are embedded in Bogsnes's narrative description of the BB management control method? What life form of being a controller is shaped by these types of language games?
2. Does the emerging life form of being a controller reflect a paradigmatic change in the way of being a controller?

Method for Narrative Analysis

In answering the research questions, we draw on elements of Ricoeur's (1983 [1984]) linguistic framework for narrative analysis and the toolkit of rhetoric. The framework involves three analytical steps. The first two steps focus on the language game embedded in the narrative text, including an analysis of the pre-narration and the plot. The third step relates the textual analysis to a world view, that is, to a paradigm.

The analysis of the pre-narration involves a pre-understanding of the network of dominating micro-stories of the language game, which are the prerequisite for the narrative's plot (Ricoeur 1983 [1984]: 54). More specifically, the narrative includes a network of micro-stories of circumstances, tools, and characters with goals that interact with the world and each other, though we are interested only in the micro-stories around events that relate to traditional management control practice, BB and the change from traditional practice to BB. In particular, we are concerned with the textual features that frame the knowledge procedures, the social interactions and the controller's character. The focus for the analysis of the micro-stories is on the compositional structure (the narrative scheme and the conceptual relationship), the symbolic or semantic features (metaphors, vocabulary, semantics domains, etc.) and the syntax (the speech-act and grammar of the sentences). Together, the textual analysis provides the basis for characterizing and interpreting the types of language games embedded in each of the micro-stories and hence their respective framing of the social interactions and the controller's character.

However, to understand the dynamic forces of change embedded in the narrative, we analyze the plot, which mediates three angles (Ricoeur 1983 [1984]: 65) of the networks of micro-stories of the language game. First, we look at the chronological change in the language games of successive events, that is, between the initial management control practice *and* the BB one. Second, we look at the plot mediating the move *from* the initial management control practice *to* BB, that is, a story of the required action for making change. Finally, we address the mediation that synthesizes the meaning of the heterogeneous micro-stories. This is the understanding of the endpoint and followability of the whole narrative into other management control situations. In other words, it is the normative implication advocated by the narrative. The analysis of the plot grasps the new way of being a controller in its wholeness, that is, it includes an account of the new BB practice, the mediation of the change to BB, and the normative implications.

In the concluding level of analysis, we look at the intersection between text and world view, that is, paradigm. In this element of our narrative analysis, we reflect upon the relation of the text to the mainstream view of realism versus the realism in the actor-based forms of constructivism as perceived by Nørreklit et al. (2006, 2010). At a meta-level, language game analysis can uncover whether the book, viewed as a communicative event, advocates a change in the paradigmatic underpinnings of the way of being a controller.

Though we have analyzed the entire book, it is not possible to present the complete analysis here. We therefore selected the parts of the text considered most critical for this chapter – they told a meaningful story of the BB idea. Also, aware that language and action are open to inter-pretation, that some interpretations are more likely than others, given criteria for language and actions, the choices become those that are most comprehensive in explaining the phenomenon (Ricoeur, 1990 [1992]: 159–60).

ANALYSIS OF THE BB WAY OF BEING THE CONTROLLER

Pre-Narration: The Micro-Stories

Bogsnes's self-narrative on BB includes a network of micro-stories cen-tered on traditional budgeting, BB and Bogsnes's career as controller. Thus, it includes micro-stories not only on change in a firm's manage-ment control approach but also on his personal change during his career. Each of the micro-stories includes an account of the management control method as well as the controller's engagement in the method. Various nar-ratives, drawing on different narrative genres, semantic fields and syntax, are used to describe the instruments, the personal characters and the social relationships. Below we present an analysis of the language games drawn upon in the network of these micro-stories around traditional budgeting, BB and Bogsnes's personal career.

The traditional budgeting framework
The micro-stories that build on traditional budgeting are organized around the budgeting procedures related to production and budget control. The stories are based on the instrument of monthly and annual departmental budgeting following the accounting calculative logic. The network of agents involved in the micro-stories includes the budget department, top management and employees. Bogsnes is present as the storyteller of the events, experienced while working in a budget department. He gives an account of the language game.

i) Budget production   The description of the traditional budget production is dominated by the narrative scheme of a one-directional, step-by-step process of number production, such as: X1 produces data and sends them to X2, who produces new data and sends them to X3, and so on until the data reach the end (Xn). The one-directional, step-by-step process is expressed with (ad)verbs such as: *starts*, *then* and *until*. When producing the budget for each organizational level, the one-directional, step-by-step process alternates up and down between the various hierarchical levels, as illustrated in the following quote:

> Another fascinating phenomenon in the annual budget game is the "elevator rides." The bigger the company, the funnier (or more tragic) it is. It starts early, with the initial data production in the front line [X1]. The numbers are then consolidated, level by level, week after week, until they one day reach top management [Xn]. For corporate budget and planning people, this is an important moment. The suit and tie is put on, and the ceremony starts. After the CEO has thanked everyone for all the hard work through long nights and weekends, the message comes: "Is this really the best we can do? I had expected higher sales, lower costs, more of this, less of that. I want you back next week with better numbers."
>
> And then the numbers are sent down the elevator again [Xn–X1]. At the lower floors, people are almost waiting at the sliding doors [X1]. Everybody knows they are coming and what the message is. And everybody is well prepared. Of course there is something to give, on costs, on manning, on sales budgets. Some of the fat is sliced off, ambitions are increased, but only a bit. And up again the numbers go [Xn]. This time the atmosphere is slightly more positive. "Great work, but is this really the best we can do?" And down again they come [Xn–X1]. . . .
>
> I would not be surprised if we talk about three to four elevator round trips in larger companies. But everybody is happy: top management [Xn], because they believe they have stretched the organization to the limit; people in the organization [X1], because they got away with it this year as well. (Bogsnes, 2009: 51)

The one-directional, step-by-step process of data production is scheduled and repeated several times up and down the hierarchy before the budget is finally approved by top management. Embedded in the step-by-step process is an assumption of a progression towards the optimal, or true, budget. The information-producing activity at the beginning and the end of the process is not described, while the interrelated activities between the levels are ones of calculation, as indicated by the verb *consolidated*. The data sent from another level is the event that causes the action towards the optimal budget, the stimulus to take a certain action. There is no insight into human motives and actions at each step. With the narrative form of the repetitive, one-directional, step-by-step process together with calculative activities, we witness the contour of a cause–event pattern of action, implying that the individual follows the systematic and predictive rules of a machine and hence a mechanical language game. The analogy of an "elevator ride" supports the vision of the budget process as a mechanical language game.

However, the quote above also includes some satiric elements produced by the use of irony, metaphors and value-laden words. More specifically, the people behind the mechanical budget process, that is, the corporate budget and planning people and the CEO, are presented as rather prominent, taking on a formal style: "The suit and tie is put on" and "After the CEO has thanked everyone for all the hard work through long nights and weekends." The formal style is linked to an action of formal power. The management's speech-acts about the status of the budget are somewhat contemptuous, as illustrated by the sarcastic questioning of the size of the budget: "Is this really the best we can do?" This attitude is reflected in the higher expectation emphasized in the claim that follows: "I had expected higher sales, lower costs, more of this, less of that."

Together the two phrases follow a scheme of thesis and antithesis in which the employees' budget expectation is rejected and replaced by the management's expectation. The two phrases are followed by directive speech-acts expressed through the instructive imperative: "I want you back next week with better numbers." The manager's instruction becomes the synthesis of the contradictions. The use of sarcasm and instruction show an aggressive approach that refutes the employees' views, not by argumentation, but by postulate. In this way, management is constructed as more knowledgeable and more powerful than the employees.

However, the management style is devoid of content, as we can see from the following phrase: "they believe they have stretched the organization to the limit." The use of the verb *believe* signals that the controllers' feelings of power and control rely on their false perceptions of the budget actions. In the view of the employees in the organization, the budget actions are ceremonial, that is, they play a double role, as the following quote indicates: "At the lower floors, people are almost waiting at the sliding doors. Everybody knows they are coming and what the message is." Metaphorical expressions such as "the lower floors" and "almost waiting at the sliding doors" are symbols of the employees as predictable and obedient.

However, phrases like "almost waiting" and "everybody knows" show that the employees can predict the action and hence are informally in control of the process. Overall, the double act of formal obedience and informal control forms the act of gaming. That the employees are the winners of the budget game is emphasized by the following claim: "they got away with it this year as well." Because the controllers' perceptions of their own power and ability to control are unrelated to reality, they appear ridiculous to the observers, as emphasized by the author's use of irony when using ambiguous words and phrases such as "fascinating phenomenon" and "the bigger the company, the funnier (or more tragic)." We witness two language games in action: the mechanical one linked to the formal organizational power and the gaming one linked to the employees and concealed from the formal power.

ii) Budget control   Another micro-story of the budget process focuses on control of the budget. The description of the employees' use of the budget is organized around container-related metaphors such as *ceiling, floor* and *bag*, as depicted in the following quote:

> A cost budget is a kind of ceiling we put on cost: "This is how much you can spend and no more. . . . We forget that the ceiling also works just as well and often better as a floor for the same costs. . . . Managers see budgets as entitlements, as bags of money handed out at the beginning of the year. . . . When a bag of budget money is handed out each autumn, an artificial border of concern is created. As long as we are well within budget, we spend "our" money with a good conscience and few concerns. Why should we not? We got that bag from someone who is supposed to be a wise and competent person, our manager at the next higher level, did we not? . . . Each department gets its own, with a lot of smaller bags inside. . . . Even in smaller companies . . . thousands of bags are handed out each year. (Bogsnes, 2009: 15–16)

Describing the approved budget using metaphors of a ceiling that also acts as floor, the first two sentences of the quote illustrate the fixed and non-dynamic dimensions of the approved budget. The *bag of money* metaphor visualizes a sort of ownership of the money. The employees' private property feelings are supported by the possessive adjective in the phrase "we spend 'our' money" and by the noun *entitlements*. Also the metaphor *border* backs up the vision of privacy. However, the use of the adjective *artificial* suggests that the sense of property is a false one. The budgeting process sets up containers that work like private bank accounts that only the employees with a budget have access to. This hinders people from adapting to changes in business conditions after the budget has been made. In this regard, employees act more like private agents than corporate ones. The phrases "good conscience" and "few concerns" describing their moral feeling suggest that the employees act without guilt. Morally confident, they consider their action approved of by the management system, which the following rhetorical question documents: "We got that bag from someone who is supposed to be a wise and competent person, our manager at the next higher level, did we not?" Such a rhetorical question creates a dilemma in that the listener is not expected to disagree, and hence accepts the action as legitimate. A disagreement would suggest that the managers are neither competent nor legitimate. In other words, the employees' argumentation about their legitimacy to act as private agents is an act of gaming. Though we are tempted to further explore the motives and actions that are hidden in such a mechanical language game, the features of this game do not address these dimensions of human behavior.

iii) Conclusion Summing up, the text describes the language game of the traditional controllers as a mechanical one in which employees' responses to the language game becomes one of gaming. So even though the controller is constructed by the language game as one who controls the organizational activities through repetitive authoritative stimuli of the employee, the gaming language constructs the employee as one who outsmarts the controller who follows formal mechanical procedures. The gaming attitude gives the employees a reflective ability to take initiatives to handle the system, while the controller is passive and neglects critique by repeating traditional dispositions.

Where the two language games meet, situations arise, as depicted through the language of sarcasm. The traditional controller is constructed as a ridiculous bellboy-like character. Also, while the budget procedure appears on the surface to be a language game centered on cost control, the mechanical nature of the game, the lack of control it engenders and the slack that results realize a language game that more likely destroys profitability. Accordingly, in analyzing the narrative of the traditional budget, we discover a controller stuck in this mechanical language game running the risk of bringing the entire organization down.

However, by forming the story around the traditional controller, Bogsnes interacts with and reflects on the problem, opposing the traditional way of being a controller. In this story, we witness the contour of a critical approach to the traditional way of being a controller.

The BB framework
BB was developed to solve some of the problems resulting from traditional budgeting. It assumes a forceful and dynamic business environment (Bogsnes, 2009: xvii). The employees are perceived as self-governed people of actions who resist subordinating themselves. Statoil's version of BB, labeled "Ambition to Action," has replaced annual budgeting. It includes a performance measurement system and some new management processes. BB does not involve giving up management accounting and planning. In fact, the book advocates contemporary calculative accounting instruments such as net present value (p. 145), forecasting (p. 131), activity-based costing (pp. 83, 72), financial and non-financial indicators (p. 72) and so on. Also, the performance measurement system accords with

ordinary performance measurement practice, as described in textbooks such as Anthony and Govindarajan (1998) and Horngren (2008). One may even argue that some of the techniques applied, such as rolling forecasting, flexible budgeting and benchmarking, are integrated parts of contemporary budgeting. Overall, BB is not about non-budgeting, but rather about another management process around accounting techniques.

The Ambition to Action process is described by the following key step-by-step procedures: 1) strategy and target setting; 2) planning involving action plans and key performance indicator (KPI) forecasts; and 3) holistic assessment of performance. First, the corporate level establishes a strategy process for the whole company based on external benchmarks. Then the business unit (BU) start their strategy process with the main targets formulated by BU management as an integrated part of the strategic process. Second, the strategic objectives are translated into action plans, and the expected outcome of those action plans is forecasted, including an estimation of the financial and organizational capacity (Bogsnes, 2009: 141). Third, a holistic performance evaluation is made, including the evaluation of both the obtained results and the mindsets. Throughout, a dynamic resource allocation process is included to ensure that the approvals of new projects during the year are within the financial and organizational capacities and that new projects can be started up any time during the year.

The various steps are not linked in a seamless mechanical process. The decoupling of the processes of target setting, forecasting and resource allocation by separating the three processes in time (Bogsnes, 2009: 120) is intentional and intended to solve some of the quality problems of traditional budgeting. Below, we analyze how the language game of some of the micro-stories around the BB framework operates at a deeper linguistic level.

The dominating micro-narratives describing Ambition to Action follow a sort of dialectical scheme that involves an exchange of viewpoint of one character (thesis, T) and the counter-notification of another character (antithesis, AT), and weaves together the two viewpoints (synthesis, ST). The dialectic is not the Marxist version traditionally used to model the historical development of the society. Thus the narratives do not follow the assumption of a deterministic development process driven by quantitative changes in the economic relationship between forces of internal contradictions which cause fundamental, qualitative changes in society (http://plato.stanford.edu/entries/marx/). In the book, the actors play an important role, intertwining the differing viewpoints of the opposing characters to reach the synthesis. The actors' interaction constitutes the synthesis overcoming the social forces of contradiction; the synthesis is highly actor driven through the management's way of managing and the use of accounting and control techniques. In this process, new types of disposition and identity are created.

In the following, we discuss how narratives around Ambition to Action follow a dialectical scheme. The micro-stories of BB include agents such as top management, the front-line manager and the controller. Below, we analyze the narratives around the following two dialectical forces in Ambition to Action: BU strategy and front-line managers, and target setting and forecasting. Also we illustrate the interactive method used by the mediating actors.

i) Strategic objectives   First, the purpose of Ambition to Action is to obtain a synthesis between two character groups in opposition: 1) the BU managers who formulate *the strategy* and interpret the forces of the business setting; and 2) *the front-line managers*, who carry out the strategy. The opposition of the two characters with respect to performance outcome is visible in the following quote:

> Ambition to Action is about translating strategies into something more concrete, helping us to execute our strategic ambitions, choices, and decisions [T]. But Ambition to Action is also about helping front-line teams perform and deliver in their daily operations [AT]. Finding the right balance between the two is important [ST]. (Bogsnes, 2009: 119)

In other words, Ambition to Action is the management process that aims to synthesize 1) the competitive strategy point of view and 2) the view of the front-line managers. The view of the BU managers is represented through strategic desires, and depicted by a vocabulary such as "strategic ambitions, choices, and decisions." The view of the front-line managers is about operational action and factual results, which are depicted by a vocabulary such as "perform and deliver in their daily operations." The opposite positions of motives and doing are also indicated by the double meaning embedded in the key term *Ambition to Action*. It encourages the organization to be 'people of action," which is about actual doing, and to be ambitious, which is about wishful desires. The use of concept balance indicates a mutual recognition of both views. However, as the term *Ambition to Action* suggests, ambition and desire to action are the overall focus of the framework. Accordingly, the BU managers' view dominates.

This management process, which synthesizes the two viewpoints, follows a dialectical process, which starts with the established strategy as formulated by the BU managers (T) and the counter-notification of Ambition to Action targets as formulated by the front-line managers during the Ambition to Action process (AT):

The starting point for Ambition to Action is the established strategy, where the necessary situation analysis, ambitions, and strategic direction are addressed. This is where we make the big choices. . . . We start with people and organization, followed by HSE [health, security and environment], ending with finance. We do this to ensure that the business reviews follow the cause-and-effect relation between the perspectives. Finance now comes last, as a consequence of the actions and deliveries on the other perspectives [T]. When making an Ambition to action, however, we start with the Finance perspective and the results we want to achieve. Then we work our way backward through a cause-and-effect relation between the different drivers that lay the foundation for good financial results [AT]. (Bogsnes, 2009: 115–16)

Embedded in the formulation of the thesis and antithesis is a dialectical procedure that caters to the opposite views of the competitive environment as interpreted by a BU manager and a front-line manager. The procedures developed by Bogsnes and his colleagues allow ambition to generate a synthesis between the two characters with opposite views of performance outcome. More specifically, the process of formulating strategy (S) and the process of formulating Ambition to Action targets (AT) are described mechanically; however, each process is driven by the two characters, respectively, starting with the viewpoint of the front-line manager in opposition to the BU manager, who formulates the norm of performance outcome. We witness this mechanical process in the step-by-step procedures, as indicated by the various directives "start," "follow," "end" and "then," and in the assumption of a "cause-and-effect relation" between the various perspectives. However, the mechanical steps and causal links go in the direction opposite to the character formulating the norm of performance outcome, that is, the BU manager. Thus, the strategy formulated by BU managers starts from "the people and organization" perspective, and similarly the Ambition to Action targets formulated by the front-line managers are initiated from the financial perspective and hence the forces of the environment. The processes are designed in such a way that the contradictory forces meet as each character takes the other character's viewpoints into account: First, the BU management, representing the financial interests of shareholders, have to understand the people and the organizational perspective. Second, front-line managers, representing the people and the organization, have to understand the financial viewpoint.

The speech-act of questioning is an instrument aimed at mediating the opposite views of strategic objectives. For example, this type of questioning is found in the story about the development of the quality of the collective strategic objectives of the units:

Here are some questions we recommend teams to ask when developing and testing the quality of their strategic objectives: Do they reflect ambition and strategy; and areas that are both important and need change? Do they provide clear guidance and direction? Are they written in a language that makes people tick without too many buzzwords? Do they support each other (cause and effect, from people and organization to finance)? Is the time horizon right, within a relevant delivery period? (Bogsnes, 2009: 122)

The questions are rhetorical, not meant for a response, but for opening the readers' minds and challenging them. In each case, leading questions are raised to convey expectations to the addressee, as suggested by the words "reflect ambition and strategy," "important and need change," "support each other" and so on. Consequently, the questions form a checklist that guides a process of self-examination used in the discussion between managers at different levels to check whether they have committed themselves to an ambitious strategy, that is, to the desire of the organization. On top of that, the questions are intended to make the organizational objectives understandable and meaningful, as the following phrases indicate: "provide clear guidance" and "language that makes people tick without too many buzzwords." Also, the expression "makes people tick" emphasizes that the employees are assumed to be both rational and emotional. Overall, the rhetorical questioning is a form of self-examination practice. In the particular examples, questions are raised to make the front-line manager reflect on his or her own practice in relation to the ideas of the BU managers. Thus this form of questioning is used to facilitate a synthesis, by making the front-line managers accountable to the overall view of the company, by strengthening the good side of the character of the front-line manager: forming the right mindset and hence establishing trustworthiness.

ii) Performance control Similarly, the dialectical scheme shapes the narrative of target setting and forecasting, where target setting and forecasting are depicted as two forces in opposition. Simultaneously, "targets must be ambitious [T] and forecasts realistic [AT]" (Bogsnes, 2009: 131):

> Because targets must be ambitious and forecasts realistic, it is quite natural to have *gaps* between the two. The purpose is of course to close such gaps, as deadlines and delivery time are approaching. A gap is nothing negative; it just shows that we are able to have two thoughts in our heads at the same time. It confirms that we are aiming high while at the same time we have a realistic view on where we believe we will end up as things look today. Having no gaps sometimes is more questionable, especially if delivery time is some time ahead. This might indicate ambitions that are too low or forecasts that are too optimistic. Yet if targets become too ambitious, gaps can become too big. This can be dangerous, because it can lead to outcomes we do not want. People might give up or do stupid things to deliver. We have therefore established a "target review" mechanism. (Bogsnes, 2009: 131)

The *target* and the *forecasts* are the thesis and antithesis. Processes of corrective action (ST) – the synthesis – close the gap between target and forecasts, shifting between the strategic viewpoint (being ambitious) and the front-line manager viewpoint (being realistic). The two measurement norms of targets and forecasts form an important part of the logic behind the BB system, a logic that differs from traditional budgeting, which includes only one norm and hence a norm including slack. On the one hand, BB challenges slack. On the other hand, by advocating realistic forecasts, BB also emphasizes the importance of forecasts being actionable, not only in talk but also in practice. The gap between the target and the forecast needs to be managed. The phrases in the quote on the corrective action for closing the gap also follow the dialectical scheme. While the need exists "to close such gaps," "a gap is nothing negative." Further, the phrases stating corrective action point to the impact of overly ambitious targets on human motivation and action: "People might give up or do stupid things to deliver."

The quote also points to a mechanism of *target review*, which is linked to the mechanism of *the holistic performance evaluation* (Bogsnes, 2009: 132). Here, we see that a speech-act of questioning is an important dimension in the performance evaluation communication between the BU manager and the front-line manager. The book lists various questions intended to guide the dialogue between the two levels of managers when talking about the performance measurement of the front-line manager (see Bogsnes, 2009: 151–2). In particular, the questions address the consistency of the results with the strategic desire of the organizations: "Did delivered results contribute toward the strategic objectives?" and go beyond the KPI measurements to look at the contextual information of the KPI: "If we take off our KPI glasses and look at what the KPI was unable to pick up, how does it look? There is normally a lot of hindsight information available. The answer might confirm what the KPI indicated or reveal a more positive or negative picture."

They also address the notion of slack: "How ambitious were the targets? Did you stretch yourself?" Thus the front-line managers are accountable for meeting the target and keeping the target challenging. Finally, some questions relate to the circumstances of the performance: "Are there changes in assumptions that should be taken into account? Did you have tailwind or headwind that had nothing to do with your own performance?" – whether the behavior behind the performance is reflective: "Were agreed – or necessary actions taken? Did you continuously establish and execute new corrective actions as needed?" – and whether the performance reflects short-term thinking, thus destroying resources important for sustained competitive corporate advantage: "Are the results sustainable? Or has there been suboptimization in order to lift short-term results?"

All said, the questions relate the conditions and motives behind the targets to the performance. The measurements do not tell the whole truth, but have to be explored and interpreted in their phenomenological context. In short, the process reflects a language game involving interactions with and reflections on the conditions and motives behind performance.

iii) Conclusion On this basis, we conclude that BB assumes rationalistic features of contemporary management accounting, but advocates that it be used together with an interactive and reflective management procedure. Accordingly, at a deeper textual level, the BB process follows a dialectical language game that weaves together opposite forces of BU managers and front-line managers, of targets and forecasts, using a management process in which the opposing viewpoints are negotiated, that is, BB contributes to the construction of a synthesis of the strategic view, as represented by BU managers, and the operational view, as represented by the front-line managers. Drawing on an interactive language game, employees are depicted as self-governing and action oriented, yet with some blindness to the viewpoint of the other. Therefore, opposing views are bridged through the speech-act of questioning. Thus BB does not couple the various organizational levels through mechanical features, but through dialogical human interaction and reflective communicative action.

The interactive and reflective forms of questioning seem to involve establishing and achieving acceptance of a common view about ambitious targets. These forms of questioning aim at bringing front-line managers' motives and actions out of the shadows of the mechanical language game into the light. However, the questioning is less about direct control and more about creating a social commitment to performance management, forming a platform of trustworthiness for the front-line manager to maneuver freely while balancing opposite forces and being accountable, aiming to establish a life form of trust and accountability.

The procedure shows the importance for management accounting of facilitating a synthesis between opposite forces of an organization through the speech-acts of questioning. Accordingly, the controller is an interactive and reflective actor who actively, through the management control method, strives to change the values, thoughts and norms of the BU managers and the front-line managers. This is the controller's life form. Bogsnes, as controller and main driver of BB, is subsequently depicted as an interactive and reflective actor. In this instance, the picture of the ridiculous character of the controller vanishes.

Bjarte Bogsnes's career

In the book, Bogsnes gives an account of his career, from graduate of the
Norwegian School of Economics and Business Administration in 1983 to
controller at Statoil in 2008. His experience derives from finance, corporate budgeting and human resources. His first work experience was in the
corporate budget department at Statoil.[6] He worked with the implementation of BB, first in Borealis[7] and later in Statoil. In these companies, he was
and has been the driving force in the development of the BB framework.

While developing the BB solution, he interacted with others who challenged and supported him, as described in a set of micro-stories. In these,
we follow Bogsnes's transformation from inexperienced graduate of
management control, to novice controller in a corporate budget department, to mature professional of management control, where today he is
a vice president at Statoil. The set of micro-stories draws on a formation
genre, as illustrated by the use of the metaphor *journey* to describe his
transformation process, and the focus on his personal growth and change
in character from immature to mature. Together, the stories tell how challenges faced early on were overcome and led to his current vision of the
ideal controller.

i) From theory to integration of theory and practice   One micro-story
describes Bogsnes's change process from theoretically disengaged student
to advocate of the BB framework. The story follows a dialectical narrative
scheme in which Bogsnes first struggles with the force of business theory
(thesis, T), and is later challenged by it when meeting the force of practice
(antithesis, AT). In the end, he resolves the challenge, intertwining the two
forces of theory and practice (synthesis, ST):

> For me, the crossroads where theory meets practice is the place to be. When
> I studied business at the Norwegian School of Economics and Business
> Administration in my hometown of Bergen, those books did not speak to me
> as strongly as they do today, and not only because I perhaps was not among
> the most frequent visitors at the study hall. I needed the painful but rewarding
> experience of trying it all out in practice, where theory hits the trenches of real
> life. This is a story from those trenches. (Bogsnes, 2009: xiii)

Today Bogsnes finds himself in a dialogical space that connects the laws
of the practical and theoretical worlds, as indicated by words and phrases
such as "crossroads" and "theory hits the trenches of real life." However,
the phrase "not among the most frequent visitors at the study hall" shows
how pure theory had never appealed to Bogsnes the student. His interest in
theory has changed, however, as emphasized in the antithesis "books did
not speak to me as strongly as they do today." The change process hap-

pened by exploring the forces together, as indicated by the phrase "trying it all out in practice." The personal change process was troublesome, though the outcome progressive, as indicated by the antithesis "painful but rewarding." We see then that his practical experiences got him to recognize the antagonistic character of traditional theory and the necessity to form a system of management control equally supported by the force of theory and practice. Thus, just as the description of the BB model follows a dialogical narrative scheme, so do the micro-stories. Again, we see the contour of the reflective–interactive language game.

ii) From conformer to actor   In another micro-story, Bogsnes elaborates on the troublesome experiences early in his career in the corporate budget department at Statoil:

> My first job was actually in the Corporate Budget Department (!) in the Norwegian oil company Statoil, back in 1983. Trust me; I know the game from the inside. Not just from that job, but also from many later finance manager jobs. I have paid my dues, almost camping in my office during the frenzy of budget peak periods. (Bogsnes, 2009: xi)

The paragraph states that Bogsnes was familiar with the game of budgeting, pointing to his "first job . . . in the Corporate Budget Department" and also to "later finance manager jobs." His familiarity is further emphasized by phrases such as "know . . . from the inside," "paid my dues" and "camping in my office." He had conformed to the mechanical language game. The phrase "paid my dues" also indicates that his experience had been troublesome. Recognizing the problems of mechanical budgeting, he may have been distressed by the culture of denial towards the problem. Suffering with problems without a solution, he was in the life form of a conformist at the beginning of his journey or formation process.

However, that changed after several years, when Bogsnes became the driver of the BB approach. The journey away from the traditional controller role was initiated by a mentor. The following micro-story describes how this mentor motivated Bogsnes to develop his BB approach:

> There might have been no journey to write about if it was not for Svein Rennemo. . . . I was reporting to Svein when I headed up Corporate Control (what a terrible name, and I picked it myself!) in the newly formed European petrochemicals company Borealis back in the mid-1990s. Svein was the CFO and later the CEO of Borealis.
>   . . .
>   "What do you expect from us?" That was the question I asked him back in 1995, when Borealis was undertaking a full-blown business process engineering. . . . I was asked to head up a part of this project called "Management

Effectiveness," and I was quite uncertain about what kind of content to put behind this name. . . . I will never forget his response. . . . Smilingly, he said to me: "Bjarte, I expect the unexpected." That was all. So much challenge, and so much trust, in so few words.

Triggered by that message, some months later we decided to abolish budgeting in Borealis. For me, those words from a great leader became the start of a long journey. Or maybe the journey started even earlier, among a group of newly appointed and very exhausted Borealis controllers[,] . . . discussing how to improve the Borealis budgeting process[,] . . . the seed of something that none of us in the room recognized, not until several months later. (Bogsnes, 2009: xi–xix)

The micro-story depicts a dialogue between the mentor Svein and student Bogsnes. The question "What do you expect from us?" raised by Bogsnes asks for a prescription for action and hence hints at the mechanical process for following orders. However, Svein's answer "I expect the unexpected" works as a force against such conventional thinking. It calls for both a creative solution and a self-reliant employee. The quote also depicts Svein as kind and determined: "Smilingly," "challenge," "trust." Interpreting Svein's management approach as anti-authoritative, Svein's question motivated Bogsnes to develop the BB solution, as the word "Triggered" emphasizes. Bogsnes and other controllers in Borealis began to develop BB as they reasoned out the inherent conflicts in theory and practice, ultimately integrating the two, finding the non-ordinary solution he had been seeking. By emancipating himself from the mechanical theoretical approach, he moved from being a conformist to being an actor. In other words, Bogsnes went through a personal formation process.

iii) Followability Since then, the BB concept has been adopted and adapted by other companies. After Borealis, Bogsnes was hired to implement BB in Statoil. However, the insight from Borealis could not be mechanically exported to other practices and people. The following micro-stories around Statoil illustrate why not: "Although we [Statoil] have been on our Beyond Budgeting journey for several years now, we still are as I write and probably also as you read" (Bogsnes, 2009: 97). "It must have been both irritating and tiring for my colleagues to listen to me banging on about the Borealis case, a company they had little relation to. Looking back, I realize how patient they were. I forgot an important principle: Everybody needs his own journey" (2009: 108).

The first quote depicts the solution in Statoil as a "journey" and hence not one that can be mechanically transferred, but adapted to the particular context. Thus integration of theory and practice is company specific and develops over time, requiring a change on the part of each company employee, as emphasized by the imperative "Everybody needs his own journey." And phrases such as "irritating and tiring for my colleagues" and "Looking back, I realize how patient they were" show how Bogsnes himself continued to reflect on his actions and relationships to others and hence continued his own process of formation. Overall, Bogsnes recognized that the formation process is a general form of being.

His ambition spread the vision to other organizations, which the following quote indicates: "I am glad that number is on the way up. Right now there are actually three of us in Norway alone. Both the world's seventh largest telecom company, Telenor, and the bank SpareBank1 Gruppen are now on the journey, with full-time project managers" (Bogsnes, 2009: 109).

iv) Conclusion On this basis, we conclude that the stories Bogsnes tells about his career draw on the reflective–interactive language game of personal formation, which Bogsnes went through as an integral part of inventing the BB procedure. The professional maturing process was full of conflicts and challenges overcome with help from an encouraging mentor. As a result of the formation process, Bogsnes emancipated himself from the mechanical language game and found a way of integrating the laws of the practical and theoretical worlds. Through several challenging experiences, Bogsnes became increasingly interactive and reflective, leading to an ideal form of a controller. Thus, he modeled the process of emancipation not only verbally, but also through action. However, other companies and people cannot mechanically import Bogsnes's BB, but must develop a BB procedure appropriate to the particular context.

Effective BB also involves an individual learning process which takes time, and leads to maturity and constructs a reflective- and interactive-oriented way of being a controller. Thus, the personal formation process of being a controller has to accompany each adaptation of BB. All this requires a reflective and interactive language game used not only in relation to others' actions, but also in relation to one's own actions, a self-reflective way of being.

Plot – Three Angles of Change

Based on the analysis of the language games embedded in these micro-stories, this section investigates the change in the way of being a controller. First, we focus on the chronological change, from initial stage of traditional budgeting to the closing stage of BB. Second, we reflect on the driving force that mediates the change in the way of being a controller. Third, we reflect on the endpoint and followability of the whole narrative, that is, the normative implications for other controllers.

i) The chronological change in the way of being a controller

The book describes the gradual change from traditional way of being a controller to the BB approach. The management control method of the traditional controller draws on a mechanical language game, which constructs the characters of the employees as smart and the controller as the foolish authority who actually fulfils the role of bellboy. The controller's mechanical thinking undermines the authority of the controller. The BB approach is the new way of being a controller. We observe a move to an interactive–reflective language game. Through the reflective–interactive language game, the controller is able to construct him- or herself as more skilled, insightful and action oriented, and can manage the actual forces of doing business. Thus the game constructs the controller as a powerful, reflective actor, no longer passive, but active – no longer a bellboy, but an actor.

Another finding is a change in Bogsnes's personal character, which he describes through a formation genre. In his early career, he modeled the character of passive controller. However, he sensed the foolishness and ignorance of this and reconstructed himself as a reflective and interactive type of controller capable of dialoguing with the dialectical forces of practice and theory. Today, he presents himself as a controller in opposition to the traditional way of being a controller and has experienced the environment as neither predictable nor amenable to control through the mechanical thinking embedded in traditional management.

ii) The way of mediating change

Traditionally, any mismatch between a new business environment and the management accounting system is resolved by a revision of the mechanical system given that the original mechanical language game becomes obsolete. But BB is not just another system that replaces a mismatch. While the conflict created by mismatch between business environment and accounting system was a necessary condition for changing the system, it was not sufficient to move it to the BB approach. The ultimate force came from the motives and actions of Bogsnes himself, who with backing from top management drove the development of the BB framework.[8] In order to find and implement a solution, he himself had to go through a personal formation process, which involved a change in his character. In other words, to change others and a system, one has to be in a different frame of mind.

iii) The normative implications for other controllers

The message of the book is that a controller should distance him- or herself from the mechanical language game of traditional management control procedures. Furthermore, the controller must be seen as an important character of the development and the ending of the problems around traditional budgeting. The traditional mechanical use of management accounting tools is ceremonial and creates only an appearance of control, making the controller look ridiculous, as if a bellboy. The consequences of this rigid budget system are slack and loss of opportunities, threatening not only the authority of the controller, but also the performance of the organization. By adopting BB, which still uses management accounting and control techniques, the controller becomes an actor constructing and communicating new types of procedures related to budgeting and the use of management accounting numbers, mediating change.

However, the normative implications (endpoint and followability) of the narrative are not that all companies should adopt Bogsnes's system, but rather that being a controller involves a reflective and interactive approach to the operational phenomenon, to others and to oneself, all of which involves dropping the mechanical way of thinking in relation to management accounting and planning; BB is about "escaping the mechanical evaluation trap" (Bogsnes, 2009: 26), which involves both a change procedure and a change in the character of the controller, which in itself involves a personal and professional transformation process.

CONCLUSION: LANGUAGE GAMES AND PARADIGMS

Our analysis of the BB narrative reveals a profound change in the way of being a controller. First, mechanical language games embedded in traditional management control methods change over time into an inter-active–reflective type of language game embedded in the BB method. As a consequence, the life form of the controller changes from bellboy in pursuit of a "true" budget to a technically skilled and reflective actor interacting with the opposite views and thoughts of the BU managers and the front-line managers. The change must be driven by the controller, who him- or herself goes through a transformation process in order to change the method and interact with others. The normative implications are that being a controller involves a reflective and interactive approach to the management control method in use, to the other organizational members and to one's own professional character. Finally, it has to be emphasized that the stories of both traditional budgeting and BB should not be perceived as a factual description of the events but as a prescription for a new "way of being a controller." Accordingly, we won't engage in a discussion around their validity, but rather the paradigm advocated by the book.

On the basis of our discourse analysis, we would argue that the language games of the book advocate a change in the paradigmatic positions of being controller, from one of mainstream realism towards a more reflective and actor-based paradigm. In particular, the book argues against a practice of management accounting that draws on the mainstream paradigm of realism, where the individual follows a mechanical pattern of action and the role of the controller is to be neutral and describe things objectively as they "really" exist "out there" (Chua, 1986; Ryan et al., 2002). Differently, the book advocates an actor-based view, which puts an individual person's motives and way of thinking in focus (Fromm, 1941). The aim of BB is to establish self-governance rooted in individual motives, reasons and wishes to accomplish. However, the individual also has to recognize the social and material world.

Accordingly, we suggest that BB assumes a practical paradigm, which resembles pragmatic constructivism (Nørreklit et al., 2006, 2010). As with pragmatic constructivism, the book emphasizes the role of the actor in the construction of reality. It emphasizes the importance of all the members of the organization in constructing a successful company in which each individual is an actor governed by his or her own mindset. BB is about how the BU and front-line managers as well as the controller can construct themselves as important company actors who interact with the powerful forces of the physical and social environment. A successful controller, in particular, has to understand and communicate with the forces of the other actors, who all aim at making things work in a practical reality.

Pragmatic constructivism does not reject the rationalistic epistemological tools, but the mainstream approach's perception of their social context and how they are to be implemented and used. It accepts that accounting is important, but adds the social dimension to the accounting process. In the view of pragmatic constructivism, traditional management methods are not leaving space for the various subjective mindsets of the individual persons and for managing the subjective mindsets for the overall interest of the organization at the same time. Pragmatic constructivism is a paradigm that leaves room for a dialectic order in which the different forces have to be balanced and the actor has to construct him- or herself in interaction with these forces. In order to do that successfully, the actor has to understand and interact in a reflective way with the forces of the others and him- or herself. Hence the actor makes them meet in a constructive way, and in the meeting there is a mutual acceptance of the forces. Also, BB advocates the particular integration of theory and practice, which is coherent with the idea of pragmatic constructivism, that the successful integration of facts, possibilities, values and communication is linked to the particular situation.

NOTES

1. Controller at Statoil in 2008.
2. While it is not unusual to hear top managers and management consultants tell their stories of success (Furusten, 1992), it is quite unique to hear a controller tell his.
3. From our research, we know that Bogsnes gives a rather factual description of his job career. We also know that a change from traditional budgeting to BB has in fact been undertaken in Statoil and that BB seems highly supported in the company.
4. Our project is financed by Statoil, and therefore it could be argued that this has made us more favorable to the BB model and hence Statoil. However, Statoil has not influenced the content of our research. Furthermore, our research is not about evaluating the BB model or what Statoil does, but to understand how management accounting changes. Finally, as Bogsnes's book is publicly accessible, and our analysis of the text is presented in a transparent way, it is possible for peers to assess our interpretations.
5. Although the meaning of a sign is not fixed, some language conventions are rather durable.
6. The largest company in Scandinavia.
7. Europe's largest petrochemicals company.
8. Who the main persons for developing BB ideas are can of course be discussed. However, by writing a book about one's experience about BB, one becomes an important person for developing ideas about BB.

REFERENCES

Anthony, R.N. and V. Govindarajan (1998), *Management Control Systems*, Burr Ridge, IL: Irwin.
Arbnor, I. and B. Bjerke (1997), *Methodology for Creating Business Knowledge*, London: Sage.
Austin, J.L. (1962), *How to Do Things with Words*, Clarendon Press, Oxford.
Bogsnes, B. (2009), *Implementing Beyond Budgeting: Unlocking the Performance Potential*, Hoboken, NJ: John Wiley & Sons.
Burns, J. and G. Baldvinsdottir (2007), "The changing role of management accountants," in T. Hopper, D. Northcott and R. Scapens (eds.), *Issues in Management Accounting*, 3rd edn., Harlow: Pearson Education, pp. 117–32.
Chua, W.F. (1986), "Theoretical constructions of and by the real," *Accounting, Organizations and Society*, **11** (6), 583–98.
Fromm, E. (1941), *Escape from Freedom*, New York: Holt, Rinehart and Winston.
Furusten, S. (1992), *Management Book: Guardians of the Myth of Leadership*, Uppsala: Department of Business Studies, Uppsala University.
Horngren, C.T. (2008), *Introduction to Management Accounting*, Upper Saddle River, NJ: Prentice Hall.
Nørreklit, L., H. Nørreklit and P. Israelsen (2006), "Validity of management control topoi – towards constructivist pragmatism," *Management Accounting Research*, **17** (1), 42–71.
Nørreklit, H., L. Nørreklit and F. Mitchell (2010), "Towards a paradigmatic foundation of accounting practice," *Accounting, Auditing and Accountability Journal*, **23** (6), 79–82.
Østergren, K. and I. Stensaker (2011), "Management control without budgets: A

field study of 'Beyond Budgeting' in practice," *European Accounting Review*, **20** (1), 149–81.

Ricoeur, P. (1983), *Temps et récit*, vol. 1, trans. Kathleen Blamey and David Pellauer (1984), *Time and Narrative*, vol. 1, Chicago, IL: University of Chicago Press.

Ricoeur, P. (1990), *Soi-même comme un autre*, trans. Kathleen Blamey (1992), *Oneself as Another*, Chicago, IL: University of Chicago Press.

Ryan, B., R.W. Scapens and M. Theobald (2002), *Research Method and Methodology in Finance and Accounting*, London: Thomson.

Saussure F. de (1960), *Course in General Linguistics*, London: Peter Owen.

Wittgenstein, L. (1953), *Philosophical Investigations*, trans. G.E.M. Anscombe, Oxford: Basil Blackwell.

PART II

Perspectives and control dimensions

8. Management control as temporal structuring

Sebastian D. Becker and Martin Messner

INTRODUCTION

The timing of activities and events plays a central role in everyday life (McGrath and Rotchford, 1983; Roe, 2009). We try to "find time" to get things done, we experience situations in which we "run out of time," we realize when it is the "right time" to do something, and we hope that "time passes" more or less quickly. In short, time is a fundamental building block of our life as human and social beings (Heidegger, 1927).

The time perspective is also important for understanding the workings and characteristics of organizations. Organization is, to a large extent, the organization of time. This is evident, for example, in the scientific management movement and its concern with time-and-motion studies, which is a root of management and organization theory (Taylor, 1911; Clegg, 2009). Similarly, many contemporary concepts and principles of management, such as just-in-time manufacturing (Schonberger, 1986; Orlikowski and Yates, 2002), time to market (Cohen et al., 1996), time-based management (Stalk and Hout, 1990) and the organizational life cycle (Cameron and Whetten, 1988), relate to the organization of time. Moreover, a number of recent managerial innovations, such as Time-Driven Activity-Based Costing (e.g., Kaplan and Anderson, 2007), real-time management (Yeh et al., 2000), improvements in accounting and information systems (Hopwood, 2009; Czarniawska, 2013) and the emerging discourse on sustainability (Orlikowski and Yates, 2002), involve some element of time and timing in organizations.

The relevance of the time dimension is reflected in organizational research that seeks to take questions of timing and temporal structuring seriously (Clark, 1985; Orlikowski and Yates, 2002). Several leading organizational journals have published special issues on time (e.g., Ancona et al., 2001; Jones et al., 2004; Hernes et al., 2013 for these issues' editorials), and edited books on the topic are also available (e.g.,

Roe et al., 2009). Despite this apparent interest in the management and organizational literature, the attention given to the relationship between time and management control has been rather limited. Only a few contributions explicitly address this relationship (e.g., Hopwood, 1989; Loft, 1989; Ezzamel and Robson, 1995; Selto et al., 1995; Mouritsen and Bekke, 1999; Anderson-Gough et al., 2001; Nandhakumar and Jones, 2001; Quattrone and Hopper, 2005). This is somewhat surprising given that management control seems to entail the control of organizational time and tempo to a significant extent. Control practices shape actors' understandings of time by defining time horizons and time periods. This happens, for example, through planning and forecasting processes in which different time horizons influence how actors coordinate their work. Furthermore, control practices allow actors to relate to different times by bringing the future and the past "into" the present. For example, a performance evaluation is a way of making sense of the past that is also expected to influence actors' behaviors in the future. Similarly, investment appraisals involve estimating future cash flows and discounting these cash flows so as to make them calculable in the present.

Against this background, this chapter aims to sensitize the reader to the fact that management accounting and control practices are inherently connected to issues of time. More specifically, we suggest viewing management control as a form of temporal structuring. We illustrate this through the example of budgeting and analyze the ways in which questions of timing and tempo are addressed in discussions of budgeting practice in the literature. In particular, we consider how the critique of budgeting found in the publications on Beyond Budgeting (e.g., Hope and Fraser, 2003a) is fuelled by certain understandings of tempo and timing. This example allows us to demonstrate that different control solutions can have notably different implications for how time is structured in organizations. This, in turn, may have important consequences for the behavior of organizational actors.

The remainder of this chapter is organized as follows. In the next section, we review some of the theoretical concepts presented in the literature that help improve our understanding of time in management accounting and control. The following section is devoted to a more in-depth analysis of developments in practice, that is, organizations' attempts to improve their temporal orientation by changing their planning and forecasting practices. Finally, we present our conclusions and provide an outlook for further research possibilities.

ORGANIZATION, CONTROL AND TIME

The Timing of Organizational Activities

Like all natural or social events, events that occur in an organization happen "in time." In other words, they follow a certain sequence and can be related to each other by referring to the notions of "past" and "future," or "early" and "late." Inherent in this understanding of time is a linear notion of time according to which time passes continuously, without a beginning or an end. Our common understanding of this "real time" of activities (Schatzki, 2006) is intimately related to the clock and the way in which it makes the constant passing of time visible to us.

An important part of "organization" lies in deciding upon the sequence in which events or actions should happen in time. Such "timing" allows organizations to coordinate activities internally and in relation to their environments. Therefore, timing is about deciding which activities must be carried out before others (e.g., producing before shipping), and which activities can or should be carried out at the same time (e.g., on-going production and on-going sales activities). In organizations, such decisions usually concern more than just individual events. This is because an important dimension of organizational life is its repetitive character (Giddens, 1984; Schatzki, 2005). The events that take place in real time can often be seen as instantiations of patterns of activity that unfold in a repetitive way. For instance, an individual unit that is produced on a shop floor is not a unique output, but just one of an entire production series. When we talk about the timing of activity in organizations, therefore, we have to acknowledge that individual actions or events are subject to temporal structures that ensure an on-going (rather than ad hoc) structuring of organizational life (Orlikowski and Yates, 2002). For example, the way in which production activities are organized in time is not something that has to be decided upon anew from case to case. Rather, the production pattern is established once for repeated enactment; that is, it is established as a repetitive cycle.

Two aspects of such temporal structures are of particular importance. First, an organization can have multiple temporal structures at the same time. One set of practices may be organized according to one temporal structure, while another may follow a different timing and tempo. For instance, managers in different departments of a firm are likely to engage in routines with contrasting temporal structures. Whereas a production manager may be used to a stable production process that continually repeats itself (e.g., a daily, eight-hour shift), a sales person could face more cyclical sales opportunities (i.e., more or less work each day or week) to which he or she has to react. Similarly, a purchasing manager engaged in negotiations with suppliers may adopt a long-term perspective, while a production worker might think more in terms of short-term cycles.

Although the co-existence of temporal structures is quite common in organizations, a complete decoupling of such structures from each other is unusual and would arguably put the idea of an integrated organization into question. Some synchronization of the temporal structures of organizational practices is needed. For instance, while production and sourcing practices may be based on different temporal structures, there is a need to coordinate these two sets of activities in order to ensure that materials are available when needed for production. In some cases, the temporal structures of one practice will have a determining influence on those of another practice; that is, one practice will act as a pacer, or *Zeitgeber*, for the other. In the literature, this phenomenon is referred to as "entrainment" (McGrath and Rotchford, 1983; McGrath and Kelly, 1986; Ancona and Chong, 1996; Bluedorn, 2000):

> The fundamental idea behind entrainment in organizational theory is that endogenous cycles exist within individuals, groups, organizations, and environments. These endogenous cycles are often influenced by other cycles within the system or outside the system so as to occur in synchrony; in entrainment language the cycles are "captured" by an external pacer so as to have the same phase, periodicity, or magnitude. These external pacers are often signalled by cues in the environment called [Z]eitgebers (Aschoff, 1979). The "captured" cycles establish an entrained rhythm that then "pulls" many other cycles into synchrony. The rhythm creates a dominant temporal ordering that serves as powerful coordination mechanism for that entity. As more and more cycles entrain to this rhythm it becomes inertial. (Ancona and Chong, 1996: 253)

Two major types of entrainment can be distinguished: tempo (or pace) entrainment and phase (or cycle) entrainment. "Tempo entrainment" refers to changes in and the alignment of speed, and can be exemplified by the speeding up of the product development process by an organization in order to match the innovation cycle determined by its competitors (Ancona and Chong, 1996). "Phase entrainment" refers to the organization of activities that would otherwise follow their own cycles into an "interwoven pattern with a common aggregate rhythm" (Ancona and Chong, 1996: 261). McGrath and Rotchford (1983) point out that in industrialized societies an individual's activities are mainly entrained to the demands of work organizations and less entrained to demands from other domains, such as the family (Zerubavel, 1979). The authors consider the example of a shift worker whose tempos and phases of activities are primarily entrained to those of the work organization, such that he or she adjusts work and leisure times according to the demands of the employer.

In other words, the shift worker's tempos and paces become "captured" by an external pacer ("primary entrainment"). Once this happens, the tempos and phases of the shift worker tend to also "pull" the tempos and phases of his or her family into synchrony such that, for example, their eating and leisure activities are made to fit the work shifts ("secondary entrainment"; Ancona and Chong, 1996). In a similar way, the fiscal year acts as a *Zeitgeber* that entrains many organizational and social practices (e.g., Ancona and Chong, 1996; Orlikowski and Yates, 2002; Ballard, 2009).

Second, as implied in the examples above, temporal structures do not exist independently of the actors who carry out those structures. Insofar as organizational actors engage in certain practices, they reproduce those practices and the temporal structures that they embody. In a university, for example, lecturers and students enact the schedule of the academic year, which is centrally defined by the university or a regulatory body. In so doing, they establish the schedule as practically relevant. The enactment of temporal structures creates a particular "time consciousness" or "time orientation" among the actors. Students and lecturers, for example, think about the passing of time in terms of the academic calendar. Similarly, accountants' time consciousness is shaped by the reporting year and by events that relate to the reporting cycle (e.g., monthly or quarterly reports). Given such differences in relevant "reference points," actors may have different perceptions of such categories as "long" and "short," or "quick" and "slow."

Management Control as Temporal Structuring

The temporal structures of organizations are, to a great extent, deliberately shaped through managerial intervention. Accounting and management control practices can play an important role in this respect, as they may influence organizational actors' time consciousness and temporal orientations. Management control aims to influence the behavior of organizational actors in order to ensure that the objectives of the organization can be fulfilled (Anthony, 1965; Merchant and Van der Stede, 2012). Accounting and control systems achieve such an influence in two main ways: by providing incentives and/or by providing information.[1] For example, a performance indicator, such as inventory turnover, can be used as a target-setting mechanism that provides managers with an incentive to improve inventory performance. Alternatively, a performance indicator could be used as a piece of information that helps managers understand what is going on in the firm and to improve, for example, return on capital employed. Both incentives and information can affect the temporal orientation of managers.

146 *Managing in dynamic business environments*

The provision of an incentive is usually linked to some standard that is defined ex ante or ex post, against which performance is evaluated.[2] The chosen performance measure can be used to incentivize managers to engage in different temporal orientations when carrying out their work. These orientations can range from a concern with short-term outcomes (e.g., quarterly earnings) to a concern with sustainability (e.g., long-term financial or environmental impact). However, the effect on temporal orientation is not only a function of what kind of performance is evaluated, but also a function of when (and how often) performance is evaluated. One example in this regard is the often documented behavior of sales managers who try to accelerate sales at the end of an evaluation period in order to meet their sales targets (Ancona and Chong, 1996). It is important to acknowledge that control systems that evaluate performance at particular points in time also provide actors with a significant degree of autonomy (Dearden, 1973). A control system that assesses performance at the end of the year allows actors to follow their own timing and tempo *during* the year. It thus gives employees the responsibility for deciding how they want to structure their everyday work and how to go about carrying out operational practices. The more detailed the performance evaluation and the more often performance is evaluated, the lower the level of autonomy given to managers. In the extreme case of a bureaucratic organization, control mechanisms specify how each and every action is to be carried out.

Control systems can also influence actors by providing information that facilitates their actions and decisions. Again, the provision of information can affect the temporal orientation and time consciousness of actors. If, for example, managers rely on an information system that mostly displays lagging indicators, they are less likely to pay attention to long-term outcomes than if they are also provided with leading indicators (Kaplan and Norton, 1992). Similarly, if sales and operations forecasts are established and discussed only for the next quarter (rather than for a longer period of time), managers are likely to focus on decisions and actions that influence the next quarter (rather than those with a longer-term effect). Of course, the provision of information can also be oriented towards the real-time needs of operational managers. In such cases, information is provided "when it is needed" and in the form in which it is requested. In this situation, control emerges as an on-going dimension of operational practice rather than as a separate practice that connects with operational practice only at certain points in time. The work of Ahrens (1997) offers a nice illustration of this contrast. Ahrens compares the ways in which management accountants in British and German breweries become involved in strategic decision making. He observes that German management accountants often describe their work in terms of a continuous cybernetic cycle. They stress that management accounting (or "controlling") follows a certain systematic procedure and that it comes into contact with operational agendas at pre-defined points (e.g., when plans have to be established or when variances need to be discussed). Ahrens (1997) observes that, in contrast to their colleagues in the German firms, management accountants in British firms tend to see their work as much more involved with operational agendas. They do not portray themselves as acting at a distance from operational managers, but rather as working in close cooperation with them. They "talk about their work as a series of responses to dynamics of their environment" (Ahrens, 1997: 573). In other words, while the German management accountants view the tempo of their activities as mainly determined by a pre-specified planning cycle, their British counterparts relate their tempo to that of operations. This helps explain why the British more easily see themselves as being pro-actively involved in operational agendas, whereas the German controllers do not craft such a role for themselves.

Whether incentives and information are considered appropriate or relevant is often judged by comparing the temporal structures inherent in control systems with those that are considered desirable for the underlying operational practices (Dearden, 1973). For instance, when it is considered desirable that firms operate in a sustainable way, a control system that incentivizes a focus on short-term results is likely to be seen as problematic. Similarly, when decisions have to be taken on a short-term basis, information that is not timely is likely to be considered unhelpful. The challenge, of course, is that there are often competing temporal demands and competing viewpoints on what is deemed desirable in an organization. For example, firms should ideally react quickly to changing circumstances, but they also need some degree of stability in their practices, which works against such flexibility (Brown and Eisenhardt, 1997). Financial managers may stress the importance of the long-term planning of cash flows, while sales managers are likely to stress the need to adjust resources to changes in market opportunities. It is in this context that control practices or systems may be subject to debate or criticism. The example of budgeting practice offers a vivid illustration of these issues, as discussed in the next section.

BUDGETING AND THE TIMING OF ORGANIZATIONAL ACTIVITY

In this section, we show how budgeting and forecasting practices are linked to issues of time. In an important study on accounting and time,

Ezzamel and Robson (1995) summarize the potential effects of accounting and budgeting practices on the temporal structuring of organizations. They argue that such practices "intervene in the processes of time experience at several levels; they help create different temporal viewpoints, they also define both the past and the future as viewed from the perspective of the present and they contribute to distinct temporal cycles within organizations" (Ezzamel and Robson, 1995: 163).

To illustrate temporal issues with regard to the management accounting and control practices associated with budgeting, the following first draws on the theoretical concept of entrainment. In a second step, this concept is applied to the practitioner discourse around budgeting, which has recently critiqued more traditional accounting and control practices from, as we argue here, a time perspective. In particular, we focus on budgeting's interdependencies with the calendar year and with other organizational activities.

Entrainment to the Calendar Year

We have suggested that budgeting can be understood from an entrainment point of view, and that management accounting and control have the potential to reinforce an organization's sense of cyclical time (Ezzamel and Robson, 1995). As the following sections show, an entrainment of and through budgeting represents an important means of control, as it implies the synchronization of the temporal structures of different organizational units.

With its typical orientation towards the fiscal or calendar year (as an external pacer, or *Zeitgeber*), budgeting is a social practice that is closely associated with an exogenous temporal structure. Once the budgeting process, as an internal activity, is captured by this external pacer (primary entrainment), budgeting itself can develop an entrained rhythm that "pulls" other cycles into synchrony (secondary entrainment). The more internal cycles entrain to this rhythm, the more the entire setup evolves into a dominant temporal ordering and, therefore, into a powerful coordination mechanism inside the organization (Ancona and Chong, 1996). Of course, budgeting is not the only accounting practice that is tied to the calendar year. Many financial reporting practices, including those influenced by financial markets or taxation authorities, are similarly connected to temporal structures established by the calendar year.

As outlined above, a multitude of temporal cycles often exist simultaneously within organizations – different organizational departments have their own rhythms defined by, at times, multiple proprietary *Zeitgebers*, which can be either external or internal. For example, a production department is subject to several external and internal *Zeitgebers*. It tends to produce according to the demand estimates that the sales department communicated to it regarding the likely sales level, which may be subject to seasonal changes. Furthermore, a production department may depend largely on the potentially cyclical availability of raw materials on world markets or on agricultural harvesting cycles. From a technological perspective, the production technology used in a production department may depend on the innovation cycle in production technology, which is also an external cycle. In addition to these more external *Zeitgebers*, a production department may depend on its organization's product development cycle, its employees' team cycles or individual career cycles (Gersick, 1988; Ancona, 1990).

For control purposes, an organization's management has an obvious interest in coordinating and thereby temporally structuring its various departments to reach its overall objectives. Given that many organizations are subject to the fiscal year for various reasons, such as financial reporting and taxation, they tend to let the fiscal year influence internal coordination mechanisms (Ancona and Chong, 1996).[3] Consequently, organizations often adopt accounting systems that express the real production and sales processes in terms of their fiscal years for planning, coordination or resource allocation (i.e., decision-facilitating) purposes. They also use such systems to set and monitor targets at certain points in time for control (i.e., decision-influencing) purposes. On the basis of the organization's fiscal year, past activities are accounted for, performance is reported, accounts are closed, and annual financial reports are written and communicated to external stakeholders for financial reporting purposes. As a result, the organization's processes and activities shift in conjunction with the fiscal year (Ancona and Chong, 1996):

> While there is no inherent reason that planning cycles, performance reviews, sales account closings, or revenue accounting should be yearly events that occur at the same point in every year, all these activities center around the . . . calendar established by the fiscal year. Performance reviews are set so that salaries and bonuses can be calculated and fed into the numbers that must be computed at the end of the fiscal year. Sales account closings peak at the end of each quarter, and particularly at the end of the fourth quarter in time to be computed in end-of-year bonuses. Division managers with profit and loss responsibilities attempt to pass off costs before the fiscal year ends so that their end-of-year performance is enhanced. (Ancona and Chong, 1996: 261)

Given a multitude of organizational processes that are entrained to the same rhythm and a multitude of organizations that are similarly entrained by the fiscal year, which in turn influences an organization's or its departments' relations with the outside world, this setup may become taken for granted and inertia may develop over time (Ancona and Chong, 1996; Orlikowski and Yates, 2002).

It seems appropriate to further examine budgeting practice in terms of its ramifications on the temporal structuring of organizations, given that much of the literature refers to this practice when describing timing in organizations (e.g., Hopwood, 1989; Gersick, 1994; Ezzamel and Robson, 1995; Ancona et al., 2001). As such, an entrainment of organizational activities and processes to the fiscal year via the budgeting process has both advantages and disadvantages. As alluded to above, one important advantage is that secondary entrainment enables organizations to reap a coordination benefit arising from the synchronization of several activities, especially if important interdependencies exist between them (McGrath and Rotchford, 1983; Ancona and Chong, 1996). A second main advantage is that an organization's primary entrainment to the fiscal year through the budgeting process can – similarly to an entrainment to internal pacers – serve as a buffer against entrainment to external pacers, such as those set by the competitive environment (Peters and Waterman, 1982; Cunha, 2009). In this regard, the prioritizing of non-competitive rhythms over competitive rhythms is argued to help organizations compete by ensuring they do not become trapped by excessive reactivity (Brown and Eisenhardt, 1997). Third, entrainment of and entraining through budgeting may reduce uncertainty and complexity for the individuals involved (Parker, 2002; Marginson and Ogden, 2005). This is because individuals are also entrained by calendar time in their personal lives and because, in general, a regular pattern of organizational activity per se has the potential to reduce uncertainty (Thompson, 1967) and to create a feeling of control (e.g., Brown and Eisenhardt, 1998) for individuals and organizations alike.

However, an entrainment to the fiscal year also has disadvantages. First, given the propensity of entrained processes to become inertial, as discussed above, an entrainment to a given cycle may become inertial. This might make an organization insensitive to external changes and unable to entrain to a new pacer in general or to a competitive pacer in particular (Ancona and Chong, 1996). This can be especially harmful in hypercompetitive environments (D'Aveni and Gunther, 1994). If, as is the case with budgeting, there is also secondary entrainment involving other internal activities, the inertia might be even more consequential. Cunha (2009) calls organizations in such situations "out-of-time" as they may "tie their work to the annual planning and review cycle, because this is the 'normal' organizational calendar" (Cunha, 2009: 232).

Second, entrainment may be dysfunctional and detrimental if it is too dominant (Ancona and Chong, 1996). For example, customer service might be organized according to the regularities of the fiscal year, which could lead to unsatisfied customers or employee stress if sales patterns deviate from the regularity of the calendar year. Whenever two activity phases are not optimally synchronized because of entrainment, they may result in work overloads, stress or unsatisfied customers (Ancona and Chong, 1996). Furthermore, with regard to sales units, the cycle of budget preparation, with its concurrent setting of targets and performance evaluations, may influence the actions of sales employees in that they may seek to move sales to months in which targets are more likely to be reached (Anderson-Gough et al., 2001; Hope and Fraser, 2003b). This may constrain long-term relationships with customers (Orlikowski and Yates, 2002).

Third, Ezzamel and Robson (1995: 164) point to potential conflicts when, for example, accounting and budgeting systems functioning with fixed temporal horizons and entrained by calendar years generate "evaluative visibilities" of results that are not in tune with the activities of the research and development department. This point is also stressed by Dearden (1973), who emphasizes that the temporal structuring implicated in management accounting and control, particularly in performance evaluations, has a significant impact on employee autonomy. The author refers to the concept of "time-span" (Jaques, 1964), which measures "the length of time [in which] an employee could use his own discretion before being reviewed and evaluated by his superior" (Dearden, 1973: 342). Clearly, the temporal structuring of organizational activities through budgeting is thereby also a measure of the autonomy created or allowed by an organization's control system. Like Ezzamel and Robson (1995), Dearden (1973) suggests that not all evaluations of performance should follow the same time period because the time span is inherently related to the job task and may therefore differ depending, for example, on the hierarchy or the level of discretion allowed.

Fourth, an entrainment to a fiscal year may foster a short-term orientation. This could put organizations at a disadvantage relative to organizations from cultures with more long-term orientations (e.g., Japan; see Hatvany and Pucik, 1981).

Criticisms of Budgeting and Its Relation to Time

While the above considerations applied more conceptual issues to a "traditional" budgeting process,[4] the following analyzes the recent critique of budgeting in which questions of time and timing seem particularly salient. Several patterns are evident in the critique of traditional budgeting. We relate these to the decision-influencing and decision-facilitating roles of accounting and control presented previously (for additional examples of the critique, see Neely et al., 2001; CIMA, 2007; Bogsnes, 2009b).

With regard to decision-influencing roles, the first criticism comes from representatives of the Beyond Budgeting approach, who argue that budgeting is part of the "command and control" culture of organizations, and that it prevents organizations from becoming more decentralized, autonomous and empowered. Their critique regarding the temporal structuring of organizations can be seen in their definition of budgeting as the "annual process that sets the performance agenda for the year ahead" (Hope and Fraser, 2001b: 10). They argue that this fixation on the annual year – an "*annual* performance trap" (Hope and Fraser, 2003a: 3, emphasis added) – has "wide behavioural implications, because it is a performance contract. The purpose is to commit people to achieving a certain result. Terms are likely to include a fixed target, time period, resources, limits of authority, reporting intervals and rewards" (Hope and Fraser, 2001b: 10). Similarly, the critique made by Jensen (2001, 2003) refers to the fact that the time interval chosen for performance measurement has a significant impact on the actions of managers. He suggests that this induces them, for example, to game the system and to move results from one period to another.

With regarding to the decision-facilitating roles of budgeting, three criticisms of budgeting are made. The first is that, in many organizations, the temporal ordering of budgeting typically foresees only one instance per year (typically a 12-month calendar year) of budget planning. In other words, the budgeting frequency is regarded as either too low or too high (Mintzberg and Waters, 1982; Hope and Fraser, 1999). For organizations with a budgeting year that begins in January, the budgeting period is typically in the late summer or autumn. This implies that resource allocations are traditionally made at only one point during the year, rather than when the need arises (Hope et al., 2011). Consequently, critics argue that organizations tend to view thinking about control as an annual, rather than a continual, event (see also Bogsnes, 2009b). Given the regularity of this event, the argument contends that this annual practice may persist, become routinized and eventually result in decreased managerial alertness (Gersick, 1994) and, more generally, in a managerial orientation towards the past rather than the future (Hope and Fraser, 2001a).

Second, depending on the circumstances and conditions defined by an organization's environment or competition, one criticism suggests that budgeting's time horizon is not linked to the "rhythm" of the business. This is applicable both in rapidly moving sectors in which an annual budgeting process demands a horizon that is too long to be budgeted and in stable sectors in which the time horizon may be too short. In both cases, managers are forced to focus too heavily on the time period prescribed by the calendar period to which the budget is entrained (Hope and Fraser, 2001a; for budgeting in the public sector, see Tarschys, 2002),[5] which has consequences for their temporal orientation (Ezzamel and Robson, 1995).

Third, and related to the above, a substantial criticism raised against budgets revolves around the fact that, once budgets have been compiled, they are not updated often enough during the budgeting period (Neely et al., 2001; Hansen et al., 2003; Hope and Fraser, 2003a). This leads to a low responsiveness on the part of the organization and to a failure to incorporate external events into the organization's budgets in real time. What lies behind this critique is the fact that clock-based views of time, which are incorporated into budgeting through entrainment to the calendar or fiscal year, interfere with an event-based view of time in which events in an organization's environment have more relevance for management and control. This is said to produce adverse results for the organization as a whole, or for particular subgroups or individuals in organizations, such that an exclusive clock-based view is considered "wrong" by some authors (Bluedorn, 2002; Roe, 2009: 295).

In light of the criticisms outlined above, organizations have developed solutions to alleviate the challenges resulting from entrainment to the fiscal or calendar year in their planning and budgeting practices. Organizations seek to improve their temporal structuring by trying to match their internal activities to those of their environments. To do so, they entrain to external, competitive pacers in order to become more effective and efficient (Marks et al., 2001; Batchelor and McCarthy, 2009; Dibrell et al., 2009). One such practice of temporal structuring is found in "year-end forecasts," which are compiled in order to continuously assess developments in a few selected line items as market conditions change. The aim of these forecasts is to give the organization a more up-to-date view (e.g., every month or every quarter) on the most likely development of the chosen line items through the end of the forecast period (i.e., the end of the budgeting period for year-end forecasts). However, given that the forecasting period for the year-end forecast grows smaller for every new forecast as the end of the budgeted year approaches, the organization will always have a detailed outlook only for the final date of the original budget period (Lamoreaux, 2011).

This problem has led firms to implement "rolling forecasts" (e.g., Player, 2009; Morlidge and Player, 2010). With generally the same aims as year-end forecasts, rolling forecasts continually roll the forecasting period forward by a constant time period (often between five and eight quarters) and are updated regularly (Hope and Fraser, 2003b; Lamoreaux, 2011). To illustrate, let us consider a setting in which the budgeting period is equal to the calendar year (January through December). A five-quarter rolling forecast prepared at the end of the first quarter would then forecast the most likely development of the chosen line items for the organization from April of the current year until the end of June of the following year.

Similarly, organizations have developed "rolling budgets," which in principle follow the same mechanism as rolling forecasts. The difference between the two is that, while forecast data in rolling forecasts aim to show the most likely development of the respective line items in the forecast period, a rolling budget also links the (typically more comprehensive) set of line items to targets (Hope and Fraser, 2003b; Lamoreaux, 2011) and to employee incentives. This adds a control and performance-evaluation element (decision influencing) to the planning, coordination and forecasting function (decision facilitating) of the rolling forecast.

Among the various options that can help improve traditional budgeting processes, rolling forecasts and rolling budgets are often believed to be the most effective solutions (Neely et al., 2003). This, in itself, evidences organizations' problems with issues of time. The practitioner literature also suggests that rolling forecasts can change the temporal orientation of managers in a number of ways. This literature argues that, as managers become skillful at preparing and interpreting rolling forecasts, they become less concerned with explaining past performance and more focused on detecting future changes in performance (Hope and Fraser, 2003b). This is because the inclusion of rolling forecasts in the managerial toolset is argued to eliminate the "rear-view mirror" effect that results from controls based on budgeted numbers (Hope and Fraser, 2001a) because managers can forecast and explain variances before these occur as well as manage by using the forecast rather than the actual results (Neely et al., 2003). Overall, rolling forecasts are argued to make planning and budgeting more forward looking and to help view planning not as a top-down, annual event but as a more continuous practice (Bogsnes, 2009b). From an entrainment perspective, however, neither year-end forecasts nor rolling forecasts shift their entrainment basis from a calendar year to individual events. Therefore, they do not completely undo the calendar-based view (Bunce et al., 2001; Bogsnes, 2009a). While a rolling forecast does move the forecast period forward, it is nevertheless bound to look into the future according to conceptions of linear time, which may be why rolling forecasts and the annual budgeting process work well together (Sivabalan et al., 2009).

One approach that prioritizes real events in an organization's environment to a greater extent is one that tries to plan and coordinate not on the basis of calendar time but according to events (Hoblitzell, 2003; Bogsnes, 2009b, 2010). This approach can be called "event-based budgeting" or "event-based forecasting" (other terms include "dynamic forecasting," see

Bogsnes, 2009a; or "event-driven dynamic planning," see Batchelor and McCarthy, 2009). Unlike rolling forecasts, these techniques work without a fixed frequency or horizon (Bogsnes, 2009a). Their use assumes that calendar time is not a particularly adequate time horizon for internal business processes and that organizations should instead orient their processes to relevant events in their environment: "We should let forecasting data flow into our systems according to their natural rhythms – when, for example, a new competitor suddenly appears, or when we postpone a scheduled maintenance shutdown, or when we decide to update our market view, or when a fire destroys a production facility" (Bogsnes, 2009a: 7).

This represents a move from entrainment to the fiscal year to entrainment to an external, competitive pacer. This, in turn, implies moving towards a subjective time in organizations following the notion that "[t]ime is in the events, and events are defined by organizational members" (Clark, 1985: 36). To date, little evidence on these issues can be found in the literature. However, Eisenhardt (1989), who studied five companies in a "high-velocity" environment, finds that the managers of these companies were able to entrain the pace of their strategic decision making to the pace of market changes. The author explains that managers did so by meeting more frequently, by using more real-time data and by simultaneously considering several alternatives in their planning activities. A contemporary example of the implementation of such event-based techniques is that mentioned for the company Statoil (Bogsnes, 2009a). Here, key questions are said to be how events should be defined and at which level this should be done. As Bogsnes (2009a) writes, the company defines events as "something that is big enough [locally] to justify a local forecast update" (2009a: 8). He suggests the company also believes that there are differences in lead time in its various departments depending on their particular *Zeitgebers* and that local knowledge is necessary to decide what an event is. Given this understanding, the introduction of "dynamic forecasting" provides organizational units with autonomy regarding their planning and forecasting processes (Batchelor and McCarthy, 2009; Bogsnes, 2009a).

These examples suggest that event-based accounting and control techniques demand certain features and skills from an organization's practices and systems as well as from individuals if relevant events in an organization's environment are to be detected or recognized. To date, some research has sensitized for such issues in relation to the sequences and trajectories of events and refers to such elements as "time-reckoning" capabilities (e.g., Clark, 1985; Clark and Maielli, 2009; see also Dodd et al., 2013). The fact that such capabilities do not lie within every organization or individual is further evidenced in a study by Das (1987). The author points to the fact that individuals active in planning need both an understanding of the competitive dynamics in a firm's environment and good foresight and visualization of longer-term developments. This does not imply a need to extrapolate from past and present data and trends, but requires the building of plans and forecasts from a unique understanding of relevant events and event trajectories in the environment. The recognition that not every manager or planner is equipped with such capabilities because of differing individual temporal orientations (e.g., Ancona and Chong, 1996) is one of the managerial implications of the studies by Das (1987) and Clark (1985). These skills may be learned over time, built up through training, or achieved through the involvement of other people or departments, such as marketing (Clark, 1985; Clark and Starkey, 1988) or management accounting. For the latter, this is also an interesting opportunity to move closer to line functions and to partner with the business in temporal ways (Ahrens, 1997). Importantly, as the example shows, admitting an event-based influence in planning and forecasting means less reliance on structures and practices, and more reliance on the autonomy of actors and their knowledge of changes in the competitive environment.

The fact that the outside world is also entrained to a *Zeitgeber*, such as calendar time, is a counter-argument for moving away from calendar-focused internal processes, as deviating from this mainstream practice may create additional costs for the organization in its relationship to its stakeholders. This might be the reason for Guild's (1998) finding[6] that a mountain resort that he studies keeps two sets of accounts – one is used to manage the organization's seasonal businesses (summer and winter) and the other is used for the purpose of financial reporting to the parent company. In addition, Cunha (2009) states that the risks for organizations that are overly entrained to events in their competitive environment ("pressed organizations") have not yet been researched. In terms of the change in temporal structuring, Cunha (2009) also mentions several problems that organizations may encounter. These mainly relate to unwritten rules, vested interests, or the inertia and persistence of organizational practices and rhythms (Cunha, 2009: 228).

As we show above, different temporal structures can both enable and constrain an organization (Orlikowski and Yates, 2002). Whether the enabling or the constraining effect is stronger is an empirical question that depends not only on the organization and its capabilities but also on its particular environment. In general, organizations have several practices available that can enable them to look for compromises or to attempt more radical change. This section has outlined a few of these practices in relation to planning and budgeting. Future research may wish to investigate the outcomes of these and other configurations for the temporal structuring of organizations.

In summary, while little academic enquiry to date has led researchers to analyze budgeting and forecasting practices from a time perspective, the significant amount of practitioner discourse around these practices provides interesting and insightful empirical reason to do so.

THE "RIGHT" TIMING IN MANAGEMENT CONTROL

In this chapter, we have demonstrated that management control is fundamentally related to questions of timing. By looking at the extant literature on temporal structuring, and by analyzing the debate around and criticisms of budgeting techniques, we have shown that accounting and control techniques not only represent the temporal structures of organizations but are also actively implicated in generating temporal structures for an organization's activities (Ezzamel and Robson, 1995). However, what does it mean to "get the timing right" in management control? Should management control practices be oriented towards a particular understanding of time?

The Beyond Budgeting debate appears to suggest that accounting practices need to be more closely oriented towards the "real-time" needs of organizations. However, this suggestion is controversial. If management control practices are made to *follow* other practices and actors within the organization, they lose their ability to temporally structure organizational activities. A purely event-based orientation may turn firms into "pressed organizations" (Cunha, 2009), and "fire-fighting" practices may no longer be helpful for planning and coordinating activities. We have also shown that there are interactions between the temporal structuring inherent in certain practices and the changes in temporal orientations of actors. Accountants have the opportunity to benefit the organization by ensuring the right timing through coordinating and synchronizing activities. However, if they become too involved in operational activities, they may lose their critical distance and independence from operational managers.

Undoubtedly, changes in temporal structuring provide management and the accounting and control function with a means to calibrate a balance between control and autonomy. However, we sensitized for the fact that also the time-reckoning capabilities of organizational actors need to be taken into account when seeking to achieve the right timing in management accounting and control. How organizations cope with the tension between timing that is accounting-driven and timing that follows the requirements of operational activities is still poorly understood. Therefore, research that examines such tensions can only be encouraged.

NOTES

1. The accounting literature often speaks of the *decision-influencing* versus the *decision-facilitating* roles of accounting (e.g., Demski and Feltham, 1976; Sprinkle, 2003).
2. This can also happen in a rather informal way or through "social controls." For instance, Anderson-Gough et al. (2001) show that socialization in audit firms involves the creation of a particular time consciousness among trainee auditors. The authors suggest that the ability to recognize the firm's demands for working "outside of the 'nine-to-five'" routine (Anderson-Gough et al., 2001: 112) is central to trainee auditors' socialization.
3. Ancona and Chong (1996: 260) mention that organizations' founders typically choose the fiscal year and that, after this decision is made, organizational activities entrain to this pacer.
4. In accordance with Anthony and Govindarajan (2007), we view "traditional budgeting" as covering one year, and as stating revenues and expenses for that year. Furthermore, we assume that managers accept responsibility for reaching the objectives formulated through budgets, that budgets are approved by the budgetee's superior and that actual performance is regularly compared to budgeted values.
5. Furthermore, budgets are criticized for being based on imprecise data on the future. However, this criticism has more to do with the type of data and/or information technologies used by organizations than with issues such as entrainment to the calendar year. The fact that the preparation of budgets takes too much time is also not related to issues of entrainment.
6. As cited by Orlikowski and Yates (2002).

REFERENCES

Ahrens, T. (1997), "Talking accounting: An ethnography of management knowledge in British and German brewers," *Accounting, Organizations and Society*, **22** (7), 617–37.

Ancona, D.G. (1990), "Outward bound: Strategies for team survival in an organization," *Academy of Management Journal*, **33** (2), 334–65.

Ancona, D.G. and C.-L. Chong (1996), "Entrainment: Pace, cycle, and rhythm in organizational behavior," *Research in Organizational Behavior*, **18**, 251–84.

Ancona, D.G., P.S. Goodman, B.S. Lawrence and M.L. Tushman (2001), "Time: A new research lens," *Academy of Management Review*, **26** (4), 645–63.

Ancona, D.G., G.A. Okhuysen and L.A. Perlow (2001), "Taking time to integrate temporal research," *Academy of Management Review*, **26** (4), 512–29.

Anderson-Gough, F., C. Grey and K. Robson (2001), "Tests of time: Organizational time-reckoning and the making of accountants in two multi-national accounting firms," *Accounting, Organizations and Society*, **26** (2), 99–122.

Anthony, R.N. (1965), *Planning and control systems: A framework for analysis*, Boston, MA: Division of Research, Graduate School of Business Administration, Harvard University.

Anthony, R.N. and V. Govindarajan (2007), *Management control systems*, 12th edn., New York: McGraw-Hill.

Aschoff, J. (1979), "Circadian rhythms: General features and endocrinological aspects," in D. Krieger (ed.), *Endocrine Rhythms*, New York: Raven Press.

Ballard, D.I. (2009), "Organizational temporality over time: Activity cycles as sources of entrainment," in R.A. Roe, M.J. Waller and S.R. Clegg (eds.), *Time in organizational research*, London: Routledge, pp. 204–19.

Batchelor, S. and B. McCarthy (2009), *In uncertain times, businesses need dynamic planning to chart course to high performance: Traditional planning gives way to "Dynamic Planning,"* New York: Accenture.

Bluedorn, A.C. (2000), "Time and organizational culture," in N.M. Ashkanasy, C.P.M. Wilderom and M.F. Peterson (eds.), *Handbook of Organizational Culture and Climate*, 1st edn., Thousand Oaks, CA: Sage, pp. 117–28.

Bluedorn, A.C. (2002), *The human organization of time: Temporal realities and experience*, Stanford, CA: Stanford Business Books.

Bogsnes, B. (2009a), "Dynamic forecasting: A planning innovation for fast-changing times," *Balanced Scorecard Report: The Strategy Execution Source*, **11** (5), 5–9.

Bogsnes, B. (2009b), *Implementing Beyond Budgeting: Unlocking the performance potential*, Hoboken, NJ: John Wiley & Sons.

Bogsnes, B. (2010), "The world has changed: Isn't it time to change the way we lead and manage?," *Balanced Scorecard Report: The Strategy Execution Source*, **12** (3), 1–7.

Brown, S.L. and K.M. Eisenhardt (1997), "The art of continuous change: Linking complexity theory and time-paced evolution in relentlessly shifting organizations," *Administrative Science Quarterly*, **42** (1), 1–34.

Brown, S.L. and K.M. Eisenhardt (1998), *Competing on the edge: Strategy as structured chaos*, Boston, MA: Harvard Business School Press.

Bunce, P., R. Fraser and J. Hope (2001), "Beyond Budgeting: The barrier breakers," in P. Horváth (ed.), *Strategien erfolgreich umsetzen*, Stuttgart: Schäffer-Poeschel, pp. 55–76.

Cameron, K.S. and D.A. Whetten (1988), "Models of organizational life-cycle: Applications to higher education," in K.S. Cameron, R.I. Sutton and D.A. Whetten (eds.), *Readings in organizational decline*, Cambridge: Ballinger, pp. 45–62.

CIMA (2007), *Beyond Budgeting*, London: Chartered Institute of Management Accountants.

Clark, P. (1985), "A review of the theories of time and structure for organizational sociology," *Research in the Sociology of Organizations*, **3**, 35–79.

Clark, P. and G. Maielli (2009), "The evolution of strategic timed-space in organizations," in R.A. Roe, M.J. Waller and S.R. Clegg (eds.), *Time in organizational research*, London: Routledge, pp. 291–313.

Clark, P.A. and K. Starkey (1988), *Organization transitions and innovation-design*, London: Pinter Publishers.

Clegg, S.R. (2009), "The ghosts of time in organization theory," in R.A. Roe, M.J. Waller and S.R. Clegg (eds.), *Time in organizational research*, London: Routledge, pp. 238–54.

Cohen, M.A., J. Eliashberg and T.-H. Ho (1996), "New product development: The performance and time-to-market tradeoff," *Management Science*, **42** (2), 172–86.

Cunha, M.P. (2009), "The organizing of rhythm, the rhythm of organizing," in R.A. Roe, M.J. Waller and S.R. Clegg (eds.), *Time in organizational research*, London: Routledge, pp. 220–37.

Czarniawska, B. (2013), "Is speed good?," *Scandinavian Journal of Management*, **29** (1), 7–12.

Das, T.K. (1987), "Strategic planning and individual temporal orientation," *Strategic Management Journal*, **8** (2), 203–09.

D'Aveni, R.A. and R.E. Gunther (1994), *Hypercompetition: Managing the dynamics of strategic maneuvering*, New York: Free Press.

Dearden, J. (1973), "'Time-span' in management control," in W.E. Thomas (ed.), *Readings in cost accounting, budgeting and control*, Cincinnati, OH: South-Western, pp. 340–53.

Demski, J.S. and G.A. Feltham (1976), *Cost determination: A conceptual approach*, Ames: Iowa State University Press.

Dibrell, C., P.S. Davis and J.B. Craig (2009), "The performance implications of temporal orientation and information technology in organization–environment synergy," *Journal of Strategy and Management*, **2** (2), 145–62.

Dodd, S., A. Anderson and S. Jack (2013), "Being in time and the family owned firm," *Scandinavian Journal of Management*, **29** (1), 35–47.

Eisenhardt, K.M. (1989), "Making fast strategic decisions in high-velocity environments," *Academy of Management Journal*, **32** (3), 543–76.

Ezzamel, M. and K. Robson (1995), "Accounting in time: Organizational time-reckoning and accounting practice," *Critical Perspectives on Accounting*, **6** (2), 149–70.

Gersick, C.J.G. (1988), "Time and transition in work teams: Toward a new model of group development," *Academy of Management Journal*, **31** (1), 9–41.

Gersick, C.J.G. (1994), "Pacing strategic change: The case of a new venture," *Academy of Management Journal*, **37** (1), 9–45.

Giddens, A. (1984), *The constitution of society: Outline of the theory of structuration*, Berkeley: University of California Press.

Hansen, S.C., D.T. Otley and W.A. Van der Stede (2003), "Practice developments in budgeting: An overview and research perspective," *Journal of Management Accounting Research*, **15** (1), 95–116.

Hatvany, N. and V. Pucik (1981), "An integrated management system: Lessons from the Japanese experience," *Academy of Management Review*, **6** (3), 469–80.

Heidegger, M. (1927), *Sein und Zeit*, Halle an der Saale: M. Niemeyer.

Hernes, T., B. Simpson and J. Söderlund (2013), "Managing and temporality," *Scandinavian Journal of Management*, **29** (1), 1–6.

Hoblitzell, T. (2003), *Best practices in planning and budgeting*, Miami, FL: Answerthink.

Hope, J. and R. Fraser (1999), "Tool of repression and a barrier to change," *Financial Times*, May 18.

Hope, J. and R. Fraser (2001a), "Figures of hate," *Financial Management*, February, 22–5.

Hope, J. and R. Fraser (2001b), "Letters: I think therefore CAM-I," *Financial Management*, **79** (September), 10–11.

Hope, J. and R. Fraser (2003a), *Beyond Budgeting: How managers can break free from the annual performance trap*, Boston, MA: Harvard Business School Press.

Hope, J. and R. Fraser (2003b), "Who needs budgets?," *Harvard Business Review*, **81** (2), 108–15.

Hope, J., P. Bunce and F. Röösli (2011), *The leader's dilemma: How to build an empowered and adaptive organization without losing control*, Hoboken, NJ: John Wiley & Sons.

Hopwood, A. (1989), "On time and accounting," Working paper, London School of Economics, London.

Hopwood, A.G. (2009), "The economic crisis and accounting: Implications for the research community," *Accounting, Organizations and Society*, **34** (6–7), 797–802.

Jaques, E. (1964), *Time-span handbook: The use of time-span of discretion to measure the level of work in employment roles and to arrange an equitable payment structure*, London: Heinemann.

Jensen, M.C. (2001), "Corporate budgeting is broken: Let's fix it," *Harvard Business Review*, **79** (10), 94–101.

Jensen, M.C. (2003), "Paying people to lie: The truth about the budgeting process," *European Financial Management*, **9** (3), 379–406.

Jones, G., C. McLean and P. Quattrone (2004), "Spacing and timing," *Organization*, **11** (6), 723–41.

Kaplan, R.S. and S.R. Anderson (2007), *Time-Driven Activity-Based Costing: A simpler and more powerful path to higher profits*, Boston, MA: Harvard Business School Press.

Kaplan, R.S. and D.P. Norton (1992), "The Balanced Scorecard: Measures that drive performance," *Harvard Business Review*, **70** (1), 71–9.

Lamoreaux, M.G. (2011), "Planning for uncertainty," *Journal of Accountancy*, **212** (4), 32–6.

Loft, A. (1989), "On time and cost accounting in the seven editions of Garcke and Fells' Factory Accounts," Working paper.

Marginson, D. and S. Ogden (2005), "Coping with ambiguity through the budget: The positive effects of budgetary targets on managers' budgeting behaviours," *Accounting, Organizations and Society*, **30** (5), 435–56.

Marks, M.A., J.E. Mathieu and S.J. Zaccaro (2001), "A temporally based framework and taxonomy of team processes," *Academy of Management Review*, **26** (3), 356–76.

McGrath, J.E. and J.R. Kelly (1986), *Time and human interaction: Toward a social psychology of time*, New York: Guilford Press.

McGrath, J.E. and N.L. Rotchford (1983), "Time and behavior in organizations," *Research in Organizational Behavior*, **5**, 57–101.

Merchant, K.A. and W.A. Van der Stede (2012), *Management control systems: Performance measurement, evaluation and incentives*, 3rd edn., Harlow: Pearson Education.

Mintzberg, H. and J.A. Waters (1982), "Tracking strategy in an entrepreneurial firm," *Academy of Management Journal*, **25** (3), 465–99.

Morlidge, S. and S. Player (2010), *Future ready: How to master business forecasting*, Chichester: John Wiley & Sons.

Mouritsen, J. and A. Bekke (1999), "A space for time: Accounting and time based management in a high technology company," *Management Accounting Research*, **10** (2), 159–80.

Nandhakumar, J. and M. Jones (2001), "Accounting for time: Managing time in project-based teamworking," *Accounting, Organizations and Society*, **26** (3), 193–214.

Neely, A., M.R. Sutcliff and H.R. Heyns (2001), *Driving value through strategic planning and budgeting*, New York: Accenture.

Neely, A., M. Bourne and C. Adams (2003), "Better budgeting or Beyond Budgeting?," *Measuring Business Excellence*, **7** (3), 22–8.

Orlikowski, W.J. and J. Yates (2002), "It's about time: Temporal structuring in organizations," *Organization Science*, **13** (6), 684–700.

Parker, L.D. (2002), "Twentieth-century textbook budgetary discourse: Formalization, normalization and rebuttal in an Anglo-Saxon environment," *European Accounting Review*, **11** (2), 305–27.

Peters, T.J. and R.H. Waterman (1982), *In search of excellence: Lessons from America's best-run companies*, New York: Harper & Row.

Player, S. (2009), *Managing through change: The power of rolling forecasts*, Ottawa: IBM Cognos Innovation Center for Performance Management.

Quattrone, P. and T. Hopper (2005), "A 'time–space odyssey': Management control systems in two multinational organisations," *Accounting, Organizations and Society*, **30** (7–8), 735–64.

Roe, R.A. (2009), "Perspectives on time and the chronometric study of what happens in organizations," in R.A. Roe, M.J. Waller and S.R. Clegg (eds.), *Time in organizational research*, London: Routledge, pp. 291–313.

Roe, R.A., M.J. Waller and S.R. Clegg (eds.) (2009), *Time in organizational research: Approaches and methods*, London: Routledge.

Schatzki, T.R. (2005), "The site of organizations," *Organization Studies*, **26** (3), 465–84.

Schatzki, T.R. (2006), "On organizations as they happen," *Organization Studies*, **27** (12), 1863–73.

Schonberger, R. (1986), *World Class Manufacturing: The lessons of simplicity applied*, New York: Free Press.

Selto, F.H., C.J. Renner and S.M. Young (1995), "Assessing the organizational fit of a just-in-time manufacturing system: Testing selection, interaction and systems models of contingency theory," *Accounting, Organizations and Society*, **20** (7–8), 665–84.

Sivabalan, P., P. Booth, T. Malmi and D.A. Brown (2009), "An exploratory study of operational reasons to budget," *Accounting and Finance*, **49** (4), 849–71.

Sprinkle, G.B. (2003), "Perspectives on experimental research in managerial accounting," *Accounting, Organizations and Society*, **28** (2–3), 287–318.

Stalk, G. and T.M. Hout (1990), *Competing against time: How time-based competition is reshaping global markets*, New York: Free Press.

Tarschys, D. (2002), "Time horizons in budgeting," *OECD Journal on Budgeting*, **2** (2), 77–103.

Taylor, F.W. (1911), *The principles of scientific management*, New York: Harper & Brothers.

Thompson, J. (1967), *Organizations in action: Social science bases of administrative theory*, New York: McGraw-Hill.

Yeh, R.T., K.E. Pearlson and G. Kozmetsky (2000), *Zero time: Providing instant customer value – Every time, all the time!*, New York: John Wiley & Sons.

Zerubavel, E. (1979), "Private time and public time: The temporal structure of social accessibility and professional commitments," *Social Forces*, **58** (1), 38–58.

9. The planning-regime concept and its application to three examples of organizational budgeting

Anatoli Bourmistrov and Katarina Kaarbøe

INTRODUCTION

In modern organizations, activities are commonly planned and organized through annual budgets. Therefore annual budgets have been thoroughly studied. The ongoing debate about the behavioral aspects of budgeting originated in the 1950s (Argyris, 1952), and gathered speed in the 1970s and 1980s (Covalevski et al., 2007). Some researchers argue that budgets are useful for organizations (Ekholm and Wallin, 2000; Libby and Lindsay, 2010), while others argue that budgets result in dysfunctional behavior (Wallander, 1999; Hope and Fraser, 2003; Neely et al., 2003). One core task of a budget is to coordinate activities among departments. Some argue that this task serves to highlight important areas in which issues need to be discussed and decisions need to be made, while more critical voices argue that such discussions become a game in which different groups act in their own self-interests. Thus, "annual budgeting" can mean different things in different contexts, leading to different planning and coordinating arrangements with a variety of behavioral consequences.

In order to improve planning in organizations, we must move away from the dichotomy of budgets as good or bad towards a discussion of when and how budgets can assist in planning, and towards an understanding of how such planning works given different types of budgets. In this chapter, we argue that use of the budget as a planning and coordinating device can be misleading. We therefore introduce the concept of "planning regimes" as a better way of characterizing relations between planning and coordination activities in organizational contexts in terms of the influence of such activities on human behavior. This is especially important in today's environment, where many contemporary organizations are questioning, changing, simplifying and even abandoning annual budgets (see, for example, Henttu-Aho and Järvinen, 2013).

In order to understand how organizations operate in different planning and coordination regimes, we introduce three organizations with different structures: one hierarchy, one conglomerate and one based on the value chain. We are mainly interested in how social and temporal embeddedness occur in different planning and coordination regimes. We suggest that planning regimes influence the design and use of budgeting for planning and coordination purposes.

Given this background, our research question is the following: *How are planning and coordination activities related to various organizational contexts?* The answer to this question is important if we are to understand how organizations plan and coordinate their activities, especially with regard to their social and temporal embeddedness. Studies in which budgeting is contextualized tend to focus on contingencies from a rather traditional perspective in which management control systems are viewed as passive tools that provide the data necessary for managers' decision making (Chenhall, 2003). Alternatively, they focus on how organizations comply with external rules and beliefs, or they explore various forms of resistance to change in budgeting systems or management control systems (Modell, 2001; Pettersen and Nyland, 2006; Boland et al., 2008) or whether national cultures influence the use of budgets (Chow et al., 1994). However, social and temporal embeddedness is not yet well understood. Therefore, within the field of management control, it will be interesting to explore the links between social and temporal embeddedness, and planning and coordination. By increasing our understanding of the social and temporal embeddedness of planning regimes, we can shed light on why the literature within budgeting is ambiguous. We can also help to develop a language for talking about budgeting.

The rest of this chapter is organized as follows. The next section provides a basis for the planning-regime concept. It includes a review of behavioral research in budgeting and the literature on embeddedness. The section thereafter introduces the three examples, which are analyzed and interpreted by applying the planning-regime concept. The chapter concludes with a discussion of the findings and this study's implications for future research.

THEORETICAL FRAMEWORK

Budgets are traditionally defined as a business plan for the short term, and they are typically expressed in financial terms. Furthermore, budgets are described as a common accounting tool that organizations use for implementing strategy (Atrill and McLaney, 2007; Horngren et al., 2012).

Budgets are often believed to be an integral part of management control systems. A budget aims at promoting *coordination and communication* among subunits within the company, provides a framework for *judging performance* and offers a way of *motivating managers* and other employees (Horngren et al., 2012).

However, budgets have been widely criticized for a number of reasons. Critics suggest that budget work is too time consuming, budgets impose a vertical command-and-control structure, they lead to centralized decision making, they stifle initiative and they focus on cost reduction rather than value creation (Wallander, 1999; Hansen et al., 2003; Hope and Fraser, 2003). In addition, budgets create responsibility centre-focused controls that are incompatible with flat, network or value chain-based organizational designs. Such controls impede employees from making the best decisions (Wallander, 1999; Hansen et al., 2003; Hope and Fraser, 2003).

The relation between budgets and human behavior has been emphasized in several studies. As early as 1952, Argyris emphasized employees' acceptance of and commitment to budgetary goals. He highlighted differences among actors in the organization, and differences in how they perceived budgets and budget work. Argyris called for an improvement in the relation between the "budget people" (management) and the factory workers. He also showed that participation is positively related to goal commitment. His studies led researchers to focus on actors in relation to budget work and on the need for participation in budget work. Numerous researchers have since tried to elucidate the significance of participation for the budget process. Some studies show that budget participation may have positive effects (Argyris, 1952; Hofstede, 1967), while others studies find that that the effects may be negative depending on contextual factors, such as reward systems (Cherrington and Cherrington, 1973), centralization (Merchant, 1981) or employee perceptions of their influence on final budget decisions, which is referred to as the importance of "voice" (Libby, 1999).

This study aims to improve our understanding of the drivers of planning and coordination in the budgeting processes, and how these drivers are related to context. For this purpose, we define a new concept – "planning regime" – which helps us to understand human behavior in relation to budgets.

"Planning Regimes" Defined

Many definitions of "regime" have been proposed in the extant literature. A regime is commonly defined as a set of conditions, most often of a political nature. Regimes are defined by political science professor Stephen

Krasner as sets of explicit or implicit principles, norms, rules and decision-making procedures around which actor expectations converge in a given issue area (Krasner, 1982). This definition is intentionally broad, and it covers human interaction in contexts ranging from formal organizations (e.g., OPEC) to informal groups (e.g., major banks). The term is typically used in studies of states, but it has also been used in the accounting field. Jones and Dugdale (2001) define an "accounting regime" as the networks of practices and dimensions over which accounting operates. They argue that accounting operates more broadly and more deeply than typically assumed.

In this study, we use the "planning-regime" concept to enhance our understanding of planning and coordination work inside organizations. Our approach is based on the idea that a firm is governed by a planning regime, which is a dynamic actor network. The focus on the relationship between planning regimes, defined as dynamic actor networks, and organizational structure is influenced by the policy network literature (Atkinson and Coleman, 1992). This literature is based on three considerations (Bleiklie, 2001). First, a regime is a network of actors. Second, this network of actors does not exclusively act to promote its own self-interest. Rather, it may be interested in a variety of factors. Third, the planning process within the dynamic regime is driven not only by goal-oriented rational action but, at times, also by rule-oriented institutionalized behavior.

The Dimensions of Budgeting Regimes

A number of questions arise with regard to the relationship between budgets and planning regimes. What dimensions characterize budgets and budget work? What contextual factors explain the outcomes of different planning and coordination activities? We argue, in contrast to textbook definitions of budgeting, which often focus solely on the technique-related part of budgeting, that we must understand not only the techniques but also the actors and their relations to one another. This is because the budgeting process can serve as an arena for learning and negotiation, and the outcomes can differ depending on the actors and their embeddedness in the context.

To construct the concept of planning regimes, we rely on two streams of literature: budgeting literature and theories about embeddedness. The budgeting literature helps us to understand when managers perceive budgets as useful, while the embeddedness literature analyzes the ways that budgets are used to coordinate activities.

In the budgeting literature, four characteristics of budgeting stand out as important for managers' use of budgets. The first two are related to the ways in which budgets are constructed or designed, while the other two concern the ways in which budgets are used or how managers control activities with budgets. First, it is important to focus on the degree of managerial participation in the budgeting process, especially in terms of how budgeting is facilitated by a system's characterization of being *top down* or *bottom up*. The bottom-up methods are called "budgetary participation." Although these receive a significant amount of attention in the literature, there is no agreement on whether participation leads to better performance relative to other methods. One explanation for this lack of consensus may be found in Clinton and Hunton's 2001 study, which shows that the link between participative budgeting and organizational outcomes does not depend solely on the level of actual participation, as suggested in earlier studies (Clinton, 1999; Chong and Chong, 2002). Instead, the degree of congruence between the perceived need for participation and the perceived degree of allowed participation is important for understanding the outcome (Clinton and Hunton, 2001). This indicates that, when local line managers feel a need to participate in the budgeting process, this is important in terms of their feeling of "ownership" of the targets. Therefore, the first important factor in understanding the local use of budgeting seems to be the level of local participation in deciding final plans and budgets (for instance, a low need to participate in contexts of top-down budgeting and a high need to participate in contexts with a bottom-up approach).

Second, budgets can be used for *resource allocation* in several ways (Bergstrand, 2009). In this regard, three main methods are described in the literature: incremental budgeting, zero-based budgeting and formula-based budgeting (mainly used in the public sector). Incremental budgeting occurs when the budget is decided well in advance, after which only minor, incremental adjustments are made. Zero-based budgeting occurs when the budget is completely re-decided each year in order to adjust for strategic considerations. Finally, formula-based budgeting takes place when a formula based on specific criteria is used to decide resource allocations. These resource-allocation methods vary in terms of the degree of renewal with regard to how resources are allocated. The degree of renewal is lowest in formula-based budgeting and highest in zero-based budgeting. In the literature resource allocation in accounting focuses either on the challenges associated with resource allocation in the public sector (Wildavski, 1979; Nahapiet, 1988) or on the balance between resource allocation and reward systems (see, for example, Fisher et al., 2002).

Third, the *type of target control* (or the degree of control tightness) is also emphasized in the literature as an important dimension in understanding variation in budget use. Studies show that, in times of economic distress, targets become tighter and budgets are used to tighten the control, while targets are looser in better times (Czarniawska-Joerges, 1988). In the literature the studies focus on whether budget goals are more or less motivating given different levels of control. The findings vary widely, with some studies showing budgets as poor motivators (Hirst and Lowy, 1990; Hirst and Yetton, 1999) and others showing them as better motivators (Merchant and Manzoni, 1989). Furthermore, the budget maker's personal qualities and previous experience seem to affect the types of goals that he or she finds motivating (Merchant and Manzoni, 1989).

Finally, *management style* is important to the use of budgets. Hopwood (1972) shows that the responses to a budget differ depending on how the budget is linked to evaluations and rewards, especially in terms of the degree of freedom managers have to define and report on targets. Hopwood (1972) divides management styles into three categories: budget constrained, profit conscious and non-accounting. In the budget-constrained style, evaluations are based on the cost-center head's ability to continually meet the budgetary goals on a short-term basis. This performance criterion is stressed at the expense of other valued and important criteria. In the profit-conscious style, evaluations are based on the ability of the head of the cost center to increase the general effectiveness of his or her unit's operations in relation to the organization's long-term purposes. Such managers are concerned with the minimalization of long-term costs at the cost-center level, which requires that accounting data be used flexibly. In the non-accounting style, data other than the accounting data are used for evaluations. Accounting data provide information on whether the budget is in balance, but they do not necessarily say anything about whether the manager is behaving so as to minimize long-term costs (Hopwood, 1972, 1973).

Social Embeddedness in Planning and Coordination

We can derive a new understanding of the use of budgeting for planning and coordination by viewing the actors in the budgeting process as embedded socially and temporally (in time). When combined with budgeting behavior theory, embeddedness theory provides a theoretical basis for the budgeting-regime concept.

"Embeddedness" refers to the fact that economic actions and outcomes are affected by actors' pair-wise relations and by the overall network (structure) of relations (Granovetter, 1973, 1992). *Relational embeddedness* reflects the nature of the pair-wise relations through strong or weak ties, which has a direct effect on individuals' economic actions. *Structural embeddedness* goes beyond immediate ties and refers to the aggregated impact of pair-wise relations. Granovetter indicates that not only do personal relations matter, but the structure of the overall network of relations is also key:

> A worker can more easily maintain a good relationship with a supervisor who has good relations with most other workers as well. If the supervisor is at odds with the others, and especially if those others are friendly with one another, they will be able to make life very difficult for the one worker who is close to the supervisor; pressures will be strong to edge away from this closeness. (Granovetter, 1992: 35)

In their attempts to understand cooperation and negotiation processes in market interaction, theories often focus on social embeddedness (McGinn and Keros, 2002). Even though previous studies of embeddedness have mainly centered on market relations, we believe that the embeddedness concept is useful for understanding how actors in the budgeting process interact and to understand the consequences of those interactions for coordination. Previous studies show that buyers turn to their friends in market-based interaction when making large, unique purchases, such as purchases of a house or a car (DiMaggio and Louch, 1998). In Uzzi's studies of the apparel industry and mid-market banking, arm's-length transactions were common, but the majority of critical translations involved close, personal relationships (Uzzi, 1997, 1999). The need for interaction in order to come to a joint understanding is also supported by Weick, who argues that negotiation requires that actors jointly make sense of the negation as it evolves (Weick, 1998).

For planning regimes, this implies that an understanding of who participates in the construction of the budget and the types of relationships these actors have with each other is key. If only relational embeddedness is associated with the budgeting process, then the importance of budgets becomes more important. In such situations, the budget is the only link between the two parties. Therefore, whether the social embeddedness is structural or relational is an important mechanism for explaining coordination between departments.

Temporal Embeddedness in Budgeting

Another mechanism that can explain coordination is temporal embeddedness. Time can be understood as objective or subjective, or it can be understood from a practice perspective (Orlikowski and Yates, 2002). The objective view understands time as clock time, which is outside the individual and cannot be influenced. In this view, the experience of time is associated with standardized time-measurement systems, such as clocks and calendars. Actors cannot change time, only adapt to it by speeding up, slowing down or prioritizing differently.

The subjective time perspective argues that time is a social construct. In other words, time differs depending on the culture. Time is experienced through interpretive processes that create meaningful temporal notions, such as events, cycles or rites of passage. Actors can actually change time or the interpretation of time; for example, they can have "quit time" (to create silence) or put something on the "fast track" (to increase speed). The interpretation of time becomes different depending on how you express time.

Finally, the practice-based perspective understands time as a constitution of ongoing human action. The experience of time arises from individuals' recurrent practices that (re)produce temporal structures, such as project schedules that are both the medium and the outcome of the practices. Actors are knowledgeable agents who reflexively monitor their actions. In so doing, they can acknowledge new or modified temporal structures in their practices, such as a new fiscal year or "casual Fridays." Such temporal structuring occurs as individuals routinely schedule and attend meetings, work toward project deadlines and organize lectures according to the academic calendar. Such temporal structurings give meaning to time in an organizational setting.

In this study, we divide time into three areas. In the objective perspective, we call time use *clock time*. In the subjective perspective, we call time use *event time*. In the practice-oriented perspective, we call time use *entrainment time*, which refers to the use of time in relation to something else. *Clock time* is consistent with a mechanical view of the world. In contrast, *event time* is conceived as qualitative, heterogeneous, discontinuous and unequivalent when different time periods are compared (Orlikowski and Yates, 2002). People often structure meetings by referring to both calendar time for routine activities (weekly meetings) and event time for exceptions (meetings related to a specific area, such as a jazz festival, i.e., an event). Tuttle (1997) refers to Ancona and Chong (1996), who define *entrainment* as "the adjustment of the pace or cycle of one activity to match or synchronize with that of another" (Tuttle, 1997: 351). Entrainment is the process of matching the individual's temporal orientation with the temporal demands of the environment. In budgeting and target setting, this is related to whether forecasts and resource allocation should be discussed weekly, monthly, in conjunction with different events or on some other basis.

We argue that both social and temporal embeddedness are important to understanding the budgeting process and the coordination between entities. In our analysis, we investigate the different budgeting regimes in terms of how the actors relate to each other (strong or weak ties) and how time is understood (clock time, event time or entrainment time). If time is understood as clock time, budgeting processes can be viewed as wasting time when discussing various common issues. If time is understood as event time, the purpose of the budget – such as learning – is more important than the clock time. Finally, if time is understood as entrainment time, it is important to find the best timing or rhythm for different budget-related events in relation to other activities.

This discussion extends the focal research question of how planning and coordination activities are related to organizational contexts by linking it to the budgeting behavior and embeddedness literature. Hence, this chapter not only describes different planning regimes but also analyzes social and temporal embeddedness in order to increase our knowledge of the drivers of coordination and planning.

PLANNING REGIMES IN THREE CASE COMPANIES

In this section, we first describe the characteristics of three planning regimes. We then analyze the regimes in terms of design (the construction of the budget) and control (how the budget is used during the year). The planning regimes are exemplified by three different organizations: Alpha, Beta and Gamma.

Alpha is a regional health enterprise in the Norwegian public specialized health care sector. The Beta group was established in 1992. It includes companies that are vertically integrated in the pulp-and-paper and cardboard business. The group controls a large pulp-and-paper factory, transportation companies, lumber and timber production facilities and forests, as well as sales offices. Since its establishment, the group has been strategically acquiring companies that are important for its vertical value chain. These companies are active in raw material supplies for pulp-and-paper production (lumber and timber), transportation and sales (especially abroad). Gamma is a group of companies with a highly diversified structure. For example, several of the companies in the group are active in the tourist business, retail stores and business centers.

These three organizations are used to illustrate the three planning regimes. The examples provided here are not in-depth case studies but rather illustrations of the different planning regimes. In this regard, they help us to understand the importance of the context, and the drivers of coordination and planning.

In the following section, we present how budgeting is handled in the three organizations. We start by discussing the budgeting regime, after which we analyze how the budget is designed and used. The budgets' designs are described along two dimensions: the type of local participation (top down, bottom up or a mix) and the degree of renewal (incremental, zero based or formula based). Use of budget for control purposes is also described along two dimensions: target setting, as depicted in the leadership style, and the level of control.

Three Planning and Coordination Regimes: "Family," "Military Unit" and "Stock Exchange"

The first planning regime, which is found in Alpha, we denote as "family." The group of enterprises to which Alpha belongs is molded together. The enterprises in this group are closely and exclusively related, and they are socially embedded in what resembles a family structure. As in a family, the members are united by a common belongingness to similar kinship – the health care business and the region. The enterprises are formally related in terms of authority structure (e.g., a parent–subsidiary relationship), but informal relations are also prevalent, as managers in these companies know each other well and have long been in close contact with one another. Furthermore, there is a high level of trust among members, the different business units are comfortable with each other and there is a great degree of legitimacy when discussing important "family" matters, such as budgets or resource coordination. Coordination is mainly organized around clock time. As in a family, where major repetitive events, such as birthdays or holidays, bring family members together, Alpha involves its members in the coordination of enterprise planning and resource allocation during major, calendar-driven events (such as regular meetings) during the year. Therefore the social embeddedness is structural, while the temporal embeddedness is based on clock time.

We refer to the second planning regime, which is found in Beta, as a "military unit." As in a military unit, the coordination of activities in enterprise Beta is organized around the mission (i.e., to earn and accumulate profit in the headquarters). Beta has a clear authority structure, and units exhibit strict subordination to orders from headquarters. Reward and punishment mechanisms have been established for following or not following the orders related to the mission. In addition to this clear relational embeddedness towards the headquarters, structural embeddedness is evident in the interdependency of each enterprise in the vertical value chain. As in a military unit, enterprises depend on each other, as their level of specialization requires them to work together to accomplish the mission.

When conducting a mission and coordinating activities a military unit is dependent upon both clock time and event time. Clock time is the more common, as the unit can coordinate activities by being accountable to headquarters for the mission's progress (e.g., regular communication meetings and updates). However, the mission is also structured around event time – it is important to pay attention to changes in the environment. Members of a military unit are expected to observe what is going on in their surroundings in order to assess the threats and initiate changes in the way the mission should be accomplished if the chain of events is different from what was initially presented in the briefing. In Beta, such changes occur, for example, when input prices change. The social embeddedness is both structural and relational, while the temporal embeddedness is based on both clock time and event time.

In Gamma, we find yet another planning regime – the "stock exchange." In the "stock exchange," the social and temporal embeddedness of the coordination and planning regime differs from the "family" and the "military unit." In the context of the group of enterprises to which Gamma belongs, the companies work independently and compete with each other, like traders on a stock exchange. The companies are not linked by a common mission. Instead, they are coordinated by competition on the marketplace, and the goal of each company is to earn money. Formal contact between traders happens only when they are engaged in a mutual transaction. Thus, for Gamma, social embeddedness is mainly relational. It develops through the use of spot contracts and through reporting to the headquarters. Gamma's temporal embeddedness is characterized as focused on entrainment time because enterprises in this example have to adapt to the market to a higher degree than those in the other examples. The focus on competition necessitates comparisons with the other companies in the conglomerate that compete under different conditions. It is vital that Gamma continually show profit. To do so, it must adjust the pace of its activities so that they are synchronized with other companies' activities. Therefore, Gamma's structural embeddedness is mainly relational, while its temporal embeddedness relates mainly to entrainment time.

ANALYSIS OF THE BUDGETING REGIMES

The different regimes have different influences on the design and use of control. In the family regime (Alpha), the budget plays an important role in creating legitimacy for the resource allocation. This description is based on how Alpha allocates resources to each hospital. Alpha uses a formula-based budgeting design, which means that each hospital should receive the same amount of financial resources in proportion to the health needs of the local population. The rationale behind this formula-based budgeting is that there should be equity among the resources available to patients. Alpha's focus is not on the hospitals (the production unit) but on the receiver of the product (health services). Based on calculations of historical events, Alpha can determine which members of the population are likely to need most health care. For example, the elderly, the handicapped and social welfare clients typically have a greater need for health care services. Consequently, hospitals with these patients receive more resources.

Alpha is part of a *hierarchical* structure composed of the Ministry of Health, the regional health enterprise (Alpha) and the local hospitals. Alpha and the local hospitals have their own boards to govern activities. The annual budgeting process starts with an order from the Ministry to Alpha, which is the regional health enterprise. This order is not detailed. Instead, it describes a mission for the health region, such as providing qualitative health care for the population in the area. In addition, the order can highlight strategic focus areas, such as psychiatric care. Together with the order, the regional authority receives a lump sum, which can be reduced if the regional enterprise does not deliver according to the order. Even though strategic focus areas influence the resource allocation, most of the allocation is decided by Alpha. The allocation of financial resources is Alpha's responsibility, and it is expected to allocate the resources in a way that will enable the region to reach the given goals. The role of each hospital is to offer health care services to patients in their area.

The resources provided by the Ministry are allocated to strategic focus areas and to meeting the population's health care demands. The former can, for example, include teaching or another focused activity. The latter are allocated through a formula-based budgeting process. This process differs from traditional budgeting focusing on planned production based on costs, volume and capacity, as formula-based budgeting does not take capacity per unit into account. The calculation is based only on the region's need for health care services. The accounting principle is similar to that of transfer pricing – the product cannot cost more than the customer wants to pay for it (in this case, the customer is the Ministry of Health).

Resources are allocated once each year on the basis of the formula-based budget. There is no need for negotiations, as the actors involved have agreed upon the formula. Participation is related to making decisions regarding the formula and plays an important role in the budget's legitimacy. The formula is changed every few years to reflect changing conditions.

In the military regime (Beta), the budget plays an important role for the entire group of companies. Structurally, the budget work is organized by headquarters around pre-defined cost and responsibility centers found in the group's *vertical value chain*. The annual budgeting process aims to develop a master plan for the whole year that will govern the activities of each enterprise in the group for the year. The primary idea behind the annual budget seems to be to increase cost control and efficiency in each of the enterprises in the value chain. The cost efficiency of units is expected to rise with respect to the total value of the group's production, transportation and sales activities. Thus, resource allocation should be optimized from the perspective of the profitability of the group as a whole, rather than from the perspective of the individual unit.

The budgetary process is complicated. It involves communication between headquarters and the various levels in the group. The budget principle is incremental budgeting. The budgeting process starts from the top with the establishment of central frames for the budgetary work. In this step, for instance, required cost cuts and transfer prices between enterprises are articulated. This information is then provided to the cost centers, top managers and key employees. At each cost center, employees are responsible for providing the information necessary for the budget's preparation in a timely manner. Each cost center's finance director is responsible for controlling the quality of the information and for the timely aggregation of the information. Finally, each enterprise's budget department is responsible for the consolidation and aggregation of budget information into the consolidated budget. The budget is then controlled by the vice-directors before it is approved by headquarters.

The budget for each enterprise should be prepared for the year, and it should include detailed quarterly and monthly targets for each budgeted item. The main parameters used to make all budgets are based on estimated production volume, (transfer) prices on products and raw materials, and a variety of established production standards and norms for each enterprise.

The budgeting system is focused on expenses, which are budgeted in detail. The necessary level of revenue is then budgeted to ensure that the entire enterprise breaks even. When preparing the budget, changes in the organizational environment are anticipated only on the input side, for example prices for raw materials and products. Average yearly production standards, norms and prices are usually used during the planning period. When the budget is prepared at the cost-center level, it incorporates only information available within the "factory fence perimeter." In other words, possible changes in the business environment are not thoroughly evaluated. However, environmental uncertainty is offset to some extent by a simple rule allowing a 3 percent deviation between the budget and actual performance.

The budget is the essence of control in Beta, and it is closely connected to the control of the efficiency of the production process, as only established production standards are executed. The implementation of the standards is monitored, and these standards can be changed on the basis of needs uncovered by the ongoing monitoring. The variance between the budget and the actual figures is another parameter monitored for each budget line. Any substantial deviation must be explained in writing in an explanatory note addressed to the enterprise director. When such a note is received, a decision is made regarding whether the employees responsible for that line of the budget should receive a lower bonus or no bonus at all. Therefore, the bonus system is closely linked to variance: the higher the deviation from the budget, the greater the punishment in the form of a bonus reduction.

In Gamma, the stock-exchange regime, the budget also plays an important role. Gamma is structured like a conglomerate. It has a sales budget and a production budget related to the pulp-and-paper production volume needed in order to produce the necessary revenue. It also has a cost budget that allows for the calculation of costs per product type as well as the full costs for all products in the product mix. In addition, Gamma has a budget for overhead expenses related to administration and supporting activities. The profitability of all types of products is also covered in the budget, which enables Gamma to assess overall profitability, make plans for profit allocation and develop programs for technical reconstruction. A prognosis is also produced for flows of raw materials, and payments related to loans, rents and taxes. The final focus of the budget is the balance sheet and cash flows for the year.

Gamma's budgeting work is mainly concentrated on the top level of the enterprise. The planning department is responsible for calculating cost per product and profit plans, while the economic department is responsible for budgeting cash flows and finalizing the balance sheet. The annual budget is controlled by the director of finance and approved by the board of directors.

When preparing the budget, the information flows to the planning department from the top and the bottom. The budgeting work begins with the gathering of information on product prices, raw material prices and necessary transport fees. These figures are estimated based on demand for the company's products and on anticipated inflation. In addition, the level of profit required by shareholders is carefully considered. Detailed calculations regarding the use of raw materials (e.g., coal, petrol products, wood and chemicals) are especially important. Such calculations are impossible without local information from the departments. Therefore, in terms of participation, deciding the budget can be viewed as a bottom-up process.

The previous budget is considered as input information for new calculations. However, all calculations are made from a zero base each year. First, all expenses are calculated. Second, the income necessary to meet the necessary profit figures is determined. For Gamma, breakeven is not enough. If the figures show that the company will only break even, the expense categories are reviewed and reduced without reducing estimated income. The plan for cutting costs is determined by revising or correcting the cost items to arrive at the planned profit figure.

"Planning Regimes" and Design

We have shown that the levels of participation and renewal differ in the three planning regimes. Alpha has designed a formula-based budgeting process, while Beta has adopted incremental budgeting and Gamma uses a zero-based budgeting system. Participation also differs across the designs. Alpha has participation in relation to creating the formula, but no participation when annually running the formula to determine the budget. Beta has a top-down process with a low level of local participation. Gamma has a bottom-up process with a high level of local participation. (See Table 9.1.)

How can we explain these differences in design elements, and why do these different designs appear? We argue that budget design depends on how a company is socially embedded. Alpha's social embeddedness is structural. The actors know each other well and have close contacts with each other. The relationship between the hospitals in Alpha's region is almost familial. In a family regime, no one is afraid of going bankrupt. Beta, on the other hand, has both structural and relational embeddedness. Its structural embeddedness is related to its vertical chain, in which all companies are needed to produce the products, while its relational embeddedness is related to its headquarters, as demonstrations of efficiency

Table 9.1   Designing the budget in the three planning regimes

Renewal\local participation	Low (increment)	Middle (formula based)	High (zero based)
Low (top down)	Military (Beta)		
Middle (historical)		Family (Alpha)	
High (bottom up)			Stock exchange (Gamma)

are necessary to avoid repercussions. This is a military planning regime. Finally, Gamma's social embeddedness is mainly relational, as there is very little contact with other companies. At the same time, the companies compete with each other. This is a survival-of-the-fittest system in which relationships with headquarters are very important. The planning regime is a stock-exchange regime.

Planning Regimes and Control

The type of planning regime influences how budgets are used and how budgets control activities. The budgeting process is divided into two dimensions: the level of control (low or high) and target-setting freedom in terms of leadership style (budget constrained, profit conscious or non-accounting).

In the military regime, control is high. Results are carefully evaluated with respect to targets and there is a focus on budget deviations, regardless of whether those deviations are negative or positive. The standard is the most important issue for control in this regime, and the leadership style is a budget-constrained style.

In the family regime, control is mixed (middle). As all parties have agreed on the resources to be allocated per patient, the level of control is high. However, different actors are involved in the establishment of the formula and control is looser. The financial directors of all hospitals and from Alpha participate in this latter task. In addition, one doctor from each hospital and a consultancy group specialized in budgeting models are involved. Furthermore, various groups work with special areas for each hospital that are not part of the regular model and receive part of the strategic resource allocation (strategic focus areas). Finally, the model is made available to all hospitals in a hearing round before the board makes a final decision. Real negotiation occurs throughout this process. Thereafter, the evaluation focuses on deviations and actions related to staying in line with the budget, although some of the evaluation is based on other parameters. In this case, management has adopted a non-accounting leadership style.

For Gamma, control is low and target evaluation is relatively loose. This is because the consequences of poor results are so serious that there is less need to closely follow up on the budgets. The leadership style in this case is profit oriented, as the focus is on the relationship between costs and revenue. (See Table 9.2.)

Why, then, does budget use for control purposes differ among organizations? We suggest that, in our case companies, such differences are related to temporal embeddedness. For the family regime, a clock-time

Table 9.2   Use of control in the three planning regimes

Level of control/freedom in target setting	Low	Middle (low/high)	High
Low (budget constrained)			Military (Beta)
Middle (profit conscious)	Stock exchange (Gamma)		
High (non-accounting)		Family (Alpha)	

understanding is sufficient, as the organization knows how many resources to use and how they should be used during the year. For the military regime, clock time and event time are relevant. In this case, event time is related to changes in the environment. Finally, for the stock-exchange regime, the temporal embeddedness also includes entrainment, which is a matching process between an individual's temporal orientation and the temporal demands of the environment. In this case, much of the focus is on competition. Comparisons are made with the other companies in the conglomerate, which compete under different conditions. This means that it is important for companies in Gamma to continually show profit. It is a matter of survival of the fittest.

CONCLUSIONS

In this chapter we wanted to answer the question about *how planning and coordination activities are related to various organizational contexts*. We have shown that the three example companies design the budget and control their activities differently. We have also shown that these differences can be explained by their social and temporal embeddedness. The three organizations represent three ideal planning regimes. These examples are used to highlight the importance of social and temporal embeddedness to our understanding of how planning and coordination activities are related to the organizational context. There might be other plausible explanations for variations in the design of budgets and control of activities in these three organization, but these examples show that planning is more than just techniques. In this regard, the planning-regime concept enhances our understanding of how embeddedness can influence planning and coordination activities in companies.

We refer to the first planning regime as a "family" regime because the design of the budget is formula based and participation occurs only during the design phase. This indicates that the social embeddedness is structural; that is, the different business units are comfortable with each other and there is a large degree of legitimacy based on the agreement made when deciding the formula. Control is high, and management has adopted a non-accounting leadership style. As there is little complexity, it is possible to use clock time to coordinate activities in this regime.

The second planning regime is a "military" regime because the design of the budget is top down and incremental. This indicates that the social embeddedness is both structural and relational. The structural element is based on the relative independence of each actor in the value chain, while the relational element is based on the importance of relations with the authority structure. Control is high, and the leadership style is budget constrained. This organization uses both clock time and event time to coordinate activities. Clock time is used to coordinate daily activities, while event time is used to respond to events in the environment.

The third regime is referred to as a "stock-exchange" regime because the budget is designed from the bottom up with a large degree of participation. The budget is zero based. In this regime, the social embeddedness is mainly relational because the companies work independently and compete with each other. Finally, the temporal embeddedness is characterized by entrainment time, even though this regime also uses clock time and event time. Entrainment time is important because the company must adapt to the market to a higher degree than in other regimes.

In the family regime, the aim of coordination is equality, and the organizational structure is a traditional hierarchy. For the military regime, the aim is cost efficiency, and it is organized as a vertical value chain. In the stock-exchange regime, the aim is to achieve maximum return on investments, and it is organized as a conglomerate. What, then, drives coordination in the three regimes? The mechanisms for coordination in the family regime are based on structural embeddedness, which is founded in agreements about what to prioritize that have been developed over an extended period of time. In the military regime, coordination is driven by cost efficiency. Finally, in the stock-exchange regime, coordination is driven by opportunity seeking and a desire for efficiency.

Reaction times also differ among the three regimes, which results in different forms of coordination. The family regime is in a stable environment where it is possible to agree on use of clock time. The military regime is mostly stable but does also change like a chock depending on external changes. It therefore uses both clock time and event time. Finally, the stock-exchange regime is dynamic and changes out of best timing, which also demands entrainment time (adjusting of the pace or cycle of one activity to match or synchronize with that of another). It has to adjust its timing in relation to how competitors act. In sum, the planning-regime concept helps us to understand the usefulness of the coordination activities and the mechanisms that drive different regimes.

We have shown that actors may adopt planning regimes depending on perceptions of social and temporal embeddedness. In family regimes, the "family" is important and these regimes have a common understanding of time. In military regimes, management decides what to do and it closely follows the activities. Nevertheless, the entire organization is viewed as important. Finally, in the stock-exchange regime, there is no common identity. Instead, these regimes adopt a "survival-of-the-fittest" understanding of reality. As the customer decides, these regimes find it important to adjust to the customer's needs and be flexible.

Our study has also highlighted the need to understand the contextual embeddedness of the planning process, which enables us to understand why different companies use different types of planning regimes. Instead of focusing on the number of companies that do or do not use budgets (Ekholm and Wallin, 2000; Libby and Lindsay, 2010), we suggest developing a deeper understanding of why organizations use budgets in different ways. As control and autonomy are understood differently in the various regimes, the design and control of budgets differ. For some companies that are structurally embedded and use clock time, there is no need for more advanced management control systems. For others that are relationally embedded and focus on entrainment time, the dynamics become very important.

From a practical perspective, this study shows that the type of planning regime has implications for the design of the budget (participation and type of budget) and for control (leadership style and level of control). When organizations allow for looser forms of control in which we might expect another type of interaction in the budgeting process, such as Beyond Budgeting, they must consider the fact that many dimensions change at the same time. For example, if Beyond Budgeting can be understood as a move towards a stock-exchange regime, it demands a consciousness of relational embeddedness, event time and entrainment time.

This, in turn, implies an increasing need to create dynamic management control systems that can handle more demanding social and temporal embeddedness. This can be achieved by combining budget work with other tools and activities on different levels in the organization. The organization must be aware of why it has adopted a particular design and what it wishes to control with it.

REFERENCES

Ancona, D. and C. Chong (1996), "Entrainment: Pace, cycle and rhythm in organizational behavior," in B.M. Staw and L.L. Cummings (eds.), *Research in Organizational Behavior*, vol. 18, Greenwich, CT: JAI Press, pp. 251–81.

Argyris, C. (1952), *The Impact of Budgets on People*, New York: Controllership Foundation.

Atkinson, M.M. and W.D. Coleman (1992), "Policy network, policy communities and the problems of governance," *Governance*, **5** (2), 154–80.

Atrill, P. and L. McLaney (2007), *Management Accounting for Decision Makers*, Harlow: Prentice Hall.

Bergstrand, J. (2009), *Accounting and Management Control*, Lund: Studentlitteratur.

Bleiklie, I. (2001), "Towards European convergence of higher education policy?," *Higher Education*, **13** (3), 9–29.

Boland, R.J., Jr., A.K. Sharma and P.S. Afonso (2008), "Designing management control in hybrid organizations: The role of path creation and morphogenesis," *Accounting, Organizations and Society*, **33** (7–8), 899–914.

Chenhall, R.H. (2003), "Management control systems design within its organizational context: Findings from contingency based research and directions for the future," *Accounting, Organizations and Society*, **28**, 127–68.

Cherrington, D.J. and Cherrington, J.O. (1973), "Appropriate reinforcement contingencies in the budgetary process," *Journal of Accounting Research*, **11**, 225–53.

Chong, V.K. and K.M. Chong (2002), "Budget goal commitment and informational effects of budget participation on performance: A structural equation modeling approach," *Behavioural Research in Accounting*, **14**, 65–86.

Chow, C.W., Y. Kato and M.D. Shields (1994), "National culture and the preference for management controls: An explorative study of the firm–labor market interface," *Accounting, Organizations and Society*, **19** (5), 381–400.

Clinton, B.D. (1999), "Antecedents of budgetary participation: The effects of organizational, situational, and individual factors," *Advances in Management Accounting*, **8**, 45–70.

Clinton, B.D. and J.E. Hunton (2001), "Linking participative budgeting congruence to organization performance," *Behaviour Research in Accounting*, **13**, 127–41.

Covaleski, M.A., J.H. Evans, J.L. Luft and M.D. Shields (2007), "Budgeting research: Three theoretical perspectives and criteria for selective integration," in C.S. Chapman, A.G. Hopwood and M.D. Shields (eds.), *Handbook of Management Accounting Research*, vol. 1, Oxford: Elsevier, pp. 587–642.

Czarniawska-Joerges, B. (1988), "Dynamics of organizational control: The case of Berol 7 AB," *Accounting, Organizations and Society*, **14** (4), 415–30.

DiMaggio, P. and H. Louch (1998), "Socially embedded consumer transactions: For what kinds of purchases do people most often use networks?," *American Sociological Review*, **63**, 619–37.

Ekholm, B.G. and J. Wallin (2000), "Is the annual budget really dead?," *European Accounting Review*, **9** (4), 519–39.

Fisher, J., J.R. Fredricksen and S.A. Peffer (2002), "The effect of information asymmetry on negotiated budgets: An empirical investigation," *Accounting, Organizations and Society*, **27**, 27–43.

Granovetter, M.S. (1973), "The strength of weak ties," *American Journal of Sociology*, **78** (6), 1360–80.

Granovetter, M. (1992), "Economic action and social structure: The problem of embeddedness," in M. Granovetter and R. Swedberg (eds.), *The Sociology of Economic Life*, Boulder, CO: Westview Press.

Hansen, S.C., D.T. Otley and W.A. Van der Stede (2003), "Practice developments in budgeting: An overview and research perspective," *Journal of Management Accounting Research*, **15** (1), 95–116.

Henttu-Aho, T. and J. Järvinen (2013), "A field study of the emerging practice of Beyond Budgeting in industrial companies: An institutional perspective," *European Accounting Review*, published online January 17, DOI: 10.1080/09638180.2012.758596.

Hirst, M.K. and S.M. Lowy (1990), "The linear additive and interactive effects of budget goal difficulty and feedback on performance," *Accounting, Organizations and Society*, **15** (5), 425–36.

Hirst, M.K. and P.W. Yetton (1999), "The effects of budget goals and task interdependence on the level of and variance in performance: A research note," *Accounting, Organizations and Society*, **24**, 205–16.

Hofstede, G.H. (1967), "The game of budget control: How to live with budgetary standards and yet be motivated by them," Ph.D. thesis, Groningen University.

Hope, J. and R. Fraser (2003), *Beyond Budgeting: How Managers Can Break Free from the Annual Performance Trap*, Boston, MA: Harvard Business School Press.

Hopwood, A.G. (1972), "An empirical study of the role of accounting data in performance evaluation," in Empirical Research in Accounting, Supplement to *Journal of Accounting Research*, **10**, 156–82.

Hopwood, A.G. (1973), *An Accounting System and Managerial Behaviour*, Farnborough: Saxon House.

Horngren, C.T., S.M. Datar and M.V. Rajan (2012), *Cost Accounting: A Managerial Emphasis*, Harlow: Pearson Education.

Jones, T.C. and D. Dugdale (2001), "The concept of an accounting regime," *Critical Perspectives on Accounting*, **12**, 35–63.

Krasner, S. (1982), "Regimes and the limits of realism: Regimes as autonomous variables," *International Organization*, **36** (2) (Spring), 497–510.

Libby, T. (1999), "The influence of voice and explanation on performance in a participative budgeting setting," *Accounting, Organizations and Society*, **24**, 125–37.

Libby, T. and R.M. Lindsay (2010), "Beyond Budgeting or budgeting reconsidered? A survey of North American budgeting practice," *Management Accounting Research*, **21** (1), 56–75.

McGinn, K.L. and A.T. Keros (2002), "Improvisation and the logic of exchange in socially embedded transactions," *Administrative Science Quarterly*, **47**, 442–73.

Merchant, K.A. (1981), "The design of the corporate budgeting system: Influences on managerial behavior and performance," *Accounting Review*, **56**, 813–29.

Merchant, K.A. and J.-F. Manzoni (1989), "The achievability of budget targets in profit centers: A field story," *Accounting Review*, **64** (3), 539–58.

Modell, S. (2001), "Performance measurement and institutional processes: A study of managerial responses to public sector reform," *Management Accounting Research*, **12** (4), 437–64.

Nahapiet, J. (1988), "The rhetoric and reality of an accounting change: A study of resource allocation," *Accounting, Organizations and Society*, **13** (4), 333–58.

Neely, A., M. Bourne and C. Adams (2003), "Better budgeting or Beyond Budgeting," *Measuring Business Excellence*, **7** (3), 22–8.

Orlikowski, W.J. and J. Yates (2002), "It's about time: Temporal structuring in organizations," *Organization Science*, **13**, 684–700.

Pettersen, I.J. and K. Nyland (2006), "Management and control of public hospitals – the use of performance measures in Norwegian hospitals: A case-study," *International Journal of Health Planning and Management*, **21** (2), 133–49.

Tuttle, D.B. (1997), "A classification system for understanding individual differences in temporal orientation among processual researchers and organizational informants," *Scandinavian Journal of Management*, **13** (4), 349–66.

Uzzi, B. (1997), "Social structure and competition in interfirm networks: The paradox of embeddedness," *Administrative Science Quarterly*, **42**, 35–67.

Uzzi, B. (1999), "Embeddedness in the making of financial capital: How social relations and networks benefit firms seeking financing," *American Sociological Review*, **64**, 481–505.

Wallander, J. (1999), "Budgeting – an unnecessary evil," *Scandinavian Journal of Management*, **15**, 405–21.

Weick, K.E. (1998), "Improvisation as a mindset for organizational analyses," *Organization Science*, **9**, 543–55.

Wildavski, A. (1979), *Speaking Truth to Power*, Boston, MA: Little, Brown.

10. Does managerial discretion affect learning from experience in organizations?

Bjarne Espedal and
Alexander Madsen Sandvik

INTRODUCTION

Every organization wants to achieve efficiency and adaptiveness. Although each of these goals is essential to the other, they might also be in opposition (March, 1991). For example, the pursuit of efficiency might trap organizations in errors of formal control to such an extent that experimentation and exploration are severely limited. As one possible solution for such errors, "Beyond Budgeting" proposes the abandonment of formal organizational control systems in favor of dynamic control systems. However, Beyond Budgeting is more than an alternative to formal control – "it is about leadership more than anything else" (Bogsnes, 2009: xii). In this regard, the purpose of this chapter is to examine the following question: How and under what conditions can leadership affect organizational adaptiveness?

Leadership theory suggests that leadership can affect an organization's ability to adapt to new demands and challenges. The theory also posits that *managerial discretion* is a necessary condition for intelligent adaptation to environmental demands (Yukl, 2002; March and Weil, 2005; Hambrick, 2007; Espedal, 2009; Northouse, 2010). When leadership has discretion, it has freedom of choice and, in turn, the chance (and power) to affect the organization's capacity to become more dynamic. However, achieving adaptiveness is not only a question of freedom of choice. In order to make appropriate decisions, leadership also needs valid knowledge. Therefore, in relation to exploration and organizational adaptiveness, freedom of choice involves the pursuit of a mixture of knowledge gleaned from analysis and experience. Thus, the leadership's ability to influence an organization's capacity to become more dynamic requires not only freedom of choice but also a capacity to learn from one's own experience and the

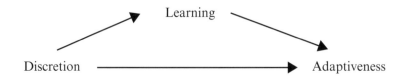

Figure 10.1   Relationships among discretion, learning and adaptiveness

experience of others (Levitt and March, 1988; March, 1999). Through such learning, the leadership might discover a need to change both organizational practice and premises for new practice (Espedal, 2008).

This chapter therefore focuses on leadership's capacity to learn from its own experience and the experience of others. It argues that such learning might mediate a positive relationship between managerial discretion and organizational adaptiveness. Discretion (autonomy) enables learning, which is beneficial for decision making and, in turn, affects adaptiveness (see Figure 10.1).

Given this point of departure, the chapter examines the relationship between discretion and learning. It specifically addresses two issues: 1) how discretion affects leadership's capacity to learn from its own experience and the experience of others in organizations; and 2) how organizational and individual determinants of discretion affect discretion and learning.

First, we outline the main features of the key concepts – managerial discretion and learning from experience. Second, the relationship between the two key concepts is discussed. Third, we examine how organizational and individual determinants of managerial discretion affect discretion and learning, after which we present a conceptual frame for a study of managerial discretion and learning in Norwegian organizations.

THEORY AND HYPOTHESES

Managerial Discretion

The freedom and the capability to make and use judgments informed by knowledge are viewed as the central hallmarks of managerial discretion. Leaders act by making choices, and they need discretion in order to make decisions and to act as they see fit in different organizational settings (March and Weil, 2005; Hambrick, 2007). Discretion is assumed to enhance a leader's impact on organizational outcomes, as the organizational constraints common to leadership are generally less severe in a context that allows for discretion. Such constraints are related to job demands, expectations, rules, control, resources, power and networks (Stewart, 1989; Hambrick, 2007). In other words, room for discretion implies a reduction in organizational limitations in the form of demands and constraints.

In addition to the organizational determinants of managerial discretion, Hambrick and Finkelstein (1987) identify individual determinants in the form of personal commitment, cognitive complexity and tolerance of ambiguity. Hence, managerial discretion is shaped not only by organizational demands and constraints, but also by individual factors that form a leader's conception of the basis and motivation for action (March and Weil, 2005). Leaders are expected to have reasons for what they do – based on this conception. These reasons inform both their choices and the justifications of those choices. They reflect a logic of action that allows some types of leadership behavior and limits the prevalence of other types. In this perspective, March and Weil (2005: 19) distinguish among: 1) a logic of consequences (achievement of individual and collective aims); 2) a logic of appropriateness (leaders act in accordance with their identities); and 3) a logic of faith and arbitrariness.

In the extant literature, the positive effects of managerial discretion are typically related to a reduction of the organizational constraints associated with organizational routines, formal control systems and job-related demands. Leaders may have low or high *formal* managerial discretion, which is determined by rules and demands, but the *perceived* discretion is more important (Tjosvold, 1986). In other words, discretion is shaped by leaders' perceptions of the determinants of managerial discretion, and these perceptions are affected by their logics of action or their conceptions of the basis and motivation for action. Thus, there might be a difference between formal and perceived discretion. On the one hand, a leader who has low formal discretion may believe that he or she has high discretion. On the other hand, a leader who has high formal discretion may believe that he or she has low discretion.

Learning from Experience in Organizations

Leaders need freedom of choice, but appropriate choices are knowledge based. An individual leader may have the opportunity and the capability to make judgments on the basis of analysis and experience. However, Tsoukas (2005) claims that the knowledge needed for decisions that affect organizational adaptiveness cannot be collected by a single individual. This is because the knowledge of the circumstances in which the leadership must act does not exist in a concentrated or integrated form, but solely as dispersed bits of incomplete knowledge. In other words, individuals in leadership roles hold related and relevant knowledge in a variety of locations. Correspondingly, Weick and Roberts (1993: 378) argue that, "no matter how visionary, how smart or how forward-looking or aggressive one's brain may be, it is no match for conditions of interactive complexity." From this point of view, any one organization is a collection of individuals, each of whom is learning, and their learning interacts. Similarly, any one organization is a part of a community of organizations in which learning processes also interact (Levitt and March, 1988). Thus, a leader can learn from his or her own experience and the experience of others, and such learning is a necessary condition for appropriate decision making.

Learning from experience in organizations is not only a question of how learning actors gain access to experience, but also a question of how learning actors react to that experience. In terms of access, a free flow of valid experience or information is the lifeblood for learning in an organization. Freedom of information, or information sharing and transparency may be outcomes of social capital, as they are associated with trust, open communication, common language and social networks (Nahapiet and Ghoshal, 1998). In addition, social capital may allow for the exchange of experiences within organizations in ways that enable the combination of actors' own experiences with those of others, as well as the combination of new experiences with old experiences, and experiences with new ideas.

In terms of creating knowledge, the bridge between experience and learning is found in interpretation. Daft and Weick (1984: 294) define interpretation as "the process through which information is given meaning" and as "the process of developing shared understandings." Learning occurs when actors reaffirm shared understandings and when they change those understandings. However, these two types of learning are contradictory (Argyris, 1999). The first type of learning is essentially learning within a perspective, while the essence of the second is escaping a perspective and implementing a different mindset. Actors are frequently good at learning within a logic of action. However, profound changes in logics that direct, motivate and legitimate behavior are difficult to achieve.

In relation to this distinction between the two types of learning, March (1991) argues that organizations have to combine the effective exploitation of existing knowledge with the creative exploration of new possibilities. The former involves a capacity to adapt existing knowledge in the sense of improving it, whereas the latter involves a capacity to search and innovate. Along these lines, leadership must provide organizational learning with enough direction to ensure that learning is regarded as significant and that it is adequately supported, while also providing participants with sufficient autonomy in the process to enable them to produce new insights. In other words, balancing exploitation and exploration means balancing efficiency and adaptiveness. However, the achievement of both efficiency and adaptiveness might be a challenge. The essence of efficiency lies in routines and in conventional behaviors bound by standards of knowledge, morality and legality. The essence of adaptiveness, on the other hand, lies in escaping routines and standards, and in the implementation of new knowledge and routines.

How Might Discretion Enable Learning?

From a learning perspective, managerial discretion may create a context that allows for exploration, which in turn is associated with new possibilities. March (1991: 71) defines exploration as "search, variation, risk-taking, experimentation, play, flexibility, discovery, and innovation." This definition is broad in scope and open to various interpretations. In subsequent work, Levinthal and March (1993: 105) restrict the scope of these activities to the knowledge domain, stating that exploration involves "a pursuit of new knowledge."

Discretion may enable the pursuit of novelty because the power and legitimacy associated with discretion protect the leadership from the uncertainty of whether new ideas will succeed. Furthermore, the leadership may have the authority to explore ideas that offer high potential in the views of external stakeholders but do not appear to be justifiable in terms of internal, organizational norms. In these ways, the leadership can sustain exploration because it has the opportunity and capability (power) to be impatient with old ideas and patient with new ideas. The leadership also needs discretion in order to create "safe play" spaces in learning processes (March, 1999: 319). Playfulness may allow leaders to temporarily suspend their mental models, logics and disbeliefs in favor of exploration and experimentation. At the same time, playfulness entails an assumption that, at some point, the playful behavior will be stopped or its learning outcomes will be integrated into an organizational learning process in a way that makes sense. Moreover, discretion may foster intrinsic motivations for knowledge sharing (Foss et al., 2009). Intrinsic motivation leads one to undertake an activity because it is in accord with personal values and pleasures associated with a change process (Ryan and Deci, 2000). Thus, as a consequence of high job autonomy, leaders may find knowledge sharing interesting, enjoying, stimulating and appropriate.

This discussion of how managerial discretion may enable learning from experience in organizations leads to our first hypothesis:

H1. Managerial discretion has a positive impact on learning from experience in organizations.

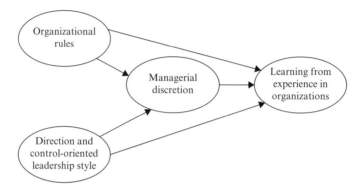

Figure 10.2   The conceptual model

This overview of discretion and learning reveals that both organizational and individual characteristics have the potential to influence freedom of choice and, in turn, affect learning. Given this view, we highlight several discretion-related issues that an organization's leaders must take into consideration when they wish to promote learning from experience. These issues are organizational rules, and leadership styles that imply a higher degree of top-down direction and control (see the conceptual model in Figure 10.2).

Organizational Rules

Organizational rules and routines are typically regarded as the primary means by which organizations accomplish much of what they do (March and Simon, 1958; Cyert and March, 1963; Thompson, 1967; Nelson and Winter, 1982). Proponents of managerial discretion suggest that the leadership has a low level of discretion if most of the management functions are built into organizational rules. Thus, the literature on managerial discretion holds a negative view of organizational rules. We argue that this view is only partly true. On the one hand, organizational rules might be a source of stability and inflexibility. On the other hand, they might be a source of learning and change.

Organizational rules as instruments of stability
Although they are recognized as essential aspects of organized work, organizational rules and routines are also seen as programs that might be executed without conscious thought. This understanding has deep roots in social theory, as reflected in writings on bureaucracy (Weber, 1947; Selznick, 1949; Gouldner, 1954; Blau, 1955; Crozier, 1964; Kaufman, 1977; Hummel, 1987). Thus, organizational rules may become a source of stability, inertia,

inflexibility and mindlessness, which may create numerous problems with regard to freedom of choice and learning. One such problem can be "over-conformity" (Merton, 1957), in which rules enforce overly strict codes of behavior that make deliberate decisions a rarity. Such decisions may be hindered by a lack of information or by the absence of impulsive, spontaneous pleasures in the leader's organizational life (Pfeffer, 1994). A second problem is "over-identification" with the rules, or inordinate and inflexible adherence to rules. This is also known as a "passion for legalism."

A third problem is "double-binding" (Argyris, 1999). Precommitment is an activity designed to help leadership to deal with threats. However, precommitment to a rule in order to be "in control" of a threat might, in itself, be a threat that leads to defensive reasoning and political games in organizations. Defensive reasoning and opportunism violate the intentions of a precommitment. If actors become aware of their impact, they will claim "that they are in a double-bind, helpless but to act as they do" (Argyris, 1999: 167). A fourth problem might be "goal displacement" (Merton, 1957: 201; Etzioni, 1964: 10), in which the leadership's need to accomplish a goal leads to precommitment to a rule and the following of this rule becomes a goal in itself.

As instruments of stability, organizational rules might limit learning, but they might also be a necessity. Most of the discussion in the literature focuses on one side: how rules may hamper freedom of choice and learning. Much less attention has been paid to the other side: how commitment to (stable) rules might be necessary for individual and contextual conditions when leadership pursues learning and adaptiveness.

March and Weil (2005) argue that commitment to (stable) rules may help an organization's leaders to act properly. In other words, they suggest that discretion and good intentions alone are not enough to achieve a desired end – leaders who have discretion will need to bind themselves in some additional way to fulfill their intentions. Therefore, binding mechanisms in the form of rules are a necessity. Leaders follow a rule and discipline themselves through a sense of self that allows them to achieve a desired end that might otherwise be attainable only with difficulty. Hence, the basis for leadership action is the logic of appropriateness, which is associated with the fulfillment of an identity (March, 1994). For example, the fulfillment of an identity may tell the leader that keeping promises is about a rule of appropriateness. Promise keeping (via duty ethics) is an important leadership issue that deals with a fundamental moral principle that touches everyday organizational life. Without some degree of truthfulness and reliability in organizations, leaders and organizational members would not be able to act and interact.

A rule-driven, uncorrupt and predictable system (bureaucracy) may also be better able to orchestrate rationality, growth and adaptiveness than a more informal, loose system (Teece, 2007). The former system might be a source of security and efficiency. As Leavitt (2003: 101) points out, "hierarchies deliver real practical and psychological value. On a fundamental level, they don't just enslave us, they also fulfill our deep needs for order and security. And they get big jobs done."

Organizational rules as an instrument of learning and change

Organizational rules are vital constituents of organizational learning and change. They can be adapted to experience or changed when experience changes (Levitt and March, 1988). They have an inherent capability to generate change merely by their ongoing performance (Feldman and Pentland, 2003). Furthermore, they are associated with dynamic capabilities (Zollo and Winter, 2002). Thus, organizational rules and routines play an important role in organizational learning and adaptation processes because they retain lessons learned in the past and they can be adapted as experience changes. Accordingly, they are necessary for the intelligent adaptation of organizations to environmental demands (Espedal, 2006, 2007).

This discussion illustrates one dilemma faced by organizational leadership. Rules and norms are both a necessity and a limitation for appropriate managerial discretion. Adherence to rules may help the leadership to act properly and thereby enable learning in organizations. However, it may also limit managerial discretion, thereby restricting learning in organizations. Thus, we arrive at the following hypotheses:

H2a. Organizational rules have a negative impact on learning from experience in organizations.

H2b. Organizational rules have a positive impact on learning from experience in organizations.

Hypothesis 2b suggests that organizational rules play an important role in organizational learning processes because they retain organizational lessons learned in the past. Rules track environmental changes and pressure, and they are an organization's cumulative repository of learning. As such, they are necessary for the intelligent adaptation of organizations to environmental demands. Given this perspective, we might expect a positive relationship between organizational rules and learning from experience in organizations. However, we can also argue that managerial discretion should partially mediate the relationship between organizational rules and organizational learning.

Organizations substitute new rules for old ones on the basis of learning from experience. Such changes involve processes of observing and interpreting organizational actions, processes of converting interpretations into organizational rules, and processes of retrieving rules from previous experiences and reconciling them with more recent experiences. Thus, rules reflect lessons learned in the past, and the knowledge embedded in them might help leaders to cope with problems, and to fulfill their needs for safety and security in new learning and change processes. Managerial discretion might be a vital part of these processes. Discretion increases leaders' freedom of choice, which might be beneficial for the continuous updating of rules. This implies:

H2c. Managerial discretion partially mediates the positive relationship between organizational rules and learning from experience in organizations.

Perceived Organizational Leadership Style

Leadership is instrumentally geared towards outcomes (e.g., Northouse, 2010). In other words, most definitions of leadership link the concept to outcomes (i.e., leadership means influencing people to work towards the attainment of specified goals). Hence, leadership implies some degree of top-down direction and control in organizations (Child, 2005: 315). The core aim of top-down direction is to properly align organizational goals with subordinate objectives. The leadership defines and communicates clear goals within the organization so that employees understand the objectives and what they need to do. Performance reviews (output control) are periodically conducted to determine how close employees are to attaining their objectives, and individuals are rewarded on the basis of those reviews.

Top-down control provides the leadership with structures and systems designed to make the organization more efficient. Control mechanisms might include: personal centralized control (power and authority); bureaucratic control (rules, budgets and accounting); output control (output standards and targets, performance indicators, incentives and rewards); HRM control (selection, training and assessment); and cultural control (identification, socialization, internalization and social control).

On the one hand, leaders are expected to serve or to build organizations. Such building emphasizes direction, top-down goal setting, goal implementation and control, all of which are associated with extrinsic motivations. On the other hand, leaders are supposed to "confront" their organizations. Such confrontations emphasize learning and adaptiveness, which are associated with autonomy and intrinsic motivations.

In terms of facilitating learning from experience, the challenge for the leadership lies in developing and maintaining a judicious combination of control in the form of guidance and support, and autonomy in order to encourage the free flow of information and motivate learning. It may be difficult to reconcile top-down direction and control with autonomy, trust, open communication and mindfulness, elements that are commonly believed to encourage learning from experience in organizations.

This challenge of finding the right balance between centralized control and local autonomy implies:

H3a. A perceived organizational leadership style that is associated with a high degree of top-down direction and control has a negative impact on learning from experience in organizations.

H3b. Managerial discretion partially mediates the relationship between direct and control-oriented leadership and learning from experience in organizations.

METHOD

Sample

For this study, a sample of 4000 Norwegian CEOs and management personnel at intermediate and lower levels in the private and public sector was randomly chosen from a variety of firms with ten or more employees. Study participants were approached by phone and asked to take part in the study. After participants had expressed their willingness to participate, they were asked to complete a survey and mail it to us in a self-addressed stamped envelope.

The final sample comprised 2910 persons, which gives a response rate of 72.8 percent. Of the respondents, 31.5 percent were women, and the average age was 48.82 years (SD = 8.82 years). On average, the participants reported having held a managerial position in the same company for eight years; and 31.5 percent reported holding a top leadership position, 36 percent reported to a top leader, 4.8 percent were managers of a unit or an advisory unit, 2.9 percent were project leaders, 22.4 percent were middle managers, and 2.3 percent were line managers or operative leaders.

Measures

We collected data at the management level. All items on the questionnaire were written in Norwegian. Participants provided their responses on five-point Likert scales, where 1 = "I fully disagree" and 5 = "I fully agree."

Organizational rules

We measured organizational rules using five items from the measure developed by Song and Perry (1993). For example, we used: "The company has a many written rules and procedures." The Cronbach's alpha for this measure was 0.83.

Direction and control-oriented leadership style

We measured direction and control-oriented leadership style using five items from the measure developed by Song and Perry (1993). For example, we used: "Little happens in this company without a manager's approval." The Cronbach's alpha for this measure was 0.72.

Managerial discretion

We measured managerial discretion using the measure developed in Hackman and Oldham's (1975) dimensions of autonomy and task variety. Items for this measure included: "The job gives me considerable opportunity for independence and freedom in how I work" (autonomy), and "The job requires me to use a number of complex, high-level skills" (variety). The aggregated score for autonomy and task variety had a Cronbach's alpha of 0.69.

Learning from experience in organizations

We measured learning from experience in organizations using the measure developed by Edmondson (1999). Items for this measure included: "We regularly take time to figure out ways to improve our team's work process" and "Team members gather all of the information they possibly can from others, such as customers or other parts of the organization." The Cronbach's alpha for this measure was 0.81.

Control measures

We controlled for "top leader," "leader level" and "public/private organization." Top leaders were defined as managers of more than 100 employees. Leader level was an indication of whether the manager was a line manager, a middle manager or at the top level. Public/private was a coded dummy variable that described whether the respondent worked for a private company or for a public organization.

Data Analysis

We used a hierarchical regression analysis in SPSS to examine the hypotheses. We also used structural equation modeling (SEM) with Mplus 7.0 to analyze the full hypothesized model (Figure 10.2) and the mediating effects (H2c and H3b). The advantage of SEM is that the hypothesized model can be tested statistically in a simultaneous analysis of the entire system of variables to determine the extent to which it is consistent with the data (Byrne, 2010). Prior to testing the model, we confirmed the dimensions using an exploratory factor analysis, as the questionnaire had been translated into Norwegian. We also used a confirmatory factor analysis to reveal the existence of coding factors in scales. The two facet scores were used as a manifest indicator of the latent managerial discretion factor. The resulting measurement model provided an adequate fit with the data ($\chi^2[201] = 1440.24$; $\chi^2/df = 7.17$, $p \leq 0.001$; CFI = 0.93; SMRM = 0.04; RMSEA = 0.05).

Finally, we used an SEM model to estimate the fit of the hypothesized model to the data. To gauge model fit, we examined the index of absolute fit, which included the chi-square values, the CFI (Bentler, 1990) and the RMSEA (Steiger, 1990). A CFI higher than 0.09 represents a well-fitting model (Medsker et al., 1994), although more recently a cutoff value closer to 0.95 has been suggested (Bentler and Yuan, 1999). An RMSEA value of less than or equal to 0.08 indicates a favorable fit, while values less than or equal to 0.10 represent a fair fit (Browne and Cudeck, 1989).

RESULTS

Descriptive statistics, coefficient alpha reliabilities and correlations for the variables used in the study appear in Table 10.1. With the exception of managerial discretion, all scale reliabilities exceeded 0.70, as recommended by Nunnally (1978).

Table 10.2 provides the results of the regressions used to test Hypotheses 1 to 3. The table reports the full equation standardized regression coefficients (βs) for all of the independent and control variables. We conducted a separate series of hierarchical regression analyses to determine the unique variance explained (ΔR^2). In those regressions, we entered each independent variable after the control variables as the last step in the regression. Table 10.2 reports the ΔR^2s and related F-values for each step in the hierarchical regression analysis.

As Table 10.2 shows, the measure of managerial discretion predicts learning from experience in organizations, which supports Hypothesis 1. In addition, organizational rules are positively associated with learning from experience, which supports Hypothesis 2. Finally, a controlling leadership style is negatively associated with learning from experience in organizations, which supports Hypothesis 3. The F-value was significant in all cases.

Table 10.1   Descriptive statistics, correlations and reliability of study variables

	N	M	SD	1	2	3	4	5	6	7
1. Managerial discretion	2895	3.74	.62	(.69)						
2. Organizational rules	2883	3.28	.88	−.18	(.83)					
3. Control leadership style	2886	1.95	.79	−.15**	.06**	(.72)				
4. Private/public	2910	1.50	.67	−.03	.00	−.05*	1			
5. Leader level	2910	.48	.81	.13**	−.07**	−.17**	−.02	1		
6. Top leader	2910	.04	.19	.06**	.01	−.09**	.06**	.62**	1	
7. Learning from experience	2882	3.30	.68	.22**	.23**	−.14**	.07**	.10**	.07**	(.81)

Note: $*p < .05; **p < .01.$

Table 10.2   Hierarchical multiple regression analysis predicting learning from experience on the basis of managerial discretion, control leadership style, organizational rules and various control variables

Variable	Learning from experience		
	B	ΔR^2	$F(6, 2834)$
Control Variable			
CEO	.07**	.00	12.07**
Leader hierarchy	.10**	.01	27.80**
Private/public	.07**	.00	12.80**
Independent Variable			
Managerial discretion	.21**	.05	45.20**
Organizational rules	.24**	.06	54.29**
Control leadership style	−.12**	.01	21.45**
Overall F		69.33**	
Total R^2		.13**	
Adjusted R^2		.13**	
N		2840	

Notes:
$*p<0.05; **p<0.01.$
The ΔR^2 and F-values were derived from hierarchical regression analyses.

The testing of Hypotheses 1 through 3 included a test of the hypothesized SEM model. The SEM results suggest that the hypothesized model fits the data well ($\chi^2[201] = 1440.24$; $\chi^2/\text{df} = 7.17$, $p \le 0.001$; CFI $= 0.93$; SRMR $= 0.04$; RMSEA $= 0.05$). Figure 10.3 presents the overall structural model with standardized path coefficients.

Hypothesis 1 states that managerial discretion has a positive impact on learning from experience in organizations. The results support this view ($\beta = 0.37$, $p < 0.001$).

Hypothesis 2 suggests that organizational rules have a 1) negative and a 2) positive impact on learning from experience in organizations. Hypothesis 2b is supported ($\beta = 0.26$, $p < 0.05$). The model also indicates the presence of indirect effects in which organizational rules are positively related to managerial discretion ($\beta = 0.07$, $p < 0.05$). Hypothesis 2c, which suggests that managerial discretion partly mediates the relationship between organizational rules and learning from experience in organizations, also receives support.

Finally, Hypothesis 3 states that a perceived organizational leadership style that is associated with a high degree of top-down direction and control has a negative impact on learning from experience in organizations. This hypothesis is also supported ($\beta = -0.06$, $p < 0.05$). Furthermore, the model indicates the presence of an indirect effect in which direction and control-oriented leadership is negatively related to managerial discretion ($\beta = -0.28$, $p < 0.001$). The model also supports Hypothesis 3b, which suggests that direction and control-oriented leadership partially mediates the relationship between managerial discretion and learning from experience.

DISCUSSION

In this study, we have addressed two issues: 1) how managerial discretion affects the leadership's capacity to learn from its own experience and the experience of others in organizations; and 2) how organizational and individual determinants of managerial discretion affect discretion and learning. We introduced and tested a model that used managerial discretion as a tool for explaining the relationships between organizational rules and control-oriented leadership, and learning from experience in organizations.

Notably, we find that organizational rules and managerial discretion enhance learning outcomes. Thus, both managerial discretion and organizational rules seem to be necessary conditions for learning from experience in organizations. This finding supports the notion that managerial

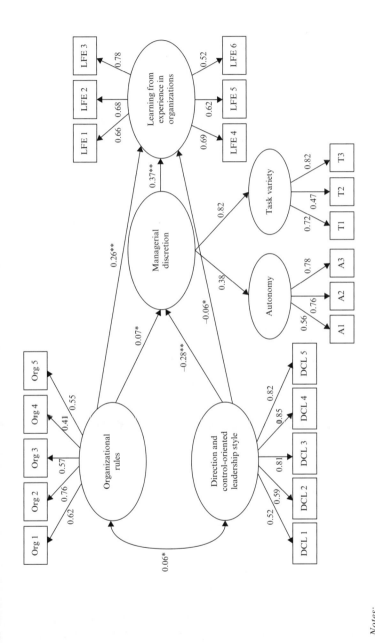

Notes:
*p < .05; **p < .01.
All paths in the structural model analysis are significant at p < 0.05.
Standard estimates are reported.

Figure 10.3 Model of the impact of organizational rules, a direction and control-oriented leadership style, and managerial discretion or learning from experience in organizations

discretion increases leaders' abilities and capacities to learn from their own experiences and the experiences of others in their organizations. Even more interestingly, the study confirms the idea that organizational rules are not only a source of stability, inflexibility and control, but also a source of learning and change. Over time, rules might change as experience changes. As a leader learns how to handle and solve a particular problem in a change process, the birth of a related rule may represent an increment of learning. Thus, rules reflect lessons learned in the past, and the knowledge embedded in them might help leaders to cope with problems, and to fulfill their needs for safety and security in new learning and change processes. From this view, leadership might require rules rather than discretion.

Another important finding is that a top-down, controlled leadership style is negatively related to both managerial discretion and learning from experience in organizations. Thus, the study confirms the notion that top-down direction and control do not enable autonomy and learning from experience in organizations.

The theoretical contributions discussed above should be interpreted in light of this study's limitations. As the data are cross-sectional, alternative explanations for the observed results may exist. There may also be ambiguity in causal direction. For example, jobs may be characterized as autonomous even in the presence of clear organizational rules and procedures. Another major concern is the possibility of spurious effects arising from the fact that the data were gathered from a common source, raising concerns about self-reported, same-source bias. In addition, all variables were collected using survey measures and are therefore subject to mono-method bias.

The sample used in the study also suffers from some important limitations. As we relied on an external survey service, we have little knowledge of who the respondents were or why they chose to participate. For example, the respondents who took part in the survey may have a higher degree of managerial discretion or they may have experienced a higher degree of learning than non-participants. We can therefore make no claims regarding the generalizability of our study. Our sample strategy also prevented us from collecting data from multiple levels or from multiple followers per leader and aggregating the data to the unit level of analysis, which is a common approach in the leadership literature (e.g., Bass et al., 2003).

These limitations aside, if the associations in our model reflect causal relationships, then our results suggest that leaders could influence learning from experience in organizations by focusing on managerial discretion and organizational rules as instruments of change. Such efforts would require awareness of the distinction between formal and perceived discretion, and awareness of organizational and individual determinants of discretion and learning. Such awareness would, in turn, most likely require mindfulness (Weick and Roberts, 1993). Mindfulness, however, represents a new leadership challenge.

REFERENCES

Argyris, C. (1999), *On Organizational Learning*, 2nd edn., Oxford: Blackwell Business.

Bass, B.M., B.J. Avolio, D.I. Jung and Y. Berson (2003), 'Predicting unit performance by assessing transformational and transactional leadership," *Journal of Applied Psychology*, **88** (2), 207–18.

Bentler, P.M. (1990), "Comparative fit indexes in structural models," *Psychological Bulletin*, **107** (2), 238–46.

Bentler, P.M. and K.-H. Yuan (1999), "Structural equation modeling with small samples: Test statistics," *Multivariate Behavioral Research*, **34** (2), 181.

Blau, P. (1955), *The Dynamics of Bureaucracy*, Chicago, IL: University of Chicago Press.

Bogsnes, B. (2009), *Implementing Beyond Budgeting*, Hoboken, NJ: John Wiley & Sons.

Browne, M.W. and R. Cudeck (1989), "Single sample cross-validation indices for covariance structures," *Multivariate Behavioral Research*, **24** (4), 445–55.

Byrne, B.M. (2010), *Structural Equation Modeling with AMOS: Basic Concepts, Applications, and Programming*, New York: Routledge.

Child, J. (2005), *Organization: Contemporary Principles and Practice*, Oxford: Blackwell.

Crozier, M. (1964), *The Bureaucratic Phenomenon*, Chicago, IL: University of Chicago Press.

Cyert, R.M. and J.G. March (1963), *A Behavioral Theory of the Firm*, Englewood Cliffs, NJ: Prentice Hall.

Daft, R.L. and K.L. Weick (1984), "Toward a model of organizations as interpretation systems," *Academy of Management Review*, **9**, 284–95.

Edmondson, A. (1999), "Psychological safety and learning behavior in work teams," *Administrative Science Quarterly*, **44** (2), 350–83.

Espedal, B. (2006), "Do organizational routines change as experience changes?," *Journal of Applied Behavioral Science*, **42**, 468–90.

Espedal, B. (2007), "Why rules rather than discretion: When the leadership intends to transform a desired policy into reality," *Journal of Organizational Change Management*, **20**, 95–108.

Espedal, B. (2008), "In the pursuit of understanding how to balance lower and higher order learning in organizations," *Journal of Applied Behavioral Science*, **44** (3), 365–90.

Espedal, B. (2009), "Maneuvering space for leadership," *Journal of Leadership and Organizational Studies*, **16** (2), 197–212.

Etzioni, A. (1964), *Modern Organizations*, Englewood Cliffs, NJ: Prentice Hall.

Feldman, M.S. and B.T. Pentland (2003), "Reconceptualizing organizational routines as a source of flexibility and change," *Administrative Science Quarterly*, **48** (1), 94–118.

Foss, N.J., D.B. Minbaeva, T. Pedersen and M. Reinholt (2009), "Encouraging knowledge sharing among employees: How job design matters," *Human Resource Management*, **48** (6), 871–93.

Gouldner, A.W. (1954), *Pattern of Industrial Democracy*, New York: Free Press.

Hackman, J.R. and G.R. Oldham (1975), "Development of the job diagnostic survey," *Journal of Applied Psychology*, **60** (2), 159–70.

Hambrick, D. (2007), "Upper echelons theory: An update" [Editorial material], *Academy of Management Review*, **32** (2), 334–43.

Hambrick, D.C. and S. Finkelstein (1987), "Managerial discretion: A bridge between polar views of organizational outcomes," *Research in Organizational Behavior*, **9**, 369–406.

Hummel, R. (1987), *The Bureaucratic Experience*, New York: St. Martin's Press.

Kaufman, H. (1977), *Red Tape: Its Origins, Uses and Abuses*, Washington, DC: Brookings Institution.

Leavitt, H.J. (2003), "Why hierarchies thrive," *Harvard Business Review*, **81** (3), 96–102.

Levinthal, D.A. and J.G. March (1993), "The myopia of learning," *Strategic Management Journal*, **14**, 95–112.

Levitt, B. and J.G. March (1988), "Organizational learning," *Annual Review of Sociology*, **14**, 319–40.

March, J.G. (1991), "Exploration and exploitation in organizational learning," *Organization Science*, **2** (1), 71–87.

March, J.G. (1994), *A Primer on Decision Making: How Decisions Happen*, New York: Free Press.

March, J.G. (1999), *The Pursuit of Organizational Intelligence*, Malden, MA: Blackwell.

March, J.G. and H.A. Simon (1958), *Organizations*, New York: John Wiley & Sons.

March, J.G. and T. Weil (2005), *On Leadership*, Malden, MA: Blackwell.

Medsker, G.J., L.J. Williams and P.J. Holahan (1994), "A review of current practices for evaluating causal models in organizational behavior and human resources management research," *Journal of Management*, **20** (2), 439–64.

Merton, R. (1957), *Social Theory and Social Structure*, New York: Free Press.

Nahapiet, J. and S. Ghoshal (1998), "Social capital, intellectual capital, and the organizational advantage," *Academy of Management Review*, **23**, 242–66.

Nelson, R.R. and S.G. Winter (1982), *An Evolutionary Theory of Economic Change*, Cambridge, MA: Belknap Press of Harvard University Press.

Northouse, P.G. (2010), *Leadership: Theory and Practice*, 5th edn., Los Angeles, CA: Sage.

Nunnally, J.C. (1978), *Psychometric Theory*, New York: McGraw-Hill.

Pfeffer, J. (1994), *Competitive Advantage through People: Unleashing the Power of the Work Force*, Boston, MA: Harvard Business School Press.

Ryan, R.M. and E.L. Deci (2000), "Self-determination theory and the facilitation of intrinsic motivation, social development, and well-being," *American Psychologist*, **55**, 68–78.

Selznick, P. (1949), *TVA and the Grassroots*, Berkeley: University of California Press.

Song, M.X. and M.E. Perry (1993), "R&D marketing integration in Japanese high-technology firms: Hypothesis and empirical evidence," *Journal of the Academy of Marketing Science*, **21**, 125–33.

Steiger, J.H. (1990), "Structural model evaluation and modification: An interval estimation approach," *Multivariate Behavioral Research*, **25** (2), 173–80.

Stewart, R. (1989), "Studies of managerial jobs and behavior: The ways forward," *Journal of Management Studies*, **26** (1), 1–10.

Teece, D.J. (2007), "Managers, markets and dynamic capabilities," in C. Helfat, S. Fingelstein, W. Mitchell, M.A. Peteraf, H. Singh, D.J. Teece and S.G. Winter (eds.), *Dynamic Capabilities: Understanding Strategic Change in Organizations*, Oxford: Blackwell, pp. 19–29.

Thompson, J.D. (1967), *Organization in Action*, New York: McGraw-Hill.

Tjosvold, D. (1986), "The dynamics of interdependence in organizations," *Human Relations*, **39**, 517–40.

Tsoukas, H. (2005), *Complex Knowledge: Studies in Organizational Epistemology*, Oxford: Oxford University Press.

Weber, M. (1947), *The Theory of Social and Economic Organizations*, Thousand Oaks, CA: Sage.

Weick, K.E. and K.H. Roberts (1993), "Collective mind in organizations: Heedful interrelating on flight decks," *Administrative Science Quarterly*, **38**, 357–81.

Yukl, G.A. (2002), *Leadership in Organizations*, 5th edn., Upper Saddle River, NJ: Prentice Hall.

Zollo, M. and S.G. Winter (2002), "Deliberate learning and the evolution of dynamic capabilities," *Organization Science*, **13** (3), 339–51.

11. The autonomy-creativity orientation of elite business school students in the US and Norway

Paul N. Gooderham, Alexander Madsen Sandvik, Siri Terjesen and Odd Nordhaug

INTRODUCTION

In staking out a new management paradigm appropriate for radically more dynamic business environments, Bogsnes (2009: 3) asks two questions: "What is it that really drives good performance?" and "How do we release creativity and innovation?" The notion is that employee creativity is increasingly important for organizations attempting to develop novel products and services, and innovative processes that build long-term competitive advantages (Zhang and Bartol, 2010).

Bogsnes (2009) argues that one key to releasing employee creativity and innovation lies in management ridding itself of a controlling "Theory X" mindset (McGregor, 1957, 1960). Theory X assumes that employees are basically lazy, lack ambition and offer little in the way of useful ideas. Instead, Bogsnes argues for the adoption of a "Theory Y" mindset, which rests on the core assumptions that employees are capable of self-direction and autonomy, and that they can be the source of many useful ideas. In this regard, Bogsnes states: "When sailing in these new waters, we need *less* traditional management and *more* leadership, less theory X and more theory Y. This is the only way to mobilize the maximum performance from everyone onboard" (2009: xvii–xviii). He also argues that the intrinsic motivation that drives creativity can be easily undermined through the use of extrinsic rewards, such as individual bonus systems. "The bonus," Bogsnes (2009: 34) contends, "*undermines* some of the interest in the job itself."

The primary aim of this chapter is to explore the degree to which elite business school students seek autonomy-creativity in their future careers.

Our interest in this group is motivated by the key roles these students are likely to hold in business organizations in the future. On the whole, they are destined to become leaders who will have a profound influence on future creativity and innovation. We define the desire for autonomy-creativity as the aspiration to find employment that provides considerable scope for creativity combined with substantial variety in work tasks, opportunities for interesting work and considerable freedom to work on one's own initiative.

The secondary aim of this chapter is to investigate the degree to which individual work-related factors, such as extrinsic rewards, constrain or promote an autonomy-creativity orientation. An additional aim is to examine whether demographic factors, such as nationality, gender and social background, have an impact on autonomy-creativity. Our study employs a sample of 463 American and Norwegian elite business school students.

THEORY

Researchers generally agree that "creativity" can be defined as the generation of ideas that are original and useful and "make sense" (Amabile, 1996). Simonton and Ting (2010) neatly summarize this definition as an equation: creativity = novelty × usefulness. This multiplicative function shows that, for creativity to occur, both novelty and usefulness are needed. Amabile (1996) suggests four major antecedents to creativity: 1) domain-relevant skills, 2) mental processes, 3) task motivation and 4) the specific context and social environment. Amabile (1998) also argues that the key to creativity is providing employees with autonomy concerning the way in which they work on strategically driven problems to enable them to make the most of their expertise and their creative-thinking skills: "The task may end up being a stretch for them, but they can use their strengths to meet the challenge" (1998: 82). Autonomy is, therefore, a critical condition for creativity (Amabile, 1988) and reflects the extent to which a job allows freedom, independence and discretion to schedule work, make decisions and choose the methods used to perform tasks (Breaugh, 1985; Morgeson and Humphrey, 2006). Amabile's theory is supported by Humphrey et al. (2007), who, in a meta-analytic study, find that autonomy is positively related to job satisfaction, growth satisfaction, internal work motivation and objective performance. In addition, Deci and Ryan (2000) show that autonomy is critical for creating self-determination and meaning.

However, do students at leading business schools actually seek work-life opportunities that confer autonomy-creativity? To the degree that they do, how is this search modified by other work-related aims? Previous research on business students' work-related values identifies materialism as a consistent motivational factor (Birkelund et al., 2000; Gooderham et al., 2004; Nordhaug et al., 2010). However, the research also indicates that materialism is only one factor among several – business students have multiple work-related values. More general research on young people's employment preferences distinguishes five work-related values: 1) bonuses and other company benefits, 2) relational culture, 3) clear goals and feedback, 4) status and 5) opportunities and career (Terjesen et al., 2007). Taken together, these values address needs for financial rewards, relational contacts, prestige and personal growth. In this study, we focus on how different work-related values, including materialism, affect the work-related value of autonomy-creativity. We explore whether those students who, for example, value extrinsic financial gains through bonuses are significantly less interested in workplaces that offer a significant degree of autonomy-creativity.

Previous research identifies the personal characteristics of openness to experience and creativity to be universal (Heine and Buchtel, 2009). However, Hofstede (1991 [1997]) shows that the desirability of achieving individual autonomy varies across national cultures. As a result, autonomy-creativity may vary among cultures. Rather than comparing across national cultures that have different levels of economic development, our study compares two cultures based in advanced economies with high standards of living: Norway and the US. In addition to culture, our analysis of the impact of demographic features on autonomy-creativity also includes gender and social class.

The significance of exploring the autonomy-creativity orientation of elite business school students is based on the theory that one's attitudes lead to behaviors. Ajzen's (1985) theory of planned behavior proposes that one's attitude towards a behavior predicts one's intention to engage in that behavior, which then leads to the behavior. This chapter considers two broad sources of variation in autonomy-creativity. The first concerns the influence of individually held work-related values. The second relates to the demographic influences of national culture, gender and socio-economic background. Taken together, our findings support McGregor's (1957, 1960) classic Theory Y assumption – that, when given the chance, employees can be trusted to seek opportunities for self-direction and creativity.

The Impact of Core Work-Related Values on Autonomy-Creativity

As indicated above, previous research suggests that, in addition to autonomy-creativity, elite business students focus on various work-related values, particularly: 1) bonuses and company benefits, 2) relational culture, 3) clear goals and feedback, 4) status and 5) opportunities and career. Some of these values relate to the job itself and the nature of work tasks, while others are concerned with the personnel policy and the social environment, which are characteristics of the employer or organization. Elite business students vary in the value they attribute to these values, some of which are associated with autonomy-creativity.

Bonuses and company benefits

Bonuses and benefits are concerned with the degree to which a job provides extrinsic consequences in the form of tangible and performance-related rewards. Kohn (1998) argues that – in contrast to "fair" compensation – incentives, bonuses, pay-for-performance plans and other reward systems distract employees and undermine their intrinsic motivation: "At least 70 studies have found that rewards tend to undermine interest in the task (or behavior) itself; this is one of the most thoroughly replicated findings in the field of social psychology" (Kohn, 1998: 35). We therefore hypothesize that:

H1. The greater the degree to which elite business students value bonuses and benefits, the less value they will place on autonomy-creativity.

Status

Although status is less tangible than bonuses and benefits, it is essentially an extrinsic reward. Given the above arguments, we hypothesize that:

H2. The greater the degree to which elite business students value status, the less value they will place on autonomy-creativity.

Relational culture

Relational culture is the degree to which the work environment is characterized by a supportive, caring employer and good collegial relations. Relational culture spans both social support (Morgeson and Humphrey, 2006) and the construct of friendship at work posited by Sims et al. (1976). Oldham and Cummings (1996) find a positive relationship between supportive supervision and employees' creative performance. Creativity takes place in a social context (Simonton, 2000), and new product development is usually the result of teamwork (Vissers and Dankbaar, 2002). Thus, Hasse (2001) argues that creative acts cannot be confined to the individual, but are the outcome of a meeting between an individual and the broader activity system. We therefore hypothesize:

H3. The greater the degree to which elite business students value relational culture, the more value they will place on autonomy-creativity.

Clear goals and feedback

Clear goals and feedback reflect the degree to which a job is characterized by clear aims (Sawyer, 1992) and clear information on task performance (Hackman and Oldham, 1976). Previous research suggests that employees are more motivated to work towards clear goals than towards vague goals such as "Do your best" (Locke and Latham, 1990, 2002). Zhang and Bartol (2010) find evidence that leadership plays an empowering role for creativity, as it positively influences employee psychological empowerment. Empowering leadership includes such aspects as helping an employee understand the importance of his or her contribution to overall organizational effectiveness. This can give an employee a feeling of greater control over the immediate work situation, and an enhanced sense that his or her own behaviors can make a difference in the work results. This, in turn, stimulates autonomy-creativity. We therefore hypothesize:

H4. The greater the degree to which elite business students value clear goals and feedback, the more value they will place on autonomy-creativity.

Opportunities and career

Amabile (1983) suggests that an individual's intrinsic task motivation plays an important role in determining behaviors that may result in creative outcomes. When individuals are intrinsically involved in their work, they are more likely to devote all of their attention to the problems they encounter (Zhang and Bartol, 2010: 112–13). When individuals have a short-term orientation in regard to their employment, they are unlikely to be intrinsically involved in their work. Accordingly they will be less able to devote themselves to engaging in creativity. The concept of work-related opportunities and career, therefore, refers to the degree to which elite business students seek job opportunities that offer long-term, as opposed to short-term, career potential.

H5. The greater the degree to which elite business students value opportunities and career, the more value they will place on autonomy-creativity.

The Impact of Demographic Variables on Autonomy-Creativity

The impact of national culture

Hofstede's (1991 [1997]) concept of uncertainty avoidance (UA) refers to the degree to which a society prefers predictability, security and

The autonomy-creativity orientation of students

stability. Societies with high levels of UA have emotional needs for written and unwritten rules. Organizations in these societies typically deploy formal rules in order to ensure that work situations are highly structured with clearly defined task roles and responsibilities. Deviant ideas and behaviors are not tolerated. Societies that are more tolerant of uncertainty report higher rates of innovation than societies that are less tolerant of uncertainty. In terms of UA, Hofstede finds no substantial difference between the Scandinavian countries, such as Norway, and the US.

More recent research into national cultures by the GLOBE group (House, 2004) includes a focus on UA. Although GLOBE's operationalization of UA is somewhat different than Hofstede's, the essential focus remains on a preference for orderliness at the expense of experimentation and innovation. Higher UA scores inhibit change and new product development. GLOBE distinguishes between values ("should be") and practices ("as is"). This distinction is important. While Hofstede's UA has significant positive correlations with GLOBE's UA values ("should be"), it has significant negative correlations with GLOBE's UA practices ("as is"). In terms of practices, GLOBE finds that the Scandinavian countries have some of the highest levels of UA, whereas the US has a mid-range score. However, in terms of UA values, GLOBE finds only minor differences between the Scandinavian countries and the US.

Given that our concern is with values rather than practices, both Hofstede's and GLOBE's rankings imply little or no differences in UA between Norway and the US. This, in turn, implies few differences in terms of autonomy-creativity. This lack of cultural differences leads us to hypothesize that:

H6. US and Norwegian elite business students have similar levels of autonomy-creativity orientation.

The impact of gender
A large body of empirical research investigates the influence of gender on work-related values, norms and beliefs (Powell, 1999), including creativity (Baer and Kaufman, 2008). The theory of gender self-schema describes how an individual's psychological construction of himself or herself is based on gender, and on the roles, norms, values and beliefs that are generally considered to be consistent with gender (Konrad et al., 2000; Eddleston et al., 2006). Thus, male-gender self-schemas are characterized by masculinity and career roles, and focus on income provision, dominance, aggression, achievement, autonomy, exhibition and endurance (Konrad et al., 2000). Female-gender self-schemas are linked to femininity

and family roles (Bem, 1981), and are associated with such values as home-making, affiliation, nurturance, deference and abasement (Konrad et al., 2000).

However, Baer and Kaufman (2008) observe that most studies on gender and creativity find a lack of differences between girls and boys, and between men and women. In some cases, especially in the area of divergent thinking, there are significant numbers of studies in which one group or the other scores higher, but these are generally counter-balanced by studies showing the opposite. Baer and Kaufman (2008) argue that a meta-analysis of the studies would indicate that women outperform men. However, they also observe that significant gender differences remain in creative productivity, and speculate that these may be due to differences in adult expectations of girls and boys, differences in opportunities available to male and female children and adults, and differences in the kinds of experiences women and men are likely to have.

Thus, although elite female business students may have a notion that their employment roles will, in part, be adapted to their future familial commitments, it is far from certain that we should expect any differences in terms of their autonomy-creativity orientation. Thus, we hypothesize:

H7. Male and female elite business students value autonomy-creativity to the same degree.

The impact of social background

A number of social scientists observe a connection between social background and creativity. In a comparison of middle- and working-class families in three societies, Strauss (1968) reports that middle-class families exhibit greater creativity than working-class families. One factor that appears to play a role in Strauss's research is the richer communication patterns evident within middle-class families. Anyon's (1980) analysis of social class and creativity points to the role of differences in educational experience. Different curricular, pedagogical and pupil evaluation practices in schools that cater for working-class and professional-class pupils emphasize different cognitive and behavioral skills. These differences contribute to the development in the children of certain relationships to authority and to the process of work. Furthermore, Bourdieu's (1984) theorizing on the concept of cultural capital suggests that students from middle-class backgrounds regard values of a purely materialistic type as vulgar. They demonstrate their "distinction" by emphasizing non-materialistic values, such as personal development. Inglehart's (1993) theory of post-materialist values is broadly supportive of this position.

Indeed, Inglehart suggests that individuals who feel confident of being able to cope materially are more inclined to emphasize expressive aspects of their future employment.

H8. Elite business students from middle-class families have a stronger orientation towards autonomy-creativity than elite business students from working-class families.

METHOD

Sample

The 463 respondents in our final sample were drawn from the final year of the bachelor's program at NHH – Norwegian School of Economics, and from final-year bachelor's students and master's students at a selection of top-tier US universities: Indiana University's Kelley School of Business, Texas Christian University (TCU), the University of Montana and Duquesne University.

Procedure

To gather the data, we employed a standardized questionnaire that contained a battery of 21 items that map job-related values. At NHH, data were collected at the end of a lecture given to 360 students in their final year of the bachelor's degree program in January 2009. Questionnaires were distributed to all of the students who attended the lecture. There were 280 completed questionnaires handed in as the students left the lecture hall. In other words, the survey was completed by nearly 80 percent of all final-year students.

Data from TCU, Duquesne, Indiana University and University of Montana students were collected at the end of lectures aimed at approximately 290 students in either the final year of their bachelor's business-degree program or in either year of their master's (MBA, MSIS) business-degree program in January and February 2009. Questionnaires were distributed to all of the students who attended the lectures. There were 230 completed questionnaires handed in as the students left their lectures, which gives a response rate of 80 percent. Of these 230 surveys, nine were removed from the sample, as most of the questions, including those on demographic factors, were not completed. Thereafter, we removed all responses from non-US nationals, leaving a sample of 183 respondents.

Measures

All items were presented in English. Participants provided their responses to each item using a ten-point Likert scale on which 1 = "not important" and 10 = "very important." The students were asked to indicate how important various job-related conditions were to them when choosing their first job or employer after having completed their business degrees.

Autonomy-creativity orientation

We measured autonomy-creativity using four key items drawn from the extant research on autonomy and problem solving (Morgeson and Humphrey, 2006): "A lot of variety in work tasks," "Interesting work," "A lot of freedom to work on your own initiative" and "Scope for creativity in the job." The Cronbach's alpha (an internal consistency estimate of reliability) for this measure was 0.73.

Bonuses and company benefits

We measured bonuses and company benefits using four items drawn from extant research on extrinsic motivation (Deci and Ryan, 1985): "Employee stock ownership," "Stock options for managers," "Individual, performance-based bonuses" and "Performance-based team bonuses." The Cronbach's alpha for this measure was 0.84.

Status

We measured status using three items: "The position has a high status," "Opportunities for a fast promotion" and "High annual earnings/salary." The Cronbach's alpha for this measure was 0.74.

Relational culture

We measured relational culture using four items drawn from extant research on social support (Morgeson and Humphrey, 2006): "Good social relations among colleagues," "Good personnel policy," "Employer cares about employees as individuals" and "There is a friendly culture." The Cronbach's alpha for this measure was 0.79.

Clear goals and feedback

We measured clear goals and feedback using three items found in previous work on goal clarity (Sawyer, 1992) and employee feedback (Hackman and Oldham, 1976; Morgeson and Humphrey, 2006). These were: "Clearly defined annual targets to work towards," "Clearly defined annual targets on which to be evaluated" and "Frequent feedback on work performance." The Cronbach's alpha for this measure was 0.77.

Opportunities and career

We measured opportunities and career using three items: "Opportunities for long-term career progression," "Opportunities to move around in the organization" and "Systematic career planning." The Cronbach's alpha for this measure was 0.67.

Analysis

In order to confirm discriminant validity, we performed an exploratory factor analysis with varimax rotation in SPSS. As we relied on self-reported measures, we retained only items with factor loadings of 0.50 (Nunnally and Bernstein, 2007) or higher on the target construct and cross-loadings of less than 0.35 (Kiffin-Petersen and Cordery, 2003). We used regression analyses to test the hypotheses in SPSS 19.0.

RESULTS

Descriptive statistics, coefficient alpha reliabilities and correlations for the variables appear in Table 11.1. All scale reliabilities exceed 0.70, as Nunnally (1978) recommended, except for opportunities and career, which has a scale reliability of 0.67. The highest correlation of the independent variables is 0.56 ($<$0.80), and collinearity statistics reported tolerance of more than 0.06 ($>$0.04) and variance inflation factors (VIF) of less than 1.65 ($<$2.5), which do not indicate a problem with multicollinearity. The exploratory factor analysis reveals that all of the items meet our criteria, providing further confirmation of the distinctiveness of each of the six factors (see the Appendix for details).

The strongest correlation between autonomy-creativity and another work-related value is found in relation to relational culture (0.45). The weakest correlations are found for bonuses and benefits (0.24) and status (0.24). However, even these correlations are statistically significant at the 0.01 level, indicating that many elite business students have a multiplicity of work-related values. Another finding evident in Table 11.1 is that the mean rating for autonomy-creativity is 7.70 on the ten-point scale, which indicates that this element is of great importance to elite business students. We also observe that the bonuses and benefits item has a mean rating of 6.0, status has a mean rating of 6.90, and clear goals and feedback has a mean rating of 7.03. Further analysis indicated that all of these mean ratings are statistically significantly lower at the 95 percent level than the mean rating for autonomy-creativity. However, relational culture has a higher mean score (8.14) than autonomy-creativity. Moreover, this mean

Table 11.1 Descriptive statistics, correlations and reliability of studied variables

	N	M	SD	1	2	3	4	5	6	7	8	9	10
1. Bonus and benefits	463	6.00	1.75	1									
2. Relational culture	463	8.14	1.20	.22**	1								
3. Clear goals and feedback	463	7.03	1.38	.39**	.38**	1							
4. Status	463	6.90	1.42	.53**	.18**	.35**	1						
5. Opportunities career	463	7.23	1.33	.40**	.39**	.46**	.44**	1					
6. Gender	460	1.32	.47	-.11*	.26**	.12*	-.11*	.08	1				
7. Nationality	460	1.40	.49	.31**	.07	.22**	.32**	.34**	.02	1			
8. Social background (both)	463	.49	.50	-.03	-.07	-.02	-.02	-.05	-.01	-.13**	1		
9. Social background (one)	463	.76	.43	.01	.02	.07	.05	.01	-.01	-.06	.56**	1	
10. Autonomy-creativity	463	7.70	1.20	.24**	.45**	.35**	.24**	.36**	.12**	.18**	.06	.05	1

Notes:
*$p < .05$; **$p < .01$.
Gender: 1 = male; 2 = female.
Nationality: 1 = Norwegian; 2 = US.
Social background: "one" indicates that either the father or the mother of the student holds at least a bachelor's degree; both indicates that both parents hold at least a bachelor's degree.

Table 11.2   Comparative distributions of job and workplace preferences

Factors	Mean		SD		T-value	DF	Sig.
	Norway	US	Norway	US			
Bonuses and company benefits	5.57	6.67	1.65	1.70	−6.89	458	.00
Relational culture	8.07	8.24	1.17	1.25	−1.50	458	.10
Autonomy and creativity	7.53	7.97	1.17	1.13	−3.89	458	.00
Clear goals and feedback	6.79	7.40	1.32	1.42	−4.72	458	.00
Status	6.52	7.46	1.40	1.26	−7.33	458	.00
Opportunities and career	6.86	7.79	1.24	1.27	−7.80	458	.00

Notes:
10 = very important, 1 = not important.
SD (standard deviation): two-tailed.

rating is statistically significantly greater at the 95 percent level than that of autonomy-creativity. In other words, while elite business students view autonomy-creativity as important, relational culture is of even more importance in their view.

Table 11.2 presents the comparative distributions for the six factors by country. They highlight country-based differences for each of the factors with the exception of relational culture. Interestingly, students from the US generally have significantly higher expectations than students from Norway. The range of means for the US students spans from 6.67 to 8.24, while the range is 5.57 to 8.07 for the Norwegian students.

Table 11.3 displays the results of the regression analysis. Model 1, which contains the five job-related values, explains 26 percent of the variance. The main explanations for this lie in the impact of relational culture, clear goals and feedback, and opportunities and career, which support Hypotheses 3, 4 and 5. As bonuses and benefits, and status have no significant impact, Hypotheses 1 and 2 are not supported.

Model 2 also includes the three demographic variables. Model 2 represents a relatively modest change in explained variance, which increases to 28 percent. In Model 2, neither nationality nor gender is significant, indicating that Hypotheses 6 and 7 are not supported. When measured as whether a single parent has a higher education, social background is not significant. However, social background in the sense of both parents

Table 11.3   Autonomy and creativity among elite business students

Variable	Autonomy and creativity			
	Model 1		Model 2	
	β	95% CI	β	95% CI
Work-related values				
Bonus and benefits	.02	[−.065, .095]	.02	[−071, .091]
Relational culture	.33**	[.228, .456]	.35**	[.241, .468]
Clear goals and feedback	.13**	[.002, .217]	.12*	[.005, .216]
Status	.06	[−.052, .143]	−.04	[−.069, .137]
Opportunities and career	.14**	[.017, .240]	.12*	[−.007, 227]
Demographic variables				
Gender			.01	[−.194, .237]
Nationality			.08	[−.022, .430]
Social background (both parents)			.13*	[.087, .515]
Social background (one parents)			−.03	[−.319, .160]
R^2	.26**		.28**	
F	32.24**	(5, 451)	19.30**	(9, 447)
ΔR^2			.02*	
ΔF			2.56*	

Notes:
*$p < .05$; **$p < .01$.
N = 456.
The ΔR^2 and F-values were derived from hierarchical regression analyses.
Bootstrap results are based on 1000 bootstrap samples.

having a higher education acquires statistical significance, which supports Hypothesis 8. In summary, Hypotheses 3, 4, 5 and 8 are supported, while Hypotheses 1, 2, 6 and 7 are not.

Although the role of social background is modest, it is nevertheless interesting to observe that it has an influence even among third- and fourth-year elite business school students, all of whom gained entry to their respective schools on the basis of similarly high educational qualifications. We tested for whether the social background of both parents interacted significantly with nationality. However, we found no significant interaction effect, meaning that the impact of social background on autonomy-creativity applies in both Norway and the US.

CONCLUSIONS

Our findings suggest a number of practical implications for employers. Among the work-related values included in our study, bonuses and benefits rank lowest. Furthermore, while this value does not have a negative impact on autonomy-creativity, it does not serve to enhance it. In other words, prospective employers of elite business school students should not invest in developing pay-for-performance schemes. Our research also indicates that status is not generally highly rated. It too has no influence on autonomy-creativity.

Instead, our findings suggest that employers should concentrate on developing work environments that emphasize what students are actually seeking: opportunities for autonomy-creativity, and a relational culture characterized by supportive managers and good social relations. Furthermore, our research indicates that the latter enhances the former. Other value orientations that promote autonomy-creativity are clear goals and feedback, and opportunities and career. In other words, elite business school students prefer to be properly mentored in the context of a long-term employment relationship.

Our findings are robust with regard to gender, and they apply to both Norway and the US. Clearly, future research should introduce more national cultures. Somewhat paradoxically, social background has some impact on autonomy-creativity. Thus, elite business school students with distinctively middle-class backgrounds are more inclined to seek autonomy-creativity. However, although this result is statistically significant, social background is a relatively minor factor in explaining differences in levels of autonomy-creativity.

Our findings are generally supportive of Bogsnes's (2009) contention that managers who seek creativity and innovation should adopt a Theory Y mindset. Given the value that elite business school students place on autonomy-creativity, the adoption of a mindset that assumes that employees are capable of self-direction and of contributing to innovation is likely to be beneficial. With regard to Bogsnes's deep skepticism toward the use of performance-related rewards, our findings suggest that those students who have pronounced extrinsic values are no less likely to value autonomy-creativity. However, our finding that an interest in these rewards has no impact on autonomy-creativity is hardly a justification for introducing such rewards. In short, these types of rewards appear to be irrelevant for autonomy-creativity.

Finally, we wish to acknowledge some of the limitations of our study, which in turn offer promising directions for future research. First, our data are cross-sectional, and our model makes assumptions with regard to causality. An improved design would enable the examination of changes in the various values over time. Second, our survey captures only students' perceptions of their personal autonomy-creativity orientation, not their demonstration of that orientation in a work environment. Future research could investigate how specific post-graduate work experiences enhance or diminish autonomy-creativity. Such research could also be extended beyond elite business school students to other groups of future employees. However, we reiterate that as elite business school students are likely to become the business leaders of the future an understanding of their work-related values and how those values relate to autonomy-creativity is critical.

REFERENCES

Ajzen, I. (1985), "From intentions to actions: A theory of planned behavior," in J. Kuhl and J. Beckmann (eds.), *Action Control*, Heidelberg: Springer, pp. 11–39.

Amabile, T.M. (1983), "The social psychology of creativity: A componential conceptualization," *Journal of Personality and Social Psychology*, **45** (2), 357–76.

Amabile, T.M. (1988), "A model of creativity and innovation in organizations," in B.M. Staw and L.L. Cummings (eds.), *Research in Organizational Behavior*, vol. 10, Greenwich, CT: JAI Press, pp. 123–67.

Amabile, T.M. (1996), *Creativity in Context: The Social Psychology of Creativity*, Boulder, CO: Westview Press.

Amabile, T.M. (1998), "How to kill creativity," *Harvard Business Review*, **76** (5), 77–87.

Anyon, J. (1980), "Social class and the hidden curriculum of work," *Journal of Education*, **162** (1), 67–93.

Baer, J. and J.C. Kaufman (2008), "Gender differences in creativity," *Journal of Creative Behavior*, **42** (2), 75–105.

Bem, S.L. (1981), "Gender schema theory: A cognitive account of sex typing source," *Psychological Review*, **88**, 354–64.

Birkelund, G.E., P.N. Gooderham and O. Nordhaug (2000), "Fremtidens næringslivsledere: Kjønn, karriere og skjebne," *Tidsskrift for samfunnsforskning*, **41** (4), 594–619.

Bogsnes, B. (2009), *Implementing Beyond Budgeting: Unlocking the Performance Potential*, Hoboken, NJ: John Wiley & Sons.

Bourdieu, P. (1984), *Distinction*, Cambridge, MA: Harvard University Press.

Breaugh, J.A. (1985), "The measurement of work autonomy," *Human Relations*, **38** (6), 551–70.

Deci, E.L. and R.M. Ryan (1985), *Intrinsic Motivation and Self-Determination in Human Behavior*, New York: Plenum.

Deci, E.L. and R.M. Ryan (2000), "The 'what' and 'why' of goal pursuits: Human needs and the self-determination of behavior," *Psychological Inquiry*, **11** (4), 227–68.

Eddleston, K.A., J.F. Veiga and G.N. Powell (2006), "Explaining sex differences in managerial career satisfier preferences: The role of gender self-schema," *Journal of Applied Psychology*, **9** (2), 437–45.

Gooderham, P.N., O. Nordhaug, K. Ringdal and G.E. Birkelund (2004), "Job values among future business leaders: The impact of gender and social background," *Scandinavian Journal of Management*, **20** (3), 277–95.

Hackman, J.R. and G.R. Oldham (1976), "Motivation through the design of work: Test of a theory," *Organizational Behavior and Human Performance*, **16** (2), 250–79.

Hasse, C. (2001), "Institutional creativity: The relational zone of proximal development," *Culture and Psychology*, **7** (2), 199–221.

Heine, S.J. and E.E. Buchtel (2009), "Personality: The universal and culturally specific," *Annual Review of Psychology*, **60**, 369–94.

Hofstede, G. (1991 [1997]), *Cultures and Organizations: Software of the Mind*, New York: McGraw-Hill.

House, R.J. (2004), *Culture, Leadership, and Organizations: The GLOBE Study of 62 Societies*, Thousand Oaks, CA: Sage.

Humphrey, S.E., J.D. Nahrgang and F.P. Morgeson (2007), "Integrating motivational, social, and contextual work design features: A meta-analytic summary and theoretical extension of the work design literature," *Journal of Applied Psychology*, **92** (5), 1332–56.

Inglehart, R. (1993), "Modernization and postmodernization: The changing relationship between economic development, cultural change and political change," Paper presented at the Conference on Changing Social and Political Values, Complutense University, Madrid, September 27 – October 1.

Kiffin-Petersen, S.A. and J.L. Cordery (2003), "Trust, individualism and job characteristics as predictors of employee preference for teamwork," *International Journal of Human Resource Management*, **14** (1), 93–116.

Kohn, A. (1998), "Challenging behaviorist dogma: Myths about money and motivation," *Compensation and Benefits Review*, **30** (2), 27, 33–7.

Konrad, A., E. Corrigall, P. Lieb and J.E. Ritchie, Jr. (2000), "Sex differences in job attribute preferences among managers and business students," *Group Organization Management*, **25** (2), 108–31.

Locke, E.A. and G.P. Latham (1990), "Work motivation and satisfaction: Light at the end of the tunnel," *Psychological Science*, **1** (4), 240–46.

Locke, E.A. and G.P. Latham (2002), "Building a practically useful theory of goal setting and task motivation: A 35-year odyssey," *American Psychologist*, **57** (9), 705–17.

McGregor, D. (1957), "The human side of enterprise," *Management Review*, **46** (11), 22–8.

McGregor, D. (1960), *The Human Side of Enterprise*, New York: McGraw-Hill.

Morgeson, F.P. and S.E. Humphrey (2006), "The Work Design Questionnaire (WDQ): Developing and validating a comprehensive measure for assessing job design and the nature of work," *Journal of Applied Psychology*, **91** (6), 1321–39.

Nordhaug, O., P.N. Gooderham, X. Zhang and Y. Liu (2010), "Elite female business students in China and Norway: Job-related values and preferences," *Scandinavian Journal of Educational Research*, **54** (2), 109–23.

Nunnally, J.C. (1978), *Psychometric Theory*, New York: McGraw-Hill.

Nunnally, J.C. and I.H. Bernstein (2007), *Psychometric Theory*, 3rd edn., New York: McGraw-Hill.

Oldham, G.R. and A. Cummings (1996), "Employee creativity: Personal and contextual factors at work," *Academy of Management Journal*, **39** (3), 607–34.

Powell, G.N. (1999), *Handbook of Gender and Work*, Thousand Oaks, CA: Sage.

Sawyer, J.E. (1992), "Goal and process clarity: Specification of multiple constructs of role ambiguity and a structural equation model of their antecedents and consequences," *Journal of Applied Psychology*, **77** (2), 130–42.

Simonton, D.K. (2000), "Creativity: Cognitive, personal, developmental, and social aspects," *American Psychologist*, **55** (1), 151–8.

Simonton, D.K. and S.-S. Ting (2010), "Creativity in Eastern and Western civilizations: The lessons of historiometry," *Management and Organization Review*, **6** (3), 329–50.

Sims, H.P., A.D. Szilagyi and R.T. Keller (1976), "The measurement of job characteristics," *Academy of Management Journal*, **19**, 195–212.

Strauss, A.M. (1968), "Communication, creativity, and problem-solving ability of middle- and working-class families in three societies," *American Journal of Sociology*, **73** (4), 417–30.

Terjesen, S., C. Freeman and S. Vinnicombe (2007), "Attracting Generation Y applicants: Organisational attributes, likelihood to apply and sex differences," *Career Development International*, **12** (6), 504–22.

Vissers, G. and B. Dankbaar (2002), "Creativity in multidisciplinary new product development teams," *Creativity and Innovation Management*, **11** (1), 31–42.

Zhang, X. and K.M. Bartol (2010), "Linking empowering leadership and employee creativity: The influence of psychological empowerment, intrinsic motivation, and creative process engagement," *Academy of Management Journal*, **53** (1), 107–28.

APPENDIX

Table 11A.1   Summary of exploratory factor analysis for characteristics of the first employer

Item	Factors					
	1	2	3	4	5	6
Employee stock ownership	.854					
Stock options for managers	.858					
Performance-based individual bonuses	.699					
Performance-based team bonuses	.663					
Good social relations among colleagues		.737				
Good personnel policy		.679				
Employer cares about employees as individuals		.754				
A friendly culture		.800				
A lot of variety in work tasks			.765			
Interesting work			.729			
A lot of freedom to work on one's own initiative			.711			
Scope for creativity in the job			.636			
Clearly defined annual targets to work towards				.866		
Clearly defined annual targets to be evaluated on				.890		
Frequent feedback on work performance				.454		
The position has a high status					.747	
Opportunities for getting fast promotion					.714	
High annual earnings/salary					.753	
Opportunities for long-terms career progression						.626
Opportunities to move around in the organization						.849
Systematic career planning						.549
Eigenvalues	6.13	2.69	1.49	1.39	1.16	1.02
% of variance	29.18	12.80	7.10	6.62	5.54	4.87
Cronbach's α	.84	.79	.73	.77	.74	.67

Notes:
N = 445.
Extraction method: principal axis factoring.
Rotation method: varimax with Kaiser normalization.
Values are those included in the final scales.
Factor loadings below 0.40 are removed.
Factor 1 – Bonuses and company benefits; Factor 2 – Relational culture; Factor 3 – Autonomy and creativity; Factor 4 – Clear goals and feedback; Factor 5 – Status; Factor 6 – Opportunities and career.

12. Systems of accountability and personal responsibility

Lars Jacob Tynes Pedersen

INTRODUCTION

A central challenge in any organization is ensuring that individuals, groups and organizational units act and perform as desired, and holding them accountable if they do not. This challenge has a *performance dimension*, as organizations need to be sure that task performance is adequate, that is, that employees undertake the tasks with which they are entrusted in a manner that promotes organizational performance. Accordingly, it is closely related to performance management and measurement (see, e.g., Kaplan and Atkinson, 1998). Moreover, this challenge has a *conduct dimension*, as organizations need to ensure that employees act in accordance with relevant norms and – when desired by the organization – with awareness of how their decisions and acts influence relevant internal and external stakeholders (e.g., Cooper and Owen, 2007; Zsolnai, 2009). These two dimensions constitute the basis for accountability. This implies that actors must be able to give accounts, explanations and justifications of what they have done and why (e.g., Munro and Hatherly, 1993; Messner, 2009), primarily with regard to performance and conduct (Benston, 1982; Jørgensen and Pedersen, 2011).

Management control systems are designed to promote accountability on all organizational levels (Macintosh and Quattrone, 2010). They do so by enabling *control after-the-fact*, that is, by scrutinizing whether actual behavior met the relevant requirements, and by creating general *awareness of control* and, thereby, accountability among organizational members, that is, by instilling people with the knowledge that future performance and conduct will be scrutinized (Kirk and Mouritsen, 1996). Both these modes of control are based on an understanding of behavior and human nature that assumes that a desired behavior can be produced through extrinsic motivations. In other words, organizations aim to motivate employees by offering rewards or the absence of negative sanctions (see Deci and Ryan, 2000). According to this logic, organizations should create a control system that: 1) identifies objectives; 2) assigns responsibilities; 3) attaches incentives and/or sanctions to various potential outcomes; 4) measures the degree to which individuals, groups and units perform as desired; and 5) rewards or punishes employees on the basis of performance.

There are several problems with this approach to accountability. First, empirical research demonstrates that the individual's intrinsic motivation is impaired to the extent that incentives are designed in a manner that leads organizational members to perceive them as *controlling*, that is, intended to control behavior (Frey, 1997; Deci and Ryan, 2000). Hence, a reliance on extrinsic sources of motivation to induce behavior may, in fact, reduce an individual's motivation. Second, when individuals perceive an incentive as controlling, they substitute intrinsic motivation with extrinsic control (Frey, 1997). This implies that the perceived locus of control with regard to the task is shifted from inside to outside the individual, which means that he or she no longer feels responsible for the task. The intervening institution (for instance, management or "the organization") is then perceived as being responsible (see also Frey and Osterloh, 2002). This perception will typically extend to responsibility for the broader effects or implications of the act carried out by the individual (see Bauman, 1994).

Let us consider a concrete example. Fitch and Saunders (1975) describe the case of the "great aircraft brake scandal," in which a young engineer realized that an airplane brake developed for the US air force failed to meet the stress requirements set for such equipment. As this constituted a considerable safety risk, the engineer warned his superiors about the risk. According to Fitch and Saunders (1975: 345), "the order received from the senior engineer who designed the brake and his superior, and his superior, was that the brake was to be 'qualified,' no matter how." The engineer's superior took the issue to management, but came back beaten. He then decided to falsify the tests rather than risk losing his job. "After all," he remarked, "we're just drawing some curves, and what happens to them after they leave here – well, we're not responsible for that" (Fitch and Saunders, 1975: 345).

In this example, the implicit incentives laid out for the young engineer and his superior are clear: Do not interfere with management's decisions and be sure to contribute to reaching the desired conclusions. The implications of the perceived responsibility, which are succinctly captured in the statement from the superior above, essentially led the two engineers to view the potentially dramatic consequences for important stakeholders as no longer being their responsibility. This example reflects part of the problem addressed in this chapter: How can personal responsibility be promoted (or impaired) by organizational systems of accountability? However, this example is a negative one – it exemplifies a situation in which management does not aim to get employees to do the right thing. In this chapter, the opposite case is also illuminated in which organizational systems of accountability can be employed with the aim of promoting responsible behavior.

This chapter, then, touches on the aim of promoting individual responsibility by organizational means, and the pitfalls and opportunities that arise in that regard. The purpose of the chapter is to explore the tension between organizational systems of accountability and the individual's sense of personal responsibility. More specifically, the chapter discusses the possibility of promoting the individual's sense of personal responsibility (Ims, 2006) or, in the language of Bovens (1998), *active individual responsibility*, by means of traditional organizational systems of accountability.

The chapter builds on previous contributions on the relationship between accountability and responsibility (e.g., Roberts, 1991, 2009; Sinclair, 1995; Shearer, 2002; Lindkvist and Llewellyn, 2003; Messner, 2007, 2009). In line with Lindkvist and Llewellyn (2003) and Roberts (1991, 2009), the problematic aspects of hierarchical accountability are emphasized with regard to the individual's inclination for intrinsically value-driven behavior. Moreover, the chapter shares the concerns of Shearer (2002), Sinclair (1995) and Messner (2007, 2009) that the economic concept of accountability in organizations displaces important dimensions of the identities and responsibilities of actors, as it facilitates a one-dimensional economic portrayal of actors, interests and relationships (see also Roberts and Scapens, 1985). Finally, this chapter shares Bovens's (1998) converse concern that an overemphasis on personal responsibility may lead to a "personalization" of the organization, thereby undermining the predictability of conduct while overloading the individual conscience.

This chapter contributes to the management control literature by: 1) exploring the psychological conditions of personal responsibility; 2) discussing the fallacies of traditional systems of accountability with regard to promoting personal responsibility; and 3) highlighting organizational implications for the design of systems of accountability. The chapter is structured as follows. First, the concepts of accountability and responsibility are presented, with an emphasis on the nature of personal responsibility. Second, problems with traditional approaches to accountability are discussed. Third, the possibility for promoting personal responsibility within systems of accountability is analyzed. Finally, the conclusions are briefly outlined.

RESPONSIBILITY AND ACCOUNTABILITY

In this section, the concepts of responsibility and accountability are investigated. First, the relationship between responsibility and accountability
is briefly discussed, and the nature and various forms of responsibility are
explored. Second, the notion of personal responsibility is analyzed from
a psychological point of view. Finally, this notion is contrasted with the
organizational practice of ensuring accountability.

The Nature and Forms of Responsibility

"Accountability" and "responsibility" are often used interchangeably.
However, they have distinct meanings. Typically, responsibility is seen as
a broader concept that encompasses what is normally considered to be the
domain of accountability. Following Bovens (1998: 24–5), we highlight
five forms of responsibility, one of which is "accountability."

First, it is common to think in terms of *responsibility as a cause*. This
reflects the idea that people, things or circumstances may cause the emergence of certain outcomes, and it gives rise to the notion of causal responsibility. Second, there is a widespread understanding of *responsibility as
accountability*, that is, moral, political and/or legal liability for (typically
harmful) outcomes of a behavior carried out by an agent. Hence, the
notion of moral responsibility is closely linked to the concept of accountability, which connotes giving an account of why a given behavior was
carried out (see Messner, 2009). Third, we may speak of *responsibility as
a capacity*, that is, the responsibility (or lack thereof) that follows from
being able to exercise a certain amount of responsibility (owing to power,
knowledge or mental ability, or a lack thereof). Fourth, it is common to
think in terms of *responsibility as a task*, that is, the obligations or functions that follow from having a particular role or position. This is closely
related to role-mediated or professional responsibility (see Ims, 2006).
Finally, we may talk of *responsibility as a virtue*, that is, the value-laden
individual character trait that inclines the individual to act responsibly.

For the purposes of this chapter, we build on the distinction between
responsibility as accountability and responsibility as a task on the one
hand, and responsibility as capacity and responsibility as a virtue on the
other hand. The former reflects the widespread organizational orientation
towards assigning responsibility for role-specific tasks to the individual,
for which he or she is held accountable (see Roberts, 1991). The emphasis,
then, lies on organizational roles and the individual's accountability for
tasks therein. This involves the possibility that the individual will be held
accountable for the choices he or she makes, which implies a need to justify

what was done. The latter, in contrast, reflects the individual's capability and active willingness to act in a manner that is in line with relevant norms or promotes desirable outcomes for internal and external stakeholders. In such cases, the emphasis lies on the power and opportunity available to the individual to make autonomous choices within the organizational context, and on the manner in which the individual realizes socio-moral values in organizational action.

The former category is largely retrospective in the sense that it is oriented towards the accountability of the decision maker for decisions and activities that have been carried out as part of his or her task behavior. It corresponds with Bovens's (1998) concept of passive responsibility, which deals with the question of who *bears the responsibility* for acts that have been carried out. The second category, however, is prospectively oriented in the sense that it focuses on the actor's action space for achieving desired outcomes or avoiding certain non-desired outcomes (see Jonas, 1984). This corresponds with Bovens's (1998) concept of active responsibility, which deals with the question of who can take responsibility or behave responsibly in order to achieve desired outcomes or prevent undesired ones. Hence, responsibility is both past and future oriented – it deals both with questions of *what was done and why* (passive/retrospective) and with questions of *what to do* (active/prospective).

It follows from the five forms of responsibility outlined above that responsibility is both *other-directed* and *self-directed*. It is other-directed in the sense that responsible action takes important norms and expectations into account (see role-mediated responsibility), as well as the interests of others, such as stakeholders (see moral responsibility). It is self-directed in the sense that we think of responsible action as reflecting the personal values (and life project) of the individual moral actor. Individuals are responsible to others *and* to themselves, although in different ways. In other words, the degree to which the individual's behavior is responsible can be assessed with regard to the expectations of others and with regard to the individual's own standards. The latter point refers to a central concept in the discourse on responsibility, namely that of personal responsibility or, in the language of Bovens (1998), active individual responsibility.

Personal Responsibility

At a deeper level than role-mediated responsibility – or, for that matter, the individual's responsibility to comply with shared socio-moral norms – is the individual's *personal sense of responsibility*. In itself, personal responsibility is about the individual's realization of his or her own beliefs and values in action. Ims (2006) argues that personal responsibility is also about reflecting on the limits of role-mediated behavior – it is the personal responsibility of the organizational member to actively take a stand on the tasks he or she is willing to execute and the obligations he or she is willing to accept (see Ims and Pedersen, 2013). In order for responsible action in organizations to mean something more than simple obedience, it must be based on a certain *sense of responsibility*. That is, the individual must actively reflect on, and take seriously, the degree to which a given action transgresses a relevant norm or carries unacceptable consequences (Bovens, 1998). Responsible choice and action, then, imply balancing goal attainment with consideration for relevant norms and the potential for negative effects on stakeholders (Zsolnai, 2009).

From a psychological point of view, personally responsible action is *self-determined behavior*. It is behavior that is intrinsically driven because it relates to issues relevant to the individual's conscience or, more broadly, has implications for his or her life project (see Williams, 1981). The suggestion that personally responsible action is self-determined implies that the volition and drive for such action spring from the individual. Hence, motivation comes from within the individual, and is derived from the beliefs and values that are important to the individual. However, according to Deci and Ryan (2000), the individual's self-determination is highly conditioned by social and cultural factors. That is, external factors can either promote or undermine the individual's self-determination.

Self-determined behavior depends on the satisfaction of three basic psychological needs: *autonomy*, *competence* and *relatedness* (Deci and Ryan, 2000). If these needs are thwarted or unfulfilled, self-determination is undermined. Deci and Ryan (2000: 231) define these three needs as follows. *Autonomy* refers to the individual's desire to self-organize experience and behavior, and to engage in activities that are concordant with one's self. Hence, the individual needs to have power and influence over his or her own action space (rather than feeling controlled), as well as the ability to express his or her own beliefs and values through action. *Competence* refers to the individual's desire to have an effect on the environment and to attain valued outcomes within it. Hence, the individual needs to be able to effectuate appropriate and consequential action given the circumstances. *Relatedness* refers to the individual's desire to be connected to others – to care and love, and to love and to be cared for. Hence, the individual needs to feel part of a larger community and to connect with people therein.

Three features of these needs are of particular relevance to personal responsibility. First, self-determination has to do with the individual's self. This signifies the *existential dimension* of personal responsibility. Second, self-determination depends on the individual's connection to others via micro- or macro-communities of which the individual is part. This signifies the *social or relational dimension* of personal responsibility, and relates to the question of why the individual is oriented towards the expectations (via norms) and interests of others. Third, the individual is concerned about the broader implications of action for the general environment. This reflects the *systemic dimension* of personal responsibility, which transcends the dyadic relationship between the "claimer of accounts" and "the giver of accounts" that characterizes accountability.

Accountability in Organizational Life

Messner (2007) argues that accountability is an intrinsically social phenomenon, as it involves an exchange between the actor and other parties who call for the actor to account for what he or she has done. This giving of accounts is central to the concept of accountability, which typically leads to the ascription of either praise or blame depending on the quality of the actor's justification for his or her actions. According to Bovens (1998), accountability entails: 1) a perception that a given actor's conduct or action (or lack thereof) has led to a harmful or violating situation or event; 2) that it is possible to ascribe some degree of causality between the actor and this event; 3) that the actor could have acted otherwise, which is a condition for being blameworthy; and 4) that the person (or collective) who acted can actually be held accountable.

All forms of role-mediated behavior in organizations are prominently characterized by accountability, as the very notion of a role implies having certain expectations of the role-holder with regard to performance or conduct. Accordingly, one of the key characteristics of organizations is that they enable and promote accountability for the individual actor, as well as for groups and larger entities (e.g., departments). Therefore, accountability is a central tool in the attempt to control behavior (see Kirk and Mouritsen, 1996; Macintosh and Quattrone, 2010).

Roberts and Scapens (1985) argue that systems of accountability embody a moral order in that they are complex systems of reciprocal rights and obligations. Such systems thus involve giving rights (e.g., decision rights and the power needed to carry out decisions) to individuals along with the relevant obligations that follow from doing so. Moreover, by being given these rights and obligations, individuals become subject to their superiors' calls for accountability related to the manner in which they manage their rights and obligations.

According to Roberts and Scapens (1985), this moral dimension of systems of accountability reflects only one of their three main structures. In addition to morality, systems of accountability also involve *meaning* and *power*. Organizational members are provided with categories of *meaning* about the organization through the system of accountability. For instance, in an organization that sets an ambitious sustainability agenda and structures the organization in order to promote the attainment of environmental goals, such aspects as sustainability and care for nature will be much more salient for organizational members than in an organization where this is not the case. Thus, systems of accountability provide structures of meaning that are relevant for organizational members with regard to the sense-making of their experiences in the organization.

The prominence of *power* in systems of accountability is reflected in positive and negative sanctions associated with organizational members' performance and conduct. This can refer to economic incentives, such as raises (e.g., based on performance), or to social incentives, such as praise or blame related to organizational action. Such incentives can be formal or informal, and they can be implicitly or explicitly communicated. Moreover, a prominent power dimension in systems of accountability relates to the calling for an account in itself. As argued by Messner (2009), a superior's call for accountability may, in fact, be seen as a form of "violence" toward the actor if, for instance, the actor is asked to account for acts that are hard to explain, or about which he or she does not have a proper recollection or understanding. Accordingly, there are limits of accountability from an ethical point of view.

In summary, systems of accountability are organizational attempts to promote responsible action among organizational members. In the following section, some of the problems associated with systems of accountability are outlined, particularly with respect to promoting personal responsibility.

PROBLEMS WITH SYSTEMS OF ACCOUNTABILITY IN ORGANIZATIONS

In this section, two main problems with systems of accountability and their potential for promoting personal responsibility are discussed. First, in light of self-determination theory (Deci and Ryan, 2000), the possibility that intrinsically important, value-driven action may be crowded out is discussed. Second, the tendency of systems of accountability to *individualize* organizational action is illuminated. For both problems, the possibility of moral disengagement on the part of the individual actor is also discussed.

If we take self-determination theory seriously, personal responsibility is a vulnerable phenomenon. It is well established that intrinsically motivated action, that is, acts that the individual would carry out even in the absence of desirable consequences, may be undermined by external intervention (Frey, 1997; Deci and Ryan, 2000). Specifically, intrinsic motivation may be crowded out if the individual experiences an attempt from the organization (e.g., from superiors) to control his or her behavior.

This issue is related to the individual's motivational psychology in general and, more specifically, to the individual's sense of responsibility. When individuals perceive an intervention as *controlling*, they substitute intrinsic motivation with extrinsic control (Frey, 1997). The psychological mechanism at play is that the individual's locus of control regarding the task shifts from inside to outside the individual. As a result, the individual no longer feels responsible for the task or its implications, but instead perceives the intervening institution as responsible (Frey and Osterloh, 2002). In terms of the distinction between accountability and responsibility, the individual may still accept accountability for the act that was carried out, but will no longer feel a sense of responsibility for what was done, how it was done or the implications for others.

It follows that individuals may act in accordance with the obligations of their jobs, thereby acting "responsibly" from the point of view of the organization, without necessarily having a sense of personal responsibility for their actions. Such actions may be attributed to both enlightened self-interest and mindless obedience (see Arendt, 1963; Milgram, 1974), but they are characterized as "shallow" from the perspective of personal values. The risk of such a disconnect between individual action and personal values is key, as it implies that organizational members can gradually "drift" into questionable practices as a result of a lack of reflection on the relevant ethical dimensions (see, e.g., Bauman, 1989; Bandura, 1999; Zimbardo, 2007; Pedersen, 2009).

This problem is particularly serious with regard to organizational actions and their consequences for the broader set of stakeholders outside the organization. The problem of systems of accountability in this regard is succinctly captured by Lindkvist and Llewellyn (2003), who argue that, when employing a comprehensive accountability system, "a floating responsibility may arise, whereby everyone has procedural accountabilities but no one has responsibility for wider consequences (moral or instrumental). In such situations an accountability system that connotes blind instrumentality may actually disconnect organizational members from wider concerns related to the effectiveness of the organization" (Lindkvist and Llewellyn, 2003: 252).

This is related to the fact that, when responsibility is diffused in an organization, personal agency is obscured, which in turn weakens the exercise of moral control. According to Bandura (1999: 198), when activities become routinized into detached sub-functions, people shift their attention from the morality of what they are doing to the operational details and efficiency of their specific jobs. In this manner, systems of accountability may promote myopia on the part of individual actors.

This leads us to the other problem of systems of accountability, which has its genesis in what is referred to as the "many hands" problem. Several people are typically involved in organizational decision making and action. It may therefore be difficult in practice to disentangle who actually did what, or who is responsible for a given course of action and its consequences (Bovens, 1998). As Bandura (1999: 198) states, "[w]hen everyone is responsible, no one really feels responsible." Moreover, collective action is typically more than the aggregate of separate actions, that is, it is nearly impossible to "distribute" praise or blame for organizational outcomes to specific individual decisions or actions (Kaptein and Wempe, 2004).

Therefore, the second problem associated with systems of accountability is the tendency of such systems to *individualize* organizational action. Accountability implies assigning role-responsibilities to individuals, who are then individually accountable for the degree to which they fulfill those expectations. However, it is far from certain that those same individuals conceive of their acts as being singularly of their own making, as several other organizational members may have taken part in or facilitated the act in question. An individualized conception of accountability may thus be at odds with individuals' understanding of organizational action.

An atomized conception of organizational actors may further undermine the individual's sense of *shared responsibility*. The basic idea of shared responsibility is that individuals within a community (e.g., within an organization) may see themselves as sharing the blame (i.e., being accountable) for harms perpetrated by or occurring within that community, with or without their active participation (May, 1992: 1). This implies an extension of the individual's accountability to include acts that the individual has not carried out himself or herself, but on which he or she may be able to exert influence. Shared responsibility implies awareness that one's personal responsibility transcends one's own choices and behavior. This may lead us to consider our roles, omissions and attitudes in light of our ethical standards in a manner similar to how we consider our actual behavior (May, 1992). This implies extending our *horizon of responsibility* and is, therefore, also relevant for personal responsibility (Ims and Pedersen, 2013). However, to the extent that organizational members are judged on the basis of individual action alone, the incentives for considering behavior as collective and, thereby, viewing responsibility as shared decrease. Thus, we may see a form of crowding out of the individual's sense of shared responsibility.

The individualization of organizational action thus has two problematic aspects. First, it moves counter to the relatedness experienced by individuals in organizations and to their understanding of organizational action as a collectively produced phenomenon. It may, therefore, undermine intrinsic motivation, while simultaneously creating a sense of unfairness among organizational members who are called to account individually for acts of a collective nature. Second, it may undermine organizational members' sense of shared responsibility, thereby narrowing their horizon of responsibility.

PROMOTING PERSONAL RESPONSIBILITY WITHIN SYSTEMS OF ACCOUNTABILITY

The question is whether systems of accountability – despite their shortcomings – can be designed in a way that enables them to promote personal responsibility among organizational members. The challenges of promoting personal responsibility in organizational life are, broadly speaking, twofold. First, there is the challenge of facilitating a sense of (personal) responsibility among employees in terms of properly executing the tasks associated with their organizational roles and showing good conduct in doing so. This reflects the emphasis on performance and conduct outlined above. Second, there is the challenge of facilitating awareness among employees of the broader implications of their acts. This relates to the issue of individual responsibility for the wider concerns that transcend the intra-organizational questions of organizational performance.

Given the discussion of the psychological conditions for personal responsibility above, we can argue that systems of accountability must provide fruitful conditions for self-determined, communal and engaged decision making and action. The practical implications of each of these three conditions for systems of accountability are explored in the following.

In order to provide fruitful conditions for self-determined behavior, systems of accountability must be designed such that they do not thwart, but rather nurture, organizational members' needs for autonomy, competence and relatedness. This implies that organizational members should not feel that the manner in which they are held accountable is merely a form of behavioral control. According to Deci and Ryan (2000), systems of accountability are a form of external intervention, which relates to the individual's extrinsic motivation. However, there are different forms of regulation based on extrinsic motivation, and they influence the individual's locus of control in different ways. On the one hand, external regulation, that is, traditional "carrot and stick" accountability systems, and introjected regulation, that is, accountability systems that provide incentives that are somewhat tied to internal benefits for the individual (e.g., status or a lack thereof), lead the individual to externalize the locus of control. Therefore, they are likely to undermine personal responsibility. On the other hand, two other forms of regulation – identified regulation, that is, accountability systems that have goals and sanctions with which the individual largely identifies or that seem consistent with the individual's beliefs and values, and integrated regulation, that is, accountability systems that are in harmony with the individual's beliefs and values with regard to goals, actions and expectations – lead the individual to internalize the locus of control. Such systems are likely to foster a sense of personal responsibility.

It is thus essential that systems of accountability aim to regulate behavior in a manner that is consistent with either identified or integrated regulation. This necessitates some degree of value alignment between the organization and its employees, as identification and integration are unlikely to be achieved if the divergence is significant Moreover, systems of accountability should be based on the principle of "Know thy employee." In other words, the manner in which the organization aims to control the behavior of its employees must be based on a proper knowledge of the employees' needs. Increasing organizational members' ownership of the goals towards which they are supposed to strive and the manner in which they are expected to do so will increase the likelihood of identification and integration. For example, in control systems in which organizational members are allowed to influence goal setting and the selection of means to achieve those goals, autonomy is higher. As a result, identification and integration are more likely.

However, such autonomy must be adapted to the competence level of organizational members, as a lack of competence may, in itself, undermine self-determination. This is again a matter of working with employees to tailor the level of autonomy and, thereby, the level of challenges to the level of any given employee's competence. This is crucial for keeping organizational members from drifting into anxiety as a result of a level of expectations for task performance that is too high (see Csikszentmihalyi, 1975).

In order to provide fruitful conditions for communal and engaged behavior, systems of accountability must be designed to: 1) cater to organizational members' need for relatedness; 2) stimulate a collective understanding of organization action; and 3) encourage awareness about the moral implications of decisions and actions. This relates, in part, to self-determination of behavior with regard to the individual's need to be connected in meaningful ways to other people in the organization.

Moreover, it relates, to some extent, to organizational members considering themselves to be "in the same boat" in the sense that they are jointly responsible for organizational outcomes to which they contribute to varying degrees and in different ways.

The former point deals with the issue raised by Messner (2009), who argues that accountability systems largely facilitate a one-dimensional economic portrayal of actors, interests and relationships. This can be caused by organizational members experiencing that evaluation is based on a narrow conception of task performance, or for that matter by promoting an overly competitive culture between organizational members. The challenge for the organization, then, is to facilitate caring relationships among organizational members, and to ensure that organizational action provides an opportunity for self-expression, recognizing that individuals are more than "performance machines."

The promotion of organizational members' experience of shared responsibility as well as a sense of responsibility for the broader implications of organizational action can, for example, be attempted through incentive systems. An interesting example is the case of Allied Electronics, which redesigned its incentive system in order to ensure that its employees were serious about achieving their relatively ambitious sustainability-related goals. New sustainability metrics and KPIs were developed, and the incentive system was tied to these metrics with considerable success (Eccles et al., 2012). Shared responsibility can be stimulated in a similar manner by, for instance, linking incentive systems to collective acts and outcomes.

In closing – and in light of the chapter's call for a focus on personal responsibility – there is also a need to recognize that there are limits to personal responsibility. This holds with regard to the interests of the organization and with regard to the well-being of individual organizational members. Bovens (1998) argues that an overemphasis on personal responsibility may lead to a "personalization" of the organization. This chapter has strongly argued that responsibility in organizations needs to be anchored in the responsibility of individuals, and that the realization of personally held values in organizational action is necessary in order to avoid the alienation and desensitization of organizational members. However, organizational members should also make second-order assessments of whether their organizations are socio-moral communities in which they experience a degree of alignment between organizational values and personal values, or if the conflict between the two sets of values is too substantial. In the latter case, organizational members constantly face decisions or acts that compromise their personal beliefs and values. For these members, it may be better to pursue a career elsewhere than to be in perpetual conflict both internally, that is, with oneself, and externally, that is, with the organization (see Ims and Pedersen, 2013).

Bovens (1998) also argues that an over-reliance on personal beliefs and values for organizational decision making and action runs the risk of undermining the predictability of conduct, which may be detrimental to the organization. Moreover, it may overload the individual conscience, as consistently being in moral conflict or moral "negotiation" in the workplace takes a significant toll on the individual. The literature on moral distress (see, e.g., Wilkinson, 1988) indicates that such overloading of the individual conscience may have serious negative consequences for the individual's well-being and health.

CONCLUSION

This chapter has explored the possibility of promoting personal responsibility within systems of accountability. The chapter's point of departure was the seemingly antithetical relationship between key characteristics of traditional systems of accountability and the psychological conditions that facilitate and foster a sense of personal responsibility among organizational members. The chapter built on the premise that it is desirable for organizational members to have a sense of personal responsibility for both their task performance and their conduct, which supports organizational goal attainment, and for the broader implications of their organizational decisions and actions, which ensures that they take the societal and environmental impact of their organizational practices into account.

We have argued that a sense of personal responsibility implies self-determination on the part of organizational members, and that this requires fulfilling their needs for autonomy, competence and relatedness in the work setting. Undermining these needs may crowd out intrinsically value-driven behavior and shift the locus of control for organizational action from inside to outside the individual. This, in turn, has dysfunctional effects with regard to fostering personal responsibility. Moreover, we have argued that an important characteristic of organization, namely the individualization of organizational action, may undermine organizational members' sense of shared responsibility – the willingness to assume responsibility for the acts of others in the organization – that the organizational members facilitate, contribute to or silently accept. Such shared responsibility is essential for creating a positive ethical climate in the organization, which implies that organizational members actively reflect on and engage in discussions about whether organizational decisions and acts can be justified. To the extent that systems of accountability individualize action in a way that undermines such relational conceptions of action and responsibility for action, the risk of questionable practices arising and diffusing in the organization arguably increases.

However, the chapter is still optimistic about the possibility of promoting personal responsibility within systems of accountability given that such systems are designed in a manner that provides fruitful conditions for self-determined, communal and engaged decision making and action. Such systems: 1) regulate behavior in a manner that involves setting goals and assigning sanctions that organizational members can accept and with which they can identify; 2) balance autonomy and competence in a way that empowers, rather than distresses, the individual; 3) employ performance and conduct evaluations that are not narrowly based on goal attainment alone; 4) facilitate caring relationships among organizational members; and 5) encompass incentive systems that relate to the collective nature of organizational action and to the broader implications of organizational outcomes, for example sustainability-related or societal outcomes. Therefore, we suggest that the organization may design systems of accountability that have the potential to foster personal responsibility. Such systems allow for the balancing of organizational actors' self-conceptions as professionals partly controlled by the organization with their self-conceptions as autonomous human beings.

REFERENCES

Arendt, H. (1963), *Eichmann in Jerusalem: A Report on the Banality of Evil*, New York: Viking Press.

Bandura, A. (1999), "Moral disengagement in the perpetration of inhumanities," *Personality and Social Psychology Review*, 3 (3), 193–209.

Bauman, Z. (1989), *Modernity and the Holocaust*, 4th edn., Cambridge, MA: Polity Press.

Bauman, Z. (1994), *Alone Again: Ethics after Certainty*, London: Demos.

Benston, G.J. (1982), "Accounting and corporate accountability," *Accounting, Organizations and Society*, 7 (2), 87–105.

Bovens, M. (1998), *The Quest for Responsibility: Accountability and Citizenship in Complex Organisations*, Cambridge: Cambridge University Press.

Cooper, S.M. and D.L. Owen (2007), "Corporate social reporting and stakeholder accountability: The missing link," *Accounting, Organizations and Society*, 32 (7/8), 649–67.

Csikszentmihalyi, M. (1975), *Beyond Boredom and Anxiety*, San Francisco, CA: Jossey-Bass.

Deci, E.L. and R.M. Ryan (2000), "The 'what' and 'why' of goal pursuits: Human needs and the self-determination of behavior," *Psychological Inquiry*, 11 (4), 227–68.

Eccles, R.G., G. Serafeim, S.X. Li and A. Knight (2012), *Allied Electronics*

Corporation Ltd: Linking Compensation to Sustainability Metrics, Cambridge, MA: Harvard Business Publishing.

Fitch, H.G. and C.B. Saunders (1975), "Blowing the whistle: The limits of organizational obedience," *Academy of Management Proceedings*, August, 345–7.

Frey, B. (1997), *Not Just for the Money: An Economic Theory of Personal Motivation*, Cheltenham, UK and Lyme, NH, USA: Edward Elgar Publishing.

Frey, B. and M. Osterloh (2002), "Does pay for performance really motivate employees?," in A. Noely (ed.), *Business Performance Measurement*, Cambridge: Cambridge University Press.

Ims, K.J. (2006), "Take it personally," in L. Zsolnai and K.J. Ims (eds.), *Business within Limits: Deep Ecology and Buddhist Economics*, Bern: Peter Lang.

Ims, K.J. and L.J.T. Pedersen (2013), "Personal responsibility and ethical action," in L. Zsolnai (ed.), *Handbook of Business Ethics: Ethics in the New Economy*, Oxford: Peter Lang.

Jonas, H. (1984), *The Imperative of Responsibility: In Search of an Ethics for the Technological Age*, Chicago, IL: University of Chicago Press.

Jørgensen, S. and L.J.T. Pedersen (2011), "Organizing for responsibility," in O. Jakobsen and L.J.T. Pedersen (eds.), *Responsibility, Deep Ecology and the Self*, Oslo: Forlag1.

Kaplan, R.S. and A.A. Atkinson (1998), *Advanced Management Accounting*, 3rd edn., Upper Saddle River, NJ: Prentice Hall.

Kaptein, M. and J. Wempe (2004), "Ethical dilemmas of corporate functioning," in L. Zsolnai (ed.), *Ethics in the Economy: Handbook of Business Ethics*, Oxford: Peter Lang.

Kirk, K. and J. Mouritsen (1996), "Spaces of accountability: Accounting systems and systems of accountability in a multinational," in R. Munro and J. Mouritsen (eds.), *Accountability: Power, Ethos and Technologies of Managing*, London: Thomson.

Lindkvist, L. and S. Llewellyn (2003), "Accountability, responsibility and organization," *Scandinavian Journal of Management*, **19**, 251–73.

Macintosh, N.M. and P. Quattrone (2010), *Management Accounting and Control Systems: An Organizational and Sociological Approach*, 2nd edn., Chichester: John Wiley & Sons.

May, L. (1992), *Sharing Responsibility*, Chicago, IL: University of Chicago Press.

Messner, M. (2007), "Being accountable and being responsible," in C. Carter, S. Clegg, M. Kornberger, S. Laske and M. Messner (eds.), *Business Ethics as Practice: Representation, Reflexivity and Performance*, Cheltenham, UK and Northampton, MA, USA: Edward Elgar Publishing, pp. 49–67.

Messner, M. (2009), "The limits of accountability," *Accounting, Organizations and Society*, **34**, 918–38.

Milgram, S. (1974), *Obedience to Authority: An Experimental View*, New York: Harper & Row.

Munro, R.J.B. and D.J. Hatherly (1993), "Accountability and the new commercial agenda," *Critical Perspectives on Accounting*, **4**, 369–95.

Pedersen, L.J.T. (2009), "Making sense of sensitivity: Moral sensitivity and problem formulation in business," Ph.D. dissertation, NHH – Norwegian School of Economics, Bergen.

Roberts, J. (1991), "The possibilities of accountability," *Accounting, Organizations and Society*, **16** (4), 355–68.

Roberts, J. (2009), "No one is perfect: The limits of transparency and an ethic for 'intelligent' accountability," *Accounting, Organizations and Society*, **34** (8), 957–70.

Roberts, J. and R. Scapens (1985), "Accounting systems and systems of accountability: Understanding accounting practices in their organisational contexts," *Accounting, Organizations and Society*, **10** (4), 443–56.

Shearer, T. (2002), "Ethics and accountability: From the for-itself to the for-the-other," *Accounting, Organizations and Society*, **27** (6), 541–73.

Sinclair, A. (1995), "The chameleon of accountability: Forms and discourses," *Accounting, Organizations and Society*, **20** (2/3), 219–37.

Wilkinson, J.M. (1988), "Moral distress in nursing practice: Experience and effect," *Nursing Forum*, **23**, 16–29.

Williams, B. (1981), *Moral Luck: Philosophical Papers 1973–1980*, Cambridge: Cambridge University Press.

Zimbardo, P. (2007), *The Lucifer Effect: Understanding How Good People Turn Evil*, New York: Random House.

Zsolnai, L. (2009), *Responsible Decision Making*, New York: Transaction Publishers.

Epilogue: Welcome to DYMACO[1]

Bino Catasús

Dear Bino,

Welcome to DYMACO as a new member of the team! It is great to have you here in our organization, and we believe, just as you do, that we can supply "opportunities for autonomy-creativity, and a relational culture characterized by supportive managers and good social relations."[2] My ambition is always to send a letter to all our new managers outlining our ideas of control in DYMACO, not least since I know of our reputation – a firm without a detailed budget.

Budgets are, as you know, about allocating resources to spaces over time. So, let me first talk about time. If you want to achieve success in DYMACO, it is paramount that you develop a skill of "timing." As you might know, Chronos was the Greek personification of time measured by equal units and without purpose, whereas Kairos was the god of the right time, that is, where time related to opportunity and intentions and was not measurable. We are a Kairos organization and not a Chronos organization, and we expect you to take opportunities without limiting yourself to a plan or, even worse, hiding behind plans already made. I want you always to ask yourself "How much value is this creating?"[3] Working at DYMACO is about reflecting on plans made, and we expect you to make calculations as to whether the future action is necessary or not. Thus, we think of you as a business person who is able to let numbers collide into calculations.

I know that keeping the budgets was the main measure of success at OLMACO and that you found budgets to be a way to "temporally structure organizational activities."[4] For me, it is "paradoxical that budgets still are among the most important tools in [organizations'] control systems,"[5] not least since we find that "the more they use budgets, the less profitable they are."[6] As we believe the world is changing at a fast pace and that the future is unpredictable, we are not different from other organizations in removing budgets.[7] In fact, our control model is built around change because we truly believe that the world is changing and that there is acuteness in integrating such a view into the control system.

In essence, when you come to work on Monday, you will notice that we "encourage managers to question their own decisions and to be continuously prepared to make changes in the desired path."[8] This means that our view is that of reflections. One may question if there is time for learning if everything is about the right timing, and you might "become too involved in operational activities . . . [and] may lose . . . critical distance and independence from [operations]."[9] Still, at DYMACO we do not believe that there is something that is too involved or too much change. In fact, the control system in DYMACO rests on the idea that the world changes faster than the organization and, therefore, we need to mobilize resources for change.

You might be concerned by this approach and believe that the world is a fairly stable place[10] and that by introducing budget rules we gain not only a source of stability and inflexibility but also a source of learning and change.[11] I do agree that yesterday was probably a very good predictor for today, but an organization that is not "already ready" will lose in comparison. One of the ways to stabilize, and in my view make the organization numb, is to rule by rules.

I think that people hide behind rules and that there is a risk that in organizing through stability we do not get the agility we aim for.[12] In fact, in DYMACO we strive for "seeing" our employees more than once a year or once a month. We have an ambition to increase the management control intensity and to have more than a singular point of control (like the financial budget). You can be sure that in DYMACO there is no place to hide.

Sometimes my friends say that DYMACO is all about social control. At DYMACO we want to achieve an "organizational identity and commitment through peer acknowledgement of professional achievements."[13] By developing a culture of transparency we want to by "careful positioning of barriers, actions and events open up to a wider observation and thereby control."[14] This means that by making things visible we strive not only to "see" you, but also that you "see" your colleagues. We want to emphasize a relational culture where you know that you are a part of the organization.

We do not aim for information flow that is hierarchical. In fact, transparency, in our idea, is a means to create trust. I know that some believe that trust is the lack of information and that "[t]here would be no need to trust anyone whose activities were continually visible and whose thought processes were transparent"[15] So I guess in that sense our ambition "implies an increasing need to . . . handle more demanding social and temporal embeddedness."[16] In today's business environment, there is no time to stop at the stoplight.

In DYMACO transparency is also strongly related to accountability, and the accountability is not, primarily, an issue giving reasons for conduct to your boss. What we want to balance is "autonomy, competence and relatedness in the work setting"[17] and making it possible to move from an ex post blame-game to an ex ante responsibility setting in dialogical, "self-determined, communal and engaged decision making and action."[18] Trust me (*sic!*), you will be made accountable, but we hope that action is internally motivated by the responsibility you have for the firm, the business unit and your colleagues. The way we try to make this work is by developing DYMACO into an organization where everything might be questioned.

As an example, we want you to collaborate with the controller, who has another role in DYMACO than s/he had in OLMACO. Here the controller "changes from bellboy in pursuit of a 'true' budget to a technically skilled and reflective actor interacting with opposite views and thoughts of the BU managers and the front-line managers."[19] The communicative culture, again, is about increasing the management control intensity. We believe that a human organization is an organization where the culture is to pose questions to everyone all the time and that by communicating with organizational members – even with the accountants – we become the organization we want to be.

I guess that you, by now, are getting a bit worried. Good. You should be. We do believe that working in DYMACO is about standing on your toes, communicating and giving feedback, delivering value from a Kairos perspective, being involved in a feedback culture in which you cannot hide behind outdated plans and, finally, being accountable for what you do. When we say human organization, we emphasize the idea that humans want and need to be observed and evaluated. DYMACO should be restless – and so should you.

Welcome on Monday.

CEO Catasús

NOTES

1. This book offers insights into the design of new, more dynamic approaches to management control. "Dynamic," says the dictionary, relates to continuous change, force and energy. Further, one broad understanding of management control is that it is a set of mechanisms that help mediate between today's situation and the future and in which the activities induce members of the organization to do certain things and to refrain from doing others. Dynamic management control is, thus, an approach to control that is hard to contest, at least from a functional perspective; it opens up the possibility of

leaving behind structures that impede creativity and make us passive. Albeit easy to accept, the demands of dynamic management control are not as innocent as they may seem. In this epilogue, I reflect on some of the characteristics of dynamic management control by imagining a letter from the CEO of DYnamic MAnagement COntrol Ltd. to the newly appointed manager. The ambition is to highlight, not least through the findings of this book, how it could be to work in such a control environment.

2.   See Chapter 11.
3.   See Figure 2.3.
4.   See Chapter 8.
5.   See Chapter 4.
6.   See Chapter 4.
7.   See Chapter 3.
8.   See Chapter 6.
9.   See Chapter 8.
10. See K. Hawley (2004), *How Things Persist*, Oxford: Clarendon Press.
11. See Chapter 10.
12. See Chapter 2.
13. See Chapter 1.
14. A.G. Hopwood (1990), "Accounting and organisation change," *Accounting, Auditing and Accountability Journal*, **3** (1), 9.
15. A. Giddens (1990), *The Consequences of Modernity*, Padstow, Cornwall: T.J. Press, p. 9.
16. See Chapter 9.
17. See Chapter 12.
18. See Chapter 12.
19. See Chapter 7.

Index

accountability systems
  overview 222–4
  problems with 229–32
  promoting personal responsibility in
    232–5
  and responsibility 225–9
accounting, multiple conceptions of
  92–3, 95, 99, 108
active individual responsibility 224, 226
activity-based costing (ABC)
  compared to Beyond Budgeting 94,
    109–10
  performance effects 64–6
  use and perceived usefulness 54–8
actor-based model 119, 136
actor, from conformer to 131–2
adaptability and efficiency 185–6,
  187–9, 193
agency theory 75–6, 78, 83, 85, 184
agility 12, 20, 59–60, 240
Aguilera, R.V. 70, 72–5, 84–5
Ahrens, T. 111, 146–7, 156
Ajzen, I. 206
Amabile, T.M. 3, 205, 208
ambiguity 71, 72, 86, 164, 187
  making sense of 95–6, 106, 108
Ambition to Action (A2A) 20–25
  ambition statements 20
  ambitions and strategies 22
  constraining effects 101–4
  implementation 25–6
  leadership implications 31
  leaving calendar year 26–31
  narrative 123–9
  in practice 97–107
  processes 23
  purposes 20
  skeptics 25–6
  successful implementation 31–2,
    99–101
  unsuccessful implementation 104–7

ambitious targets 13, 78, 98,
  99–100, 120, 121, 127–8, 129,
  229
Ancona, D.G. 144, 145, 146, 148, 149,
  150, 151, 170
Anglo-American shareholder model
  73, 88
Anthony, R.N. 35, 124
antithesis 121, 124, 125–6, 127–8,
  130–31
Anyon, J. 210
Arbnor, I. 114, 117
Argyris, C. 2, 163, 165, 188, 191
Aschoff, J. 144
Atkinson, M.M. 166
Augier, M. 4
Austin, J.L. 117
autonomy
  learning effects 185, 186, 187, 190,
    191, 193–4, 199, 200
  needs 227
  struggles with 31
  and temporal structuring 151
  Statoil 16, 17
autonomy-creativity orientation
  appendix 221
  implications for employers and
    research needs 217–18
  study method 211–13
  study results 213–16
  theory 205–11
awareness of control 222
Ax, C. 4, 52, 71

Baer, J. 209, 210
balanced scorecards (BSC)
  compared to Beyond Budgeting 94,
    109–10
  implementation 79
  merits of 81, 83
  performance effects 64–6

creativity *see* autonomy-creativity
    orientation
Crowley, M. 2
Cudeck, R. 196
cultural capital 210
Cummings, A. 207
Cunha, M.P. 150, 156, 157
customer orientation 95
customer profitability accounting
    performance effects 64–6
    use and perceived usefulness 54–8
customer service, temporal structuring
    150–51
Czarniawska-Joerges, B. 168

Daft, R.L. 188
Dankbaar, B. 207
Das, T.K. 155–6
Davis, G.F. 72
Davis, J.H. 83
Dearden, J. 146, 147, 151
decentralization 39–42, 44, 45, 49–50,
    61, 83, 84, 86, 94, 152
Deci, E.L. 189, 205, 212, 227, 229, 232
decision-facilitation roles of budgeting
    149, 151–3
decision-influencing roles of budgeting
    149, 151–2
demographic factors, impact on
    autonomy-creativity 206, 208–11,
    213–18
dialectics 124, 125–6, 127, 128, 129,
    130, 134
diffusion, management models 71–2
DiMaggio, P. 169
discourse analysis 119–35
    method 118–19
discourse theory 116–17
Donaldson, L. 83
"double binding" 191
dual control systems in practice 104–7
Dugdale, D. 166
Duncan, R.B. 36
dynamic resource allocation 15–19
    putting into practice 98–107
dysfunctional behavior 2–3, 60–62, 63,
    84, 150–51, 163

Eccles, R.G. 234
economic value added (EVA) models 71

Edmondson, A. 195
education, impact on autonomy
    creativity 210, 215–16
efficiency and adaptability 185, 188–9,
    193
Eisenhardt, K.M. 147, 150, 155
Ekholm, B.-G. 34, 37, 39, 92
"elevator ride" metaphor 120–21
embeddedness theory 168–71
empowerment 3, 4, 81, 152, 208, 236
endogenous cycles 144–5
engaged behavior, conditions for 233–4
entrainment 144–8
    to calendar year 148–56
entrainment time 170–71, 173, 179, 180
environmental uncertainty
    literature review and hypotheses
        development 35–8
    research conclusions 46–7
    study method 38–42
    study results 42–5
Espedal, B. 192
event time 170–71, 173, 179, 180
event-based forecasting 13–14, 15, 27,
    28–30, 79, 153, 154–6, 157
    putting into practice 98–107
evolutionary approach 82
existential dimension of responsibility
    227
existing knowledge 188–9
external benchmarking 5, 15, 102, 124
external communication 26–7, 149
external cycles/pacers 144–5, 148–9,
    150, 153, 155
extrinsic motivation/reward 193, 222–3,
    230, 232–3
    impact on autonomy-creativity 204,
        206, 207, 212, 213–18
Ezzamel, M. 34, 148, 151, 157

"family" planning and coordination
    regime 171, 172, 179–80
    budget design 177–8
    budget role 173–4
    use of control 178–9
feedback, link with autonomy-
    creativity 208, 212, 213–18
Feldman, M.S. 192
financial incentives, control through
    1–5